DAVENPORT
EDUCATING ACROSS THREE CENTURIES

Copyright © 2016 Thomas Brown, Ed.D and Margaret Moceri

All rights reserved. No part of the content of this book may be reproduced without the written permission of Davenport University, 6191 Kraft Avenue, Grand Rapids, Michigan, 49512. Published in the United States by Davenport University.

Library of Congress Cataloging-in-Publication Data
Brown, Thomas Ed.D. and Margaret Moceri
Davenport University: Educating across three centuries / Thomas Brown and Margaret Moceri
p. cm.
Includes index.
ISBN: 978-0-692-64175-0
1. Davenport University (Grand Rapids, Mich.)—History. 2. Davenport University (Grand Rapids, Mich.)—History—Pictorial works. I. Title.

Printed in Michigan by University Litho, 4150 Varsity Drive, Ann Arbor, Michigan, 48108

Book cover design by Susan Bakkila

Foreword

Less than one year after General Robert E. Lee surrendered to General Ulysses S. Grant at Appomattox to end the American Civil War, a small college was started in Grand Rapids that has grown to become one of the finest higher educational institutions of its kind in America. Today, its name is Davenport University.

As a former president and chancellor of Davenport for nearly a quarter-century, I had the pleasure of a front row seat—watching, leading, and working with the leadership team of Davenport University. Although I never had the opportunity to meet Mr. Davenport, I did have the opportunity to succeed his son-in-law, Robert W. Sneden, as president when he retired in 1977.

What a time to follow a leader of such greatness. Dr. Sneden learned "the school business" from the master, Mr. Davenport. Mr. Davenport led the school through the Great Depression, World War II, and post-war prosperity; Dr. Sneden built upon experienced shoulders to bring a nationally accredited institution to enormous success.

When I was selected to succeed Dr. Sneden, I, too, could stand on the shoulders of an incredible leader. A pattern was emerging as new presidents launched their own successful tenures from the innovations and accomplishments of their predecessors.

Randolph Flechsig followed me and was a very creative president who reinvigorated the university by building a new campus, reintroducing athletics, and implementing many new and more sophisticated policies and procedures to govern the institution.

Current president Dr. Richard Pappas has built upon the combined legacies of all the former presidents and leadership teams to create a dynamic institution for the 21st century. He has initiated a highly effective planning system, new degree programs, and the university's first doctorate program.

Max DePree, former CEO of Herman Miller, Inc., titled his book *Leadership Is an Art*. Davenport University, from its modest beginnings to the flourishing institution it has become today, has demonstrated that, indeed, leadership is an art. I believe that *Davenport: Educating Across Three Centuries* demonstrates also that Davenport continues to practice the art of becoming. Since the early days of its existence, our university has been an ever-changing and evolving institution, insisting always on new levels of greatness.

Institutional histories are typically of greatest interest to those associated, in one way or another, with that institution. For this updated and expanded edition, the authors intended a much broader appeal, however. Reading this book can prove to be a valuable lesson about vision, planning, management, measuring results, and innovation. It is living history—a compelling journey of learning experiences, thoughtful observations, and even fascinating glimpses into our community's growth and development.

I hope you will join me in feeling great pride in Davenport University's 150 years in education!

Cordially,

Donald W. Maine

Donald W. Maine, LL.D
Chancellor Emeritus
Davenport University

Preface to the Second Edition

Davenport: Educating Across Three Centuries is the second edition to *Davenport: History of an Institution*, published in 1991. The original volume coincided with the 125th anniversary of Davenport College; this version commemorates Davenport University's sesquicentennial.

The quarter century between these two milestones has been epochal. In 1991, the Internet was in its infancy and the term "dot-com" nonexistent. The concept of social media was still a dozen years away, and the number of worldwide cell phone owners—around 12 million—barely registers compared with today's 4 billion users. By these metrics 1991 begins to appear quaint—even rustic.

In that same time span, Davenport University itself has changed immeasurably, bearing scant resemblance to the Davenport College of 1991 (much less the Davenport Institute of 1960, or the Davenport-McLachlan Institute of 1925). This makes the case for producing an updated edition both more evident and more compelling.

There are few institutions locally that can claim a continuous record of operation that parallels the development of Grand Rapids itself. Grand Rapids Business College (the predecessor of Davenport University) was established just 30 years after Grand Rapids was first settled. Davenport is among the oldest colleges in Michigan, public or private. It has not merely endured; it has prospered, even during times when similar institutions were failing.

Davenport's story is notable for more than its longevity, however. Its influence is deeply embedded in the narrative of this region. Generations of Davenport alumni have gone on to direct companies, establish businesses, serve on boards, volunteer in their communities. Through its leaders, its graduates, its programs, and its presence, Davenport has been instrumental in the evolution of West Michigan as a center of economic and civic development. This second edition expands on these vital connections.

There are also important ways in which 150 years have not affected Davenport's core commitments—where its earliest principles have even anticipated contemporary questions. M.E. Davenport spent his entire career developing and refining what he called "practical education," an alloy that combined specific career preparation with a background in humanities and sciences. From this approach he formed an economical but eloquent motto: "Make a Living, Make a Life, Make a Contribution." Mr. Davenport believed, quite ardently, that an enriched life depended on the interplay of all three elements.

Steep escalations in tuition and student debt have kindled vigorous debate about the true 'value' of a college degree. Value, however, has always been part of Davenport's culture no matter whether the Age is Industrial or Digital. It is the fundamentals from the university's earliest days—predictive curricula, commitment to students and community, visionary leadership—that make it relevant across centuries.

1866-1910

THE INSTITUTION DEBUTS

Ohio native Conrad Swensberg establishes a new educational enterprise in post-Civil War Grand Rapids when both Swensberg and the city itself were barely 30 years old. His business training school thrives—until changes in leadership bring a reversal of fortune.

1910-1959

A NEW BEGINNING

A young business teacher pursues a promising job lead and instead finds himself aboard a sinking ship. Despite sobering odds, Michael Edward Davenport and his family rebuild the ailing institution into the largest private business training school in Michigan.

SPECIAL SECTION:
The University of Grand Rapids, 1936–1945

1959-1977

FROM INSTITUTE TO COLLEGE

Family leadership continues under Robert W. Sneden—bringing a major change in corporate structure, a new campus, and a milestone accomplishment that takes Davenport to the next level.

1977-2000

COMING OF AGE

Davenport's first nonfamily president is chosen, and Donald Maine sets the school on a course toward becoming the largest independent four-year college in Michigan. The first bachelor's degrees are awarded, and Davenport enters the Digital Age with online classes and a graduate school.

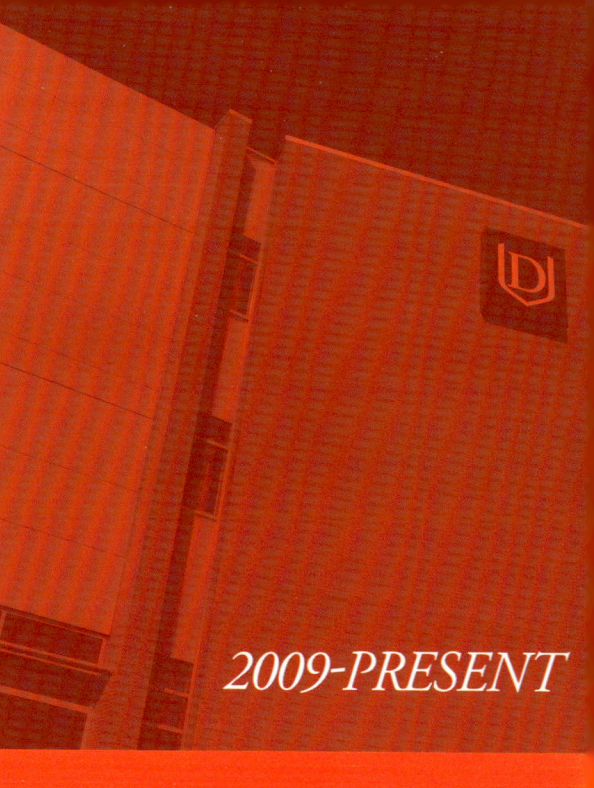

2000-2009

THE NEW MILLENNIUM

Davenport launches its university era with a new residential campus, a revived athletic program, and accelerated focus on the high-demand fields of business, technology, and health professions.

2009-PRESENT

VISION FOR CONTINUED EXCELLENCE

Under the leadership of Dr. Richard Pappas, the university advances with a bold vision for institutional quality, optimal student outcomes, and 21st century educational innovation.

SPECIAL SECTION:
Distinguishing Davenport

Prologue

DAVENPORT UNIVERSITY CAN CLAIM dual origins: its founding in 1866 and a re-establishment nearly 45 years later. It was the second incarnation that produced today's Davenport—but at the time, circumstances looked far more like the end of an era than the beginning.

Late in the fall of 1910, Michael Edward Davenport arrived for work as usual at Valley City Commercial School, where he taught bookkeeping, penmanship, commercial law, and several other subjects. It was apparent immediately that something was wrong—students and staff milled the corridors amid the news that the college's proprietor had decided—without warning—to cease operations mid-term, leaving students with unfinished courses and faculty with months of unpaid back salary.

Hoping to salvage some completion from the chaos, the stranded students and their instructors asked Davenport if he would take over management long enough to finish the fall term. Though just 25 years old and brand new to the staff, he agreed.

The school had only a few dozen remaining students, three faculty members (including Davenport himself), no operating cash, and a five-thousand dollar debt—a staggering figure in that day. By any estimation, both its balance sheet and its outlook were abysmal.

As the school teetered precariously between former vigor and imminent failure, its most difficult moment would eventually prove to be one of its most fortunate.

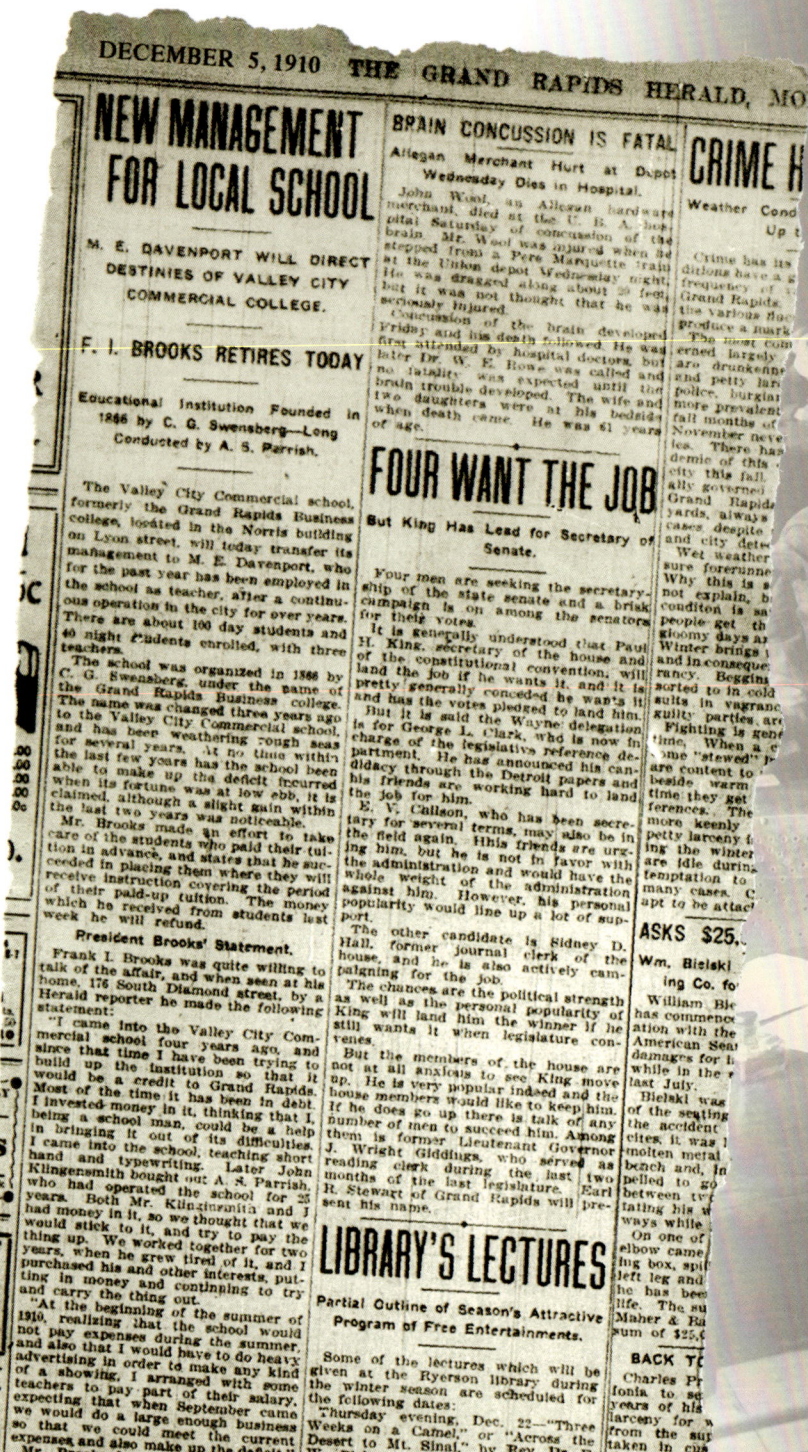

Davenport: Educating Across Three Centuries | The Institution Debuts

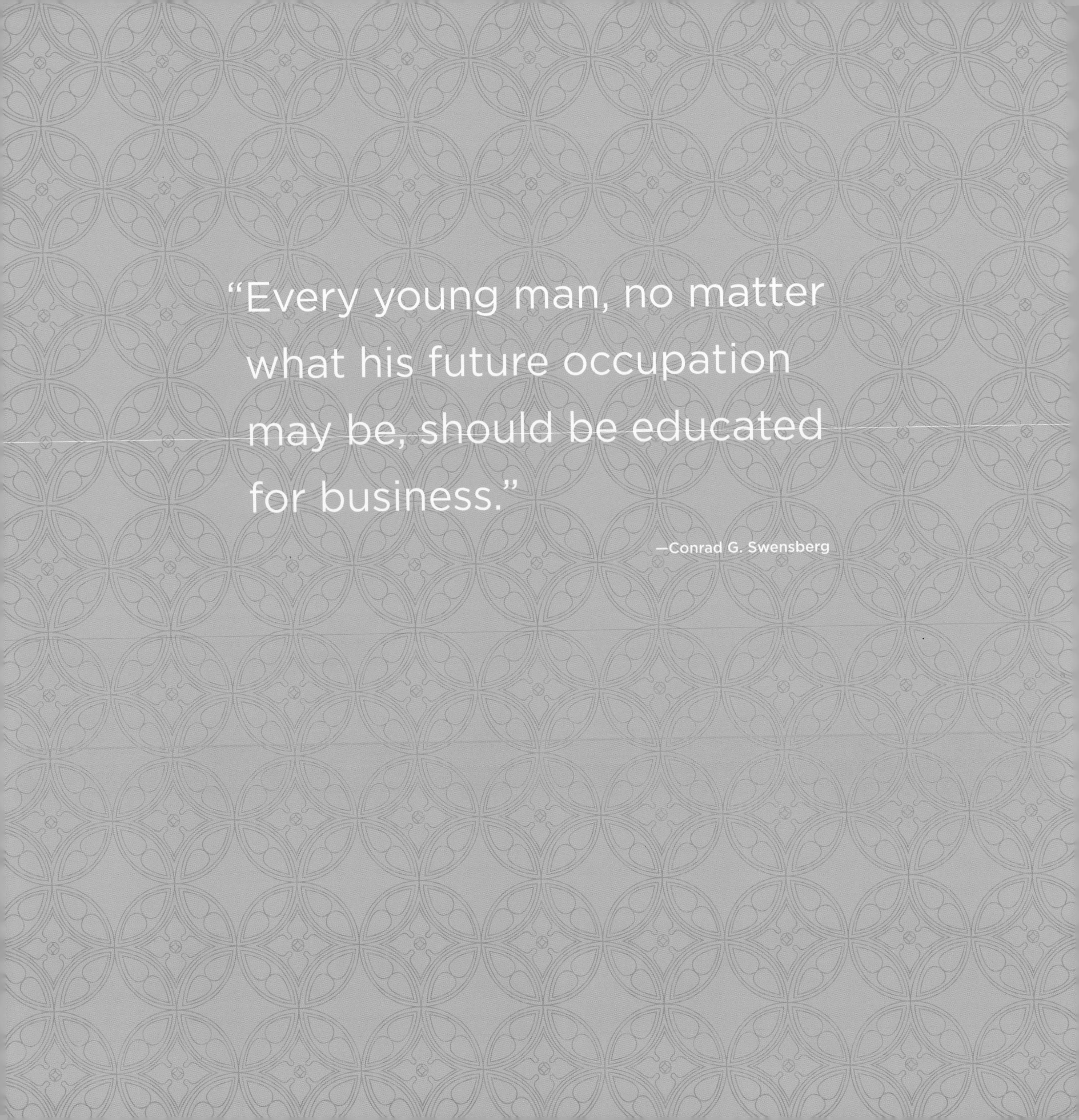

"Every young man, no matter what his future occupation may be, should be educated for business."

—Conrad G. Swensberg

THE INSTITUTION DEBUTS
1866–1910

The Headwaters

IT WAS LATE IN 1865 WHEN CONRAD G. SWENSBERG, recently discharged from the Union Army, came north from his home state of Ohio scouting locations for a new enterprise. The Civil War had ended just a few months earlier. The city of Grand Rapids, little more than a frontier outpost when Swensberg was a child, was swiftly developing into the commercial and industrial hub of West Michigan. To Swensberg, it was the ideal environment for what he had in mind.

Although it would be another ten years until the typewriter was introduced at the Centennial Exhibition in Philadelphia, the Industrial Age was already transforming the American economy. Steam power, railroads, and westward expansion were constantly redrawing the country's frontiers, as the nineteenth century's scions of finance and industry—Vanderbilt, Carnegie, Rockefeller, Morgan—established the empires that would turn the United States into a world powerhouse.

Swensberg anticipated the need for skilled professionals to staff the offices of these new corporations. In Grand Rapids, he also discovered a gap in the available options for training. Various "writing schools"—predecessors to the commercial college that concentrated exclusively on penmanship—had existed since Grand Rapids was first settled. None of these institutions had survived long, however, and Swensberg seized an opportunity.

According to the *Grand Rapids Telegram-Herald*, although he'd arrived in Michigan with "no capital but his character," Swensberg was able to rent space in the Luce Building at the corner of Monroe and Justice (later renamed Ottawa Avenue). On an upper floor he opened Grand Rapids Business College, the first business education institution of its kind in the city. Advertisements invited "young men who desire to perfect themselves by a commercial education" to send for the school catalog. Women were not yet encouraged to apply; office positions were still held exclusively by men.

Coming north from his native Ohio "with no capital but his character," Conrad G. Swensberg chose Grand Rapids to establish his business training academy.

Opening Day

January 25, 1866, was the first day of classes at GRBC, known also as the Commercial College and Telegraphic Institute. Sixteen students registered for courses in four areas: bookkeeping, penmanship, business law, and arithmetic—the core office skills of the day.

In addition to the typical business school curriculum, Swensberg had introduced a variation on the typical commercial school theme: a preparatory department offering classes in German, French, and the cognate then called the "English branches." His reason for including humanities was strategic. Commercial schools, established essentially as small businesses, were attracting many "venture entrepreneurs," and the field included its share of charlatans. Educated at Oberlin College, Swensberg valued learning as well as training and from the outset was determined that his academy would be distinguished from the dubious organizations.

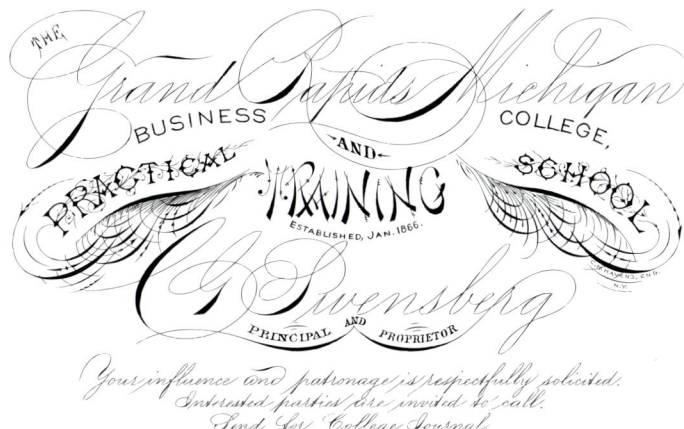

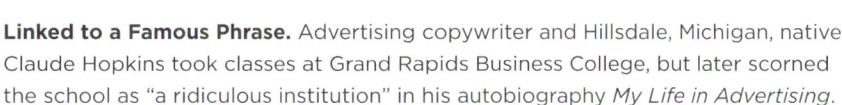

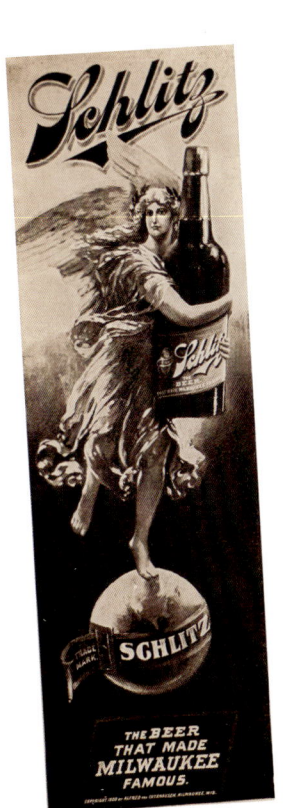

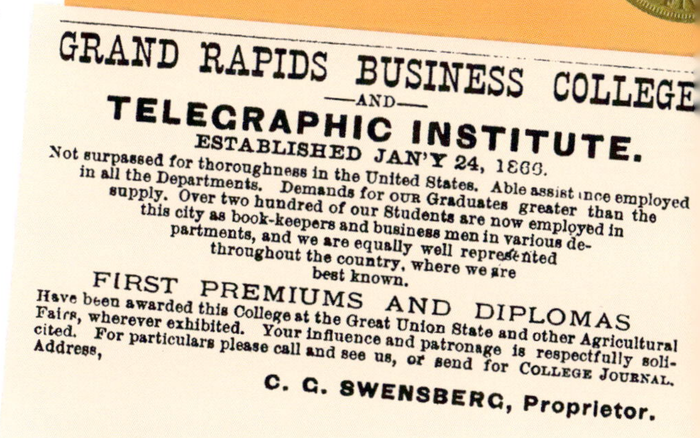

1827
Fur trader Louis Campau establishes a settlement on the Owashtanong (Grand) River.

1838
Village of Grand Rapids chartered by state of Michigan.

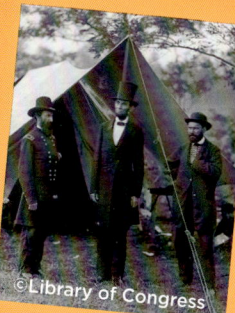

1861-65
U.S. Civil War

1866
January 25: first day of classes at Grand Rapids Business College under the leadership of founder Conrad Swensberg.

1876
Typewriter introduced at World's Fair in Philadelphia.

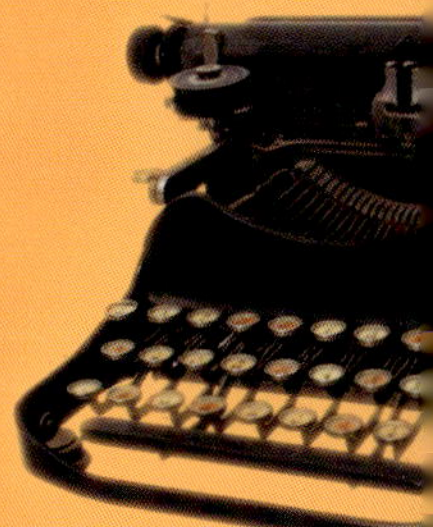

1877
Calvin College and Theological Seminary opens.

1886
Grand Rapids School Furniture (forerunner of American Seating Company), incorporated.

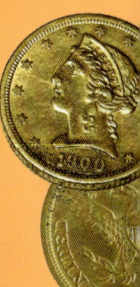

1886
The Dominican Sisters of Grand Rapids established a novitiate normal school which would evolve into Aquinas College.

Linked to a Famous Phrase. Advertising copywriter and Hillsdale, Michigan, native Claude Hopkins took classes at Grand Rapids Business College, but later scorned the school as "a ridiculous institution" in his autobiography *My Life in Advertising*.

Starting his career at Bissell Carpet Sweeper, Hopkins later broke salary records when he was hired at Chicago's Lord & Thomas agency (later Foote, Cone, & Belding) for $185,000—the equivalent of about $2 million today. Famous as "the world's highest-paid copywriter," he also wrote the book *Scientific Advertising*, long considered a classic text in the profession.

Arguably more indelible was the motto he coined for the Schlitz Brewery Company: "The Beer That Made Milwaukee Famous."

GRAND RAPIDS BUSINESS COLLEGE
—AND—
TELEGRAPHIC INSTITUTE.
ESTABLISHED JAN'Y 24, 1866.
Not surpassed for thoroughness in the United States. Able assistance employed in all the Departments. Demands for OUR Graduates greater than the supply. Over two hundred of our Students are now employed in this city as book-keepers and business men in various departments, and we are equally well represented throughout the country, where we are best known.

FIRST PREMIUMS AND DIPLOMAS

Have been awarded this College at the Great Union State and other Agricultural Fairs, wherever exhibited. Your influence and patronage is respectfully solicited. For particulars please call and see us, or send for COLLEGE JOURNAL. Address,

C. G. SWENSBERG, Proprietor.

"There is perhaps no other institution in Grand Rapids of so much value to the city and its citizens at this particular period as the Grand Rapids Commercial College and Telegraphic Institute."

—Local historian Charles Tuttle

Early Prominence

With GRBC's first well-prepared graduates, the superiority of Swensberg's approach became evident to business and industry leaders throughout the city and soon throughout Michigan. From its earliest days, the college combined its educational mission with character-shaping values. State Senator Henry S. Clubb noted that Swensberg's concern for his students was more than academic. "He has shown a genuine interest in their welfare," Clubb wrote, "not merely insisting on their perfection in the arts of penmanship and bookkeeping, but in their general character and conduct."

Eventually, schools emulating Swensberg's model began to appear around Grand Rapids, including J.U. Leon's Business College and Shorthand Institute, and Professor J.W. Welton's College, all offering various courses in bookkeeping, mathematics, and other office skills. Most had short lifespans and posed no serious challenge to GRBC's dominance.

GRBC's original location in the Luce Building on Monroe west of Ottawa Avenue (then called Justice). The city of Grand Rapids was just 30 years in existence, with unpaved streets, wood plank sidewalks, and a population of 7,000.

In 1875, Swensberg moved his school one block east to the just-completed Ledyard Building (opposite), one of the more prestigious addresses in the city. The move not only gave the growing college more space, it made a statement about its rising reputation.

LOCATION
1866
LUCE BUILDING

CLASSES
Practical Penmanship, Practical Arithmetic, Bookkeeping, Business Penmanship & Composition

16 ENROLLMENT

TUITION
$5 for 30 Penmanship Lessons; $50 for 6-month Bookkeeping Course

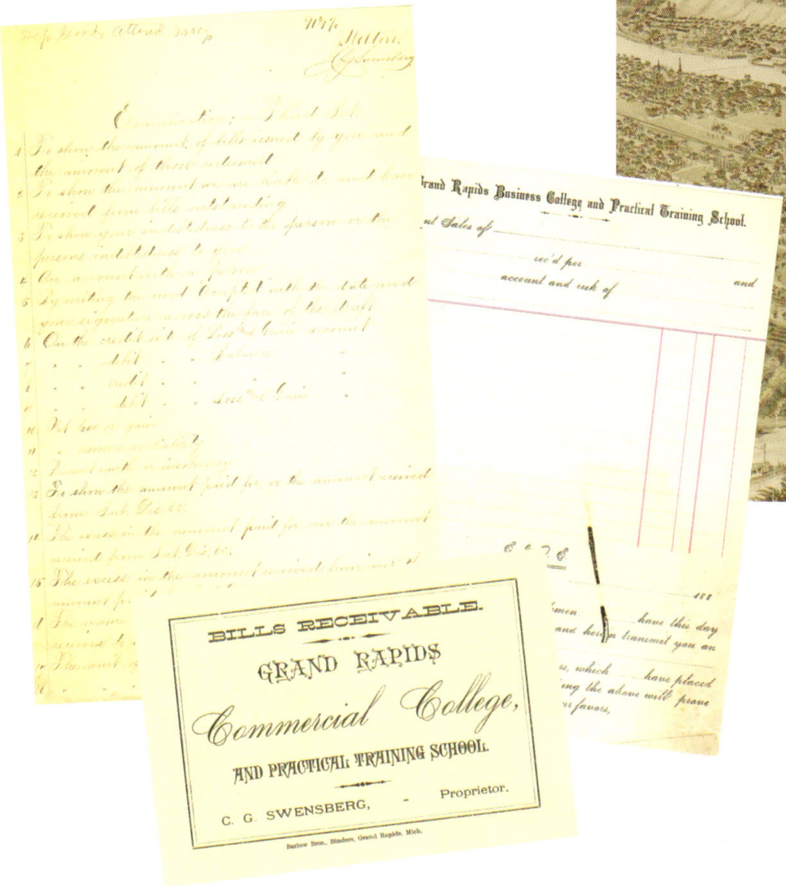

Established in 1827 as a trading post by Louis Campau, Grand Rapids was officially incorporated as a city on May 1, 1850. By the mid-1870s, lumber driven down the Grand River helped supply a world-renowned furniture industry and affirmed the city's position as the commercial hub of West Michigan.

Practice journal sheets and other training materials modeled on office procedures of the day helped students master tasks in the classroom they would be expected to perform in the workplace.

Davenport: Educating Across Three Centuries | The Institution Debuts   15

The Young Professor Conrad Swensberg

Born near Cassel, Germany, in 1835, Conrad Swensberg emigrated to America with his family in 1846, where they farmed first in Ohio and then in Iowa. Following his parents' death, young Conrad left the family homestead and worked with the Iowa Survey, marking off plats for townships, villages, and cities in the sparsely settled Northwest Territory. Eventually he returned to Ohio and enrolled in Oberlin College. Illness kept him out of combat in the Civil War, but he was able to enlist as a commissary sergeant with Ohio's 127th Infantry.

After the war, Swensberg moved to Grand Rapids and within a month had established the Grand Rapids Business College. The barbers next door affectionately dubbed him "the young professor."

As Swensberg's enterprise grew into one of the best commercial colleges in the Midwest, Swensberg himself emerged as a prominent business and civic leader. His influence as an owner, organizer, or director helped establish several companies around the city, including Valley City Milling, Phoenix Furniture, Grand Rapids Street Railway Company (which named a streetcar after him), and the Bissell Carpet Sweeper Company (most of whose charter principals were GRBC graduates). Swensberg also assisted with the creation of the *Grand Rapids Telegram-Herald*, the forerunner of the *Grand Rapids Herald*, which would continue in circulation until 1959. In addition, he helped organize the YMCA and in that facility opened the first free reading room for the public benefit.

He was also well regarded by friends. Wrote an Ohio acquaintance, "His charities are unmeasured, his courtesies are constant, and he is warmly esteemed in every community where he has lived. On the walls, desks, and shelves of his well-appointed offices we see indications of business, of friendship, of taste, of manliness, of good sense, and of large-hearted generosity." Said another: "He is exemplary in his habits and has a quiet, unassuming way that makes for him many staunch friends. Mr. Swensberg does not believe it necessary to sink the man in order to make the merchant."

Conrad Swensberg

The Grand Rapids Herald

GRAND RAPIDS, MICH., WEDNESDAY, JANUARY 23, 1893

Politically active since young adulthood, Swensberg was described as an ardent Republican from the time of the party's origins in the 1850s. He served as an election return delegate in Iowa when Abraham Lincoln was elected president.

Swensberg married in 1875, but his wife, Hattie Drake of Ohio, died just three years later. Swensberg remained a widower the rest of his life. The couple had one daughter.

When Swensberg died of heart failure on October 5, 1897, flags around the city were lowered to half-mast, and the city council included on its October 8th agenda a resolution to attend his funeral en masse.

As a leader in shaping a young city, Swensberg is remembered in many capacities. But he holds an even greater place in the history of Davenport University for establishing a precedent of quality that inspired a distinguished heritage.

Lasting Impressions. During Grand Rapids' formative years Swensberg's influence was highly visible in communications, transportation, industry, and civic development. Among the many institutions he helped establish or develop were the Bissell Carpet Sweeper Company (above at its original factory on upper Monroe Avenue, site of the present-day DeVos Convention Center), Phoenix Furniture Company, the YMCA (then located in the Federal Square building), the Grand Rapids Street Railway Company, and the *Grand Rapids Herald*.

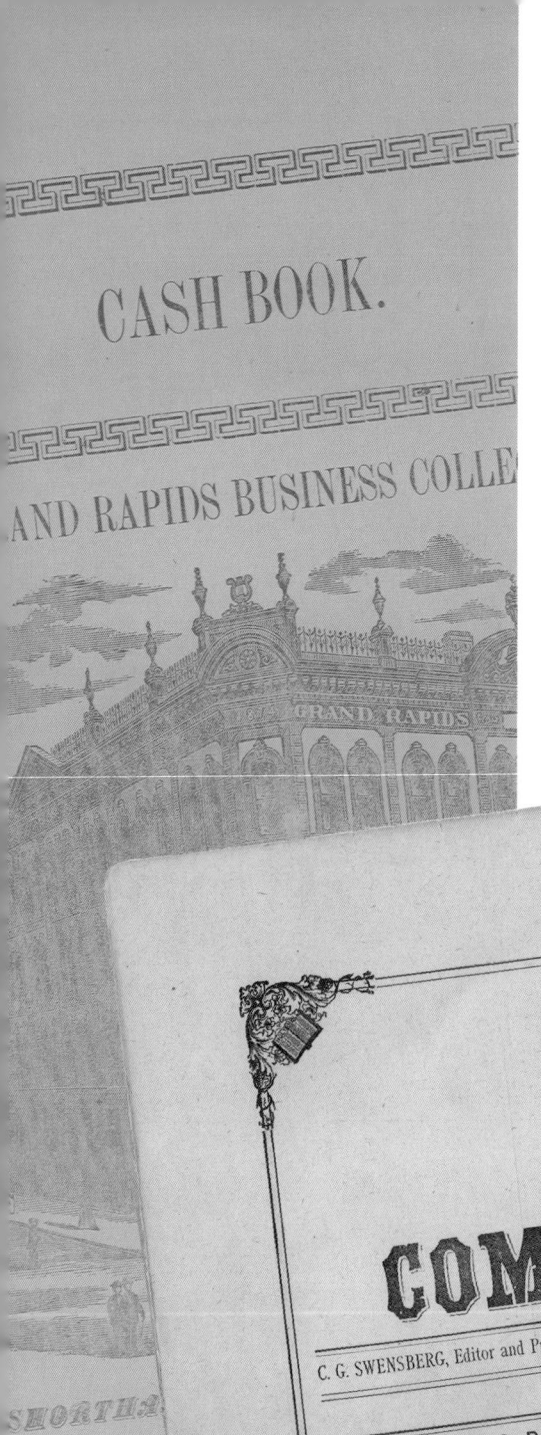

Swensberg's Successor

After devoting more than twenty years to building his college into a solid enterprise, Swensberg retired in 1888, appointing as his successor Aaron S. Parish. Parish had once taught on the GRBC faculty before moving to Peoria, Illinois, to establish his own business school.

Described by the *Grand Rapids Evening Leader* as a "progressive man whose mottoes are progression and practicality," Parish had the credentials of a competent leader who at first appeared to manage the school well. But as the twentieth century began, GRBC entered a period of instability of both management and location.

"Invincible Determination with a Right Motive, Energy, Industry, Thorough Instruction, Fair and Honorable Dealings with Everyone."

—GRBC Motto as stated in *The 1886 Grand Rapids Commercial College Journal.*

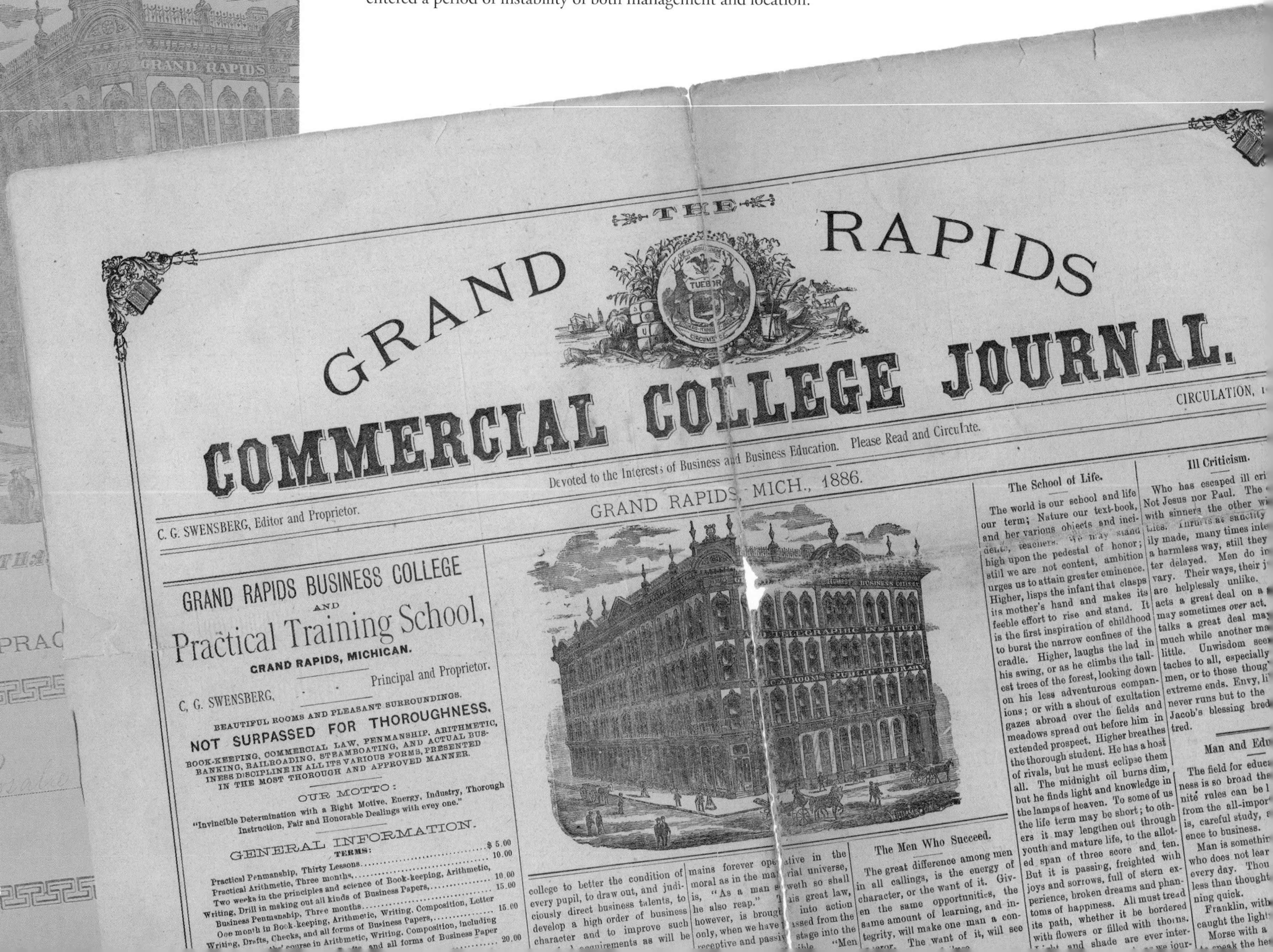
THE GRAND RAPIDS COMMERCIAL COLLEGE JOURNAL.

Devoted to the Interests of Business and Business Education. Please Read and Circulate.

CIRCULATION,

C. G. SWENSBERG, Editor and Proprietor.

GRAND RAPIDS, MICH., 1886.

GRAND RAPIDS BUSINESS COLLEGE AND Practical Training School, GRAND RAPIDS, MICHICAN.

C. G. SWENSBERG, Principal and Proprietor.

BEAUTIFUL ROOMS AND PLEASANT SURROUNDINGS.

NOT SURPASSED FOR THOROUGHNESS.

BOOK-KEEPING, COMMERCIAL LAW, PENMANSHIP, ARITHMETIC, BANKING, RAILROADING, STEAMBOATING, AND ACTUAL BUSINESS DISCIPLINE IN ALL ITS VARIOUS FORMS, PRESENTED IN THE MOST THOROUGH AND APPROVED MANNER.

OUR MOTTO:

"Invincible Determination with a Right Motive, Energy, Industry, Thorough Instruction, Fair and Honorable Dealings with evey one."

GENERAL INFORMATION.

TERMS:

Practical Penmanship, Thirty Lessons.......$ 5.00

Practical Arithmetic, Three months.......10.00

The School of Life.

Ill Criticism.

The Men Who Succeed.

Man and Edu

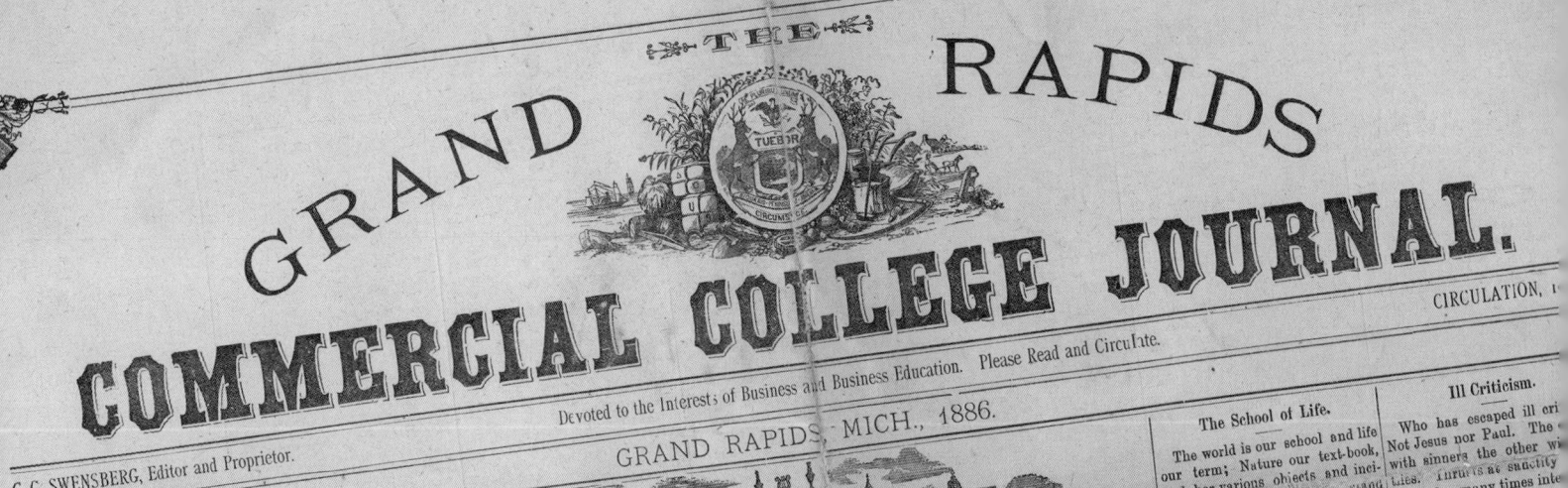

The First Change in Leadership — Aaron S. Parish

Born and educated in upstate New York, Aaron Parish moved with his family to Ingham County, Michigan, in 1858, when he was 17. The itinerant pattern of his late teens suggest a typical young adult seeking a career direction; after a few years in Michigan, he returned to New York to enroll in classes at a commercial college in Oswego County. After graduating he taught at several business colleges throughout the Midwest—including Grand Rapids Business College, where he worked for Conrad Swensberg.

In 1876 he left Grand Rapids for Peoria, Illinois, where he purchased Cole's Business College. For the next dozen years he operated the school as Parish's Business College, then returned to GRBC to take over as Swensberg's hand-picked successor.

By all accounts Parish maintained, at least initially, the prosperous foundations established by Swensberg, despite the appearance of several other office training schools in the city during the late 19th century. Local newspapers spoke somewhat dismissively of these other colleges—calling them the result of a "mushrooming" effect—but expressed continued high regard for the Grand Rapids Business College under Parish's leadership. After spending a day shadowing classes in 1890, a reporter from the *Grand Rapids Evening Leader* wrote, "The college is a veritable business world, where the same business transactions that are going on in the various branches of the city's business are carried out, with as much responsibility and precision, by the students." Eventually, most of the competitors failed, including one (Western Michigan College) amidst the taint of financial scandal.

But as the twentieth century got underway, GRBC's course became unsteady. Late in 1907 Parish sold his interests in the college to two faculty members, John F. Klingensmith and Frank L. Brooks. Before parting, he changed the school's name to Valley City Commercial College.

Grand Rapids city directories indicate that during the years following his retirement from education, Mr. Parish engaged in other enterprises, including a livery (presumably stables or carriages) and real estate. There is no record of children in his marriage to wife, Susan. In his later years, declining health kept Parish confined to his home, where he died in 1925.

Aaron Smith Parish

The Grand Rapids Herald

OCTOBER 2, 1890 — Weather: Crisp and Seasonal — Special Supplement

THOUSANDS THRONG TO GRAND RAPIDS!

Our fair city of Grand Rapids, the "Furniture City", is playing host to many visitors from across this great nation of ours.

As travelers descend from comfortable Pullman cars they are greeted by helpful porters in the gracious passenger lobby of the **GRAND RAPIDS AND INDIANA RAILROAD COMPANY STATION**. Pausing only a moment for directions they are whisked out to Campau Square - the hustling and bustling heart of our proud and hard-working community.

As the visitor takes in this magnificent vista perhaps he is impressed with our efficient street railways, our many busy shops, or perhaps just the general air of friendliness of our industrious citizens on their way home from a productive day in shop, office or factory.

MODERN FUNERALS

More and more modern families are utilizing the good services of the **DURFEE AND LEAVENWORTH FUNERAL PARLOR**. The old fashioned custom of viewing the departed loved one in the confines of the family domicile are giving way to more up-to-date practices. Messrs. Durfee and Leavenworth make all of the arrangements in a tasteful and discreet manner, thus, freeing the grieving loved ones from a small portion of the sad burden that the passing of a dear one brings.

PRINTERS OPTIMISTIC FOR RECORD PROFITS

The **VAN DORT PRINT SHOP** hums with activity as presses print advertisements, calenders, hand-bills, stationery, and other such typical projects of a small "job shop". Fair Grand Rapids has a growing printing industry which helps to spread the good word of our fine products and wares to buyers far and wide.

SANITARY PACKAGING

Industrious representatives of our

Grand Rapids was known worldwide for its artisan-quality furniture, and the business environment was populated by companies such as Stickley that would become—quite literally—household names. At its peak, the furniture industry supported 68 different manufacturers employing 13,000 skilled craftsmen and assemblers.

In the early 1900s, Grand Rapids Business College was located in the Norris Building at Lyon Street and Ottawa Avenue. It is the highlighted structure in the left of the photo. The former Grand Rapids City Hall occupies Lyon between Ottawa and Ionia. In the foreground is the Commerce Building, known then as the Furniture Temple.

Headed for Oblivion

In 1906, Parish made the curious decision to change the name of Grand Rapids Business College, once synonymous with success, to Valley City Commercial School. The following year he retired, appointing faculty member John F. Klingensmith to succeed him. Klingensmith later formed a partnership with fellow instructor Frank L. Brooks to jointly manage the school.

Details of the next few years are obscure and even conflicting. A *Grand Rapids Press* report about the leadership transition praised Klingensmith's "good work as [a] teacher in the bookkeeping department through many years of service" and described Brooks as "an active business man and an enthusiastic instructor." The article went on to claim that the school was experiencing strong enrollment and more employer demand for its graduates than it could supply.

The narrative was much different three years later. Covering Valley City's impending collapse in 1910, the *Grand Rapids Herald* stated that the operation had been "weathering rough seas for several years." Brooks himself told the newspaper that when he joined the faculty in 1906—shortly before Parish retired—the school was already operating in debt, implying that its diminishment began while still in Parish's hands.

The accelerating cadence of American commerce and industry and its booming office culture demanded more sophisticated support systems, both in technology and talent. While it was more important than ever that training keep pace, the school's leaders may have overlooked essential curriculum upgrades.

Meanwhile, the rise of a powerful competitor, McLachlan Business University (MBU), was encroaching on Valley City's influence. Founded in 1892 as Columbia Business College and later purchased by a talented and ambitious young businessman named Malcolm McLachlan, the school under his leadership had gained a regional reputation. The management troubles at Valley City allowed MBU to overtake its education rival.

J. F. Klingensmith

F. L. Brooks

Faltering Management. Partners John Klingensmith and Frank Brooks presided over a steady decline in the organization, despite at least two years of effort that included infusing the operational budget with personal assets. Although Brooks outlasted his partner, he was unable to reverse the college's downward slide.

A Young Teacher Takes Over

By 1910, Klingensmith had grown discouraged with the school's deepening deficits and turned the entire operation over to Brooks, who attempted to keep the school going on his own. But as the fall term got underway, tuition and students failed to materialize at the levels Brooks had hoped. Faculty, who had agreed to deferred salary arrangements pending the start of fall classes, remained unpaid.

Brooks gave up. Without bothering to notify staff, he prepared to shutter the operation. Valley City Commercial School was just hours away from closing its doors for good when a young, just-hired faculty member named Michael Edward Davenport stepped up.

Michael Edward Davenport

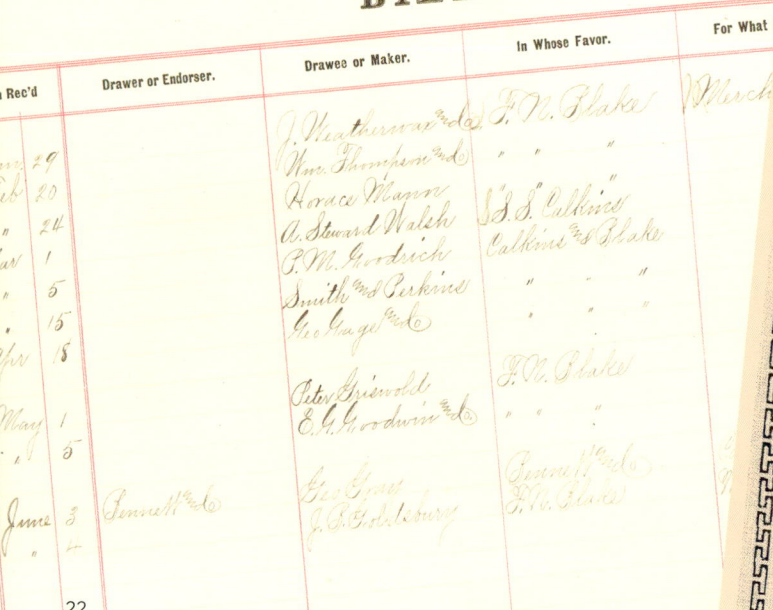

Early 20th century advertisements show a rapidly rising business and commercial culture. Many names, such as Herpolsheimer, would become iconic in the community.

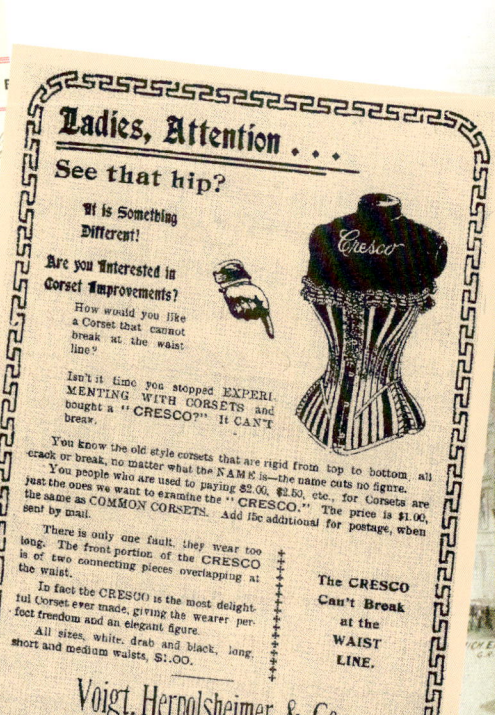

City on the Move. Grand Rapids at the turn of the 20th century bustled with streetcars, pedestrians, carriages, and commerce.

Photo courtesy Grand Rapids Public Library Historical Collection

○ *1888*
Swensberg retires and turns GRBC over to Aaron Parish.

○ *1892*
McLachlan Business University founded.

○ *1897*
Conrad Swensberg dies.

○ *1905*
Star Furniture Company founded in Zeeland, Michigan, (renamed Herman Miller Company in 1923).

○ *1907*
The name Valley City Commercial School replaces Grand Rapids Business College. Parish sells school to Frank Brooks and John Klingensmith.

○ *1910*
M.E. Davenport arrives from Carthage College in Illinois as a new faculty hire.

○ *1910*
Brooks prepares to go out of business; Davenport assumes management of school.

In the late 1800s John Robert Gregg brought his shorthand system to the United States from Great Britain, and by 1935 it was offered in 96 percent of public high schools teaching shorthand in this country.

Origins of the Independent Business School

Tutorial-based business instruction has been offered since colonial times, and in pre-Revolutionary America courses in bookkeeping first appeared in public academies. But until the early 19th century office skills, like other trades, were learned on the job. Students who wanted a commerce or business career left school to apprentice for employers.

The private business school is the oldest of vocational institutions. The first "commercial school" in institutional form is widely credited to Benjamin Franklin Foster, who founded Foster's Commercial Academy in Boston in 1832—long before vocational business education appeared in academic colleges or public secondary schools. Foster's program revolutionized the teaching of the skills once acquired only through private tutorials or the lengthy apprentice system.

Several other schools followed Foster's lead in the antebellum years. Expanding trade, manufacturing, commerce, finance, and production created an entirely new clerical profession to process the paperwork. "As enterprises grew in complexity, so did the office function," says author Judy Graf-Klein in *The Office Book*. By the 1850s there were 15 to 20 career-training schools in the country's major industrial centers. Duff's Mercantile College (known today as Everest Institute) in Pittsburgh, Pennsylvania, is credited as the oldest private career school in the nation.

Several developments in the second half of the 19th century catalyzed the need for qualified office employees and therefore institutions to train them. First was the invention of the typewriter. The possibilities offered by this remarkable instrument sparked the imaginations of educator/entrepreneurs who recognized its potential impact on office efficiency and expansion.

Other machines followed, including the dictaphone and the calculator. The development of shorthand coincided with the introduction of these labor-saving devices, and vocational schools filled with students seeking training in the new technologies.

Tools of the Trade. When the first commercial academies appeared in the early 19th century, penmanship was a fundamental skill, used not only for formal business correspondence, but also for everyday record-keeping in receipt books and accounting journals. Courses such as Zaner-Bloser and the Palmer Method emphasized whole-arm movements to produce the graceful strokes of ornamental penmanship. Calligraphy pens with replaceable tips were standard office supplies.

New methods also allowed women to enter the workforce in droves, usurping positions once held by men who were reluctant to abandon "longhand" procedures. The number of clerical workers in America increased tenfold between 1880 and 1920.

Nourished by this phenomenal growth, office-training schools of one kind of another were soon appearing across the country. In Michigan, nearly every city with a population of more than 3,000 could boast a business college. Most suffered a high mortality rate, but many solid organizations flourished for decades. Most evolved from sole proprietorships to corporations; from there, the majority made the transition from profit to nonprofit. Accreditation introduced uniform expectations for educational quality that encouraged the better institutions to prevail.

Whether known as a commercial academy, business institute, or college of commerce, independent business schools shared a singleness of purpose: teaching salient skills and offering job preparation in an expedient, effective manner.

Artisan handwriting remained into the early 20th century, but rapidly the mechanical replaced the manual. Beginning with the typewriter, labor-saving machines dramatically transformed the way work got done in the "modern" office. Calculating and adding machines, dictaphones, and duplicating equipment all were common in offices by the end of World War I.

"Make a living,
Make a life,
Make a contribution."

—M.E. Davenport

A NEW BEGINNING
1910–1959

Rescue and Reinvention

WHEN FRANK BROOKS ABRUPTLY DEPARTED, Davenport had been teaching at Valley City for barely three months. He'd come to Grand Rapids at the suggestion of Woodbridge N. Ferris, founder and president of Ferris Institute (now Ferris State University). Ferris mentored Davenport while he was a student, and later a teacher, in the institute's business department. The friendship profoundly influenced Davenport's own educational ideas; Ferris Institute had become known as the "opportunity school" by making a post-secondary education available to thousands who would not otherwise have access to a college experience. M.E. Davenport later modeled his own college on that concept.

Davenport accepted an instructor's position at Valley City Commercial College and relocated to Grand Rapids from Illinois, where he was on the faculty of Carthage College. He was expecting a thriving organization where he could develop his teaching skills; he was to be gravely disappointed.

Instead of a flourishing enterprise, Davenport discovered a school on the brink of collapse. The curriculum had been allowed to atrophy. Students and faculty were demoralized, and the school's ledgers were awash in red ink.

That Davenport was tempted to follow Brooks out the door was understandable. Certainly there were more promising—and less quixotic—opportunities for a talented young man of 25. Choosing instead to rebuild Valley City was the first of many decisions that would cast Davenport as an education pioneer.

GRAND RAPIDS BUSINESS INSTITUTE.

This school, which is one of the oldest in Michigan, was formerly known as the Grand Rapids Business University, and is now under new management, Mr. E. Davenport, a man of pleasant personality, great ability and thorough comprehension of the needs of young men and women, who wish to enter business life in some capacity or other. Many young men particularly, and young women, too, find it a pleasure as well as a help to enter some institute outside their home city. The Grand Rapids Business Institute, a very thorough, up-to-the-minute school for training young people in shorthand, bookkeeping, accounting, etc., offers great advantages in the shape of a most successful and thorough system and able teachers. The whole line of study is comparatively easy, but calls for close application and serious thought. When the course is mastered a position is found for the student if he or she is ready and qualified to fill one. Many Grand Rapids leading business men, bookkeepers and a few bankers are former students of the Grand Rapids Business Institute. The cost of tuition is very reasonable. Board and rooms for out-of-town students can be secured through Mr. Davenport. In this issue this school makes a free offer to industrious young people. It is a scholarship coupon. Look for it. The fall term opens Sept. 5, but students can enter later as well. Address Mr. E. Davenport, Grand Rapids Business Institute, Grand Rapids, Mich.

After graduating from Ferris Institute, M.E. Davenport (back row, in cap) taught at Carthage College in Illinois. Later he returned to Michigan and took over the failing Valley City Commercial College. Over the next several years, classrooms steadily refilled with students as a staff of four (including Davenport's new wife, Mabel Engle) worked to put the school back on its feet.

○ **1910**
M.E. Davenport partners with brother Forrest in the management of Grand Rapids Business Institute.

○ **1912**
The Metal Office Furniture Company (predecessor to Steelcase, Inc.) formed by Peter M. Wege and Walter Idema.

○ **1913**
Henry Ford introduces first true assembly line.

○ **1914**
Grand Rapids Junior College founded.

○ **1914**
M.E. Davenport marries Mabel Engle, who joins the faculty at GRBC.

○ **1914–18**
World War I

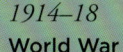

○ **1918**
L.V. Eberhard, at age 16, opens on Wealthy Street near Fuller Avenue the first store in what would become the first chain of locally owned groceries in Grand Rapids: Eberhard's. He also founded the grocery cooperative Grand Rapids Wholesale Grocery Company — now Spartan Stores, Inc.

○ **1918**
Grand Rapids Business Institute relocates to 215 Sheldon Boulevard and adds "Davenport" to its name.

Forrest Davenport

A Family Enterprise

In an effort to disassociate from the failed image of Valley City Commercial College, one of Davenport's first decisions was to restore the school's former name, Grand Rapids Business College. He then contacted his brother Forrest in Cleveland—who provided the only outside capital yet invested in the school—and together they began what amounted to a salvage operation. For $500 they purchased the college's assets, including fifty battered desks, its typewriters, and its debt. For the next five years the brothers ran the college as teachers, administrators, registrars, recruiters, and maintenance men. For their backbreaking effort they budgeted themselves a salary of ten dollars a week, provided there was that much cash available.

After conditions stabilized, Forrest returned to the family farm in Montcalm County, leaving M.E. and new wife, Mabel Engle Davenport, whom he'd married in 1914, to continue the rescue effort. Year by year, the couple worked the institute toward solvency, rebuilt the curriculum, increased enrollments, and regained for Grand Rapids Business College its lost esteem. Each taught a full load of classes in addition to their administrative responsibilities. "Individual instruction from the owners of the school" was promoted as a key attribute of a Davenport education. Students could enroll at any time and enter classes any Monday.

M. E. and Forrest Davenport are featured in a college brochure (left). It took the brothers five years to erase the school's operating deficit. They budgeted themselves weekly salaries of $10 apiece and had decided they couldn't afford wives until they were earning $15 per week.

M. E. Davenport

Mabel Engle Davenport

H. M. Heaney

A. E. Howell

Michael and Mabel Davenport hired two additional faculty members, H.M. Heaney and Arthur E. Howell. Mrs. Davenport managed the administrative office and taught shorthand and typing. M.E. Davenport, Heaney, and Howell taught bookkeeping, general business, mathematics, and banking.

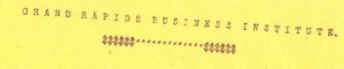

Combining a teaching workload with administrative duties, Mabel Engle Davenport (seated behind desk) registers a new student for classes.

What Goes Around: After leaving Davenport, instructor H.M. Heaney became a partner at Michigan Business and Normal College in Battle Creek. Later he returned to Grand Rapids to establish Heaney's Commercial College, in direct competition with his former employer. His enterprise was acquired by Davenport in 1944 and later sold. Under new ownership, Michigan Business College became Argubright Business College.

Arthur Howell, meanwhile, purchased Muskegon Business College and renamed it Howell's School of Business. Eventually the name was changed back to MBC, which became Baker College.

32   Davenport: Educating Across Three Centuries | A New Beginning

Legacies   Mabel Engle Davenport

After her daughter finished eighth grade—an educational crossroads in the early 20th century—Mabel Engle's mother offered her a choice: she could either continue her education through high school or get a job. Mabel decided to continue on to Grand Rapids Central High and enroll in the college preparatory department, after which she would pursue a teaching degree. At the age of 14, she had chosen her life's direction.

After graduating in 1909, Mabel enrolled in Kent County Normal, the local teacher training institution. She began her career as an elementary teacher at Townline School on South Division Avenue (still in existence as part of Kentwood Public Schools), and later at Michigan Oaks School.

She met Michael Edward Davenport through business acquaintances, and the couple married in 1914. She seemed a natural to assist her husband in the management of Grand Rapids Business Institute—her English and language skills were impeccable, and she was an excellent typist. To augment her talents, she enrolled in Gregg Shorthand School in Chicago, then returned to chair the college's shorthand department.

She became an early example of working mother, who helped set a struggling college on its feet, nurtured it to robust health despite multiple adversities, and served on its faculty—all while raising three children.

Her competency was not surprising to those who knew her. She had mastered self-sufficiency early from a strong mother who raised four children virtually alone. Mabel's father, William Engle—a talented carpenter but an absentee husband—was with the family only occasionally. The responsibility for raising two sons and two daughters fell squarely on his wife, Jennie Engle, whose expertise as a seamstress and a practicing midwife helped support the family.

Mabel's personality combined a Victorian refinement with modern sensibilities. Behind a demure exterior was an astute and decisive educator who easily matched her husband's capacity for prodigious work. She shared many affinities with "Ed": a love of students, a dedication to learning, and monumental energies.

She continued to work for Davenport-McLachlan until the early 1930s and served for years as patroness of Alpha Iota business sorority. She also managed the family farm in Crystal, Michigan, hiring help, keeping the books, and cooking for the hired hands.

Teaching contract terms in the early 20th century included, along with basic courses, "the subject of physiology and hygiene with special reference to the effects of alcoholic drinks and narcotics." In other words, lessons in reproductive health and substance abuse.

Becoming Davenport

By 1918, the student body had grown from 25 to 150, gaining on rival McLachlan Business University in both enrollment and prestige. The Davenports had added two additional faculty members and at last could abandon the dilapidated and rat-infested Norris Building the college had occupied since 1900. Davenport bought a building at 215 Sheldon Boulevard and turned it into a combination headquarters for the school and residence for his family. Shortly after, he renamed the college Davenport Business Institute (DBI).

With World War I at an end, America began re-channeling its energies into domestic priorities. A growing economy and a surge of returning veterans kept DBI's momentum strong.

By 1918, Davenport had found an ideal new home for both his school and his family at 215 Sheldon, a residence joined with a commercial building. A change in stationery shows that Davenport also had enough confidence in the school's momentum to put his own name on it. Eventually he dropped Grand Rapids Business Institute from the letterhead altogether and proceeded under the Davenport name alone.

34 Davenport: Educating Across Three Centuries | A New Beginning

WOODSTOCK

UNDERWOOD

L. C. SMITH

Keys to Success. The typewriter not only revolutionized the industrial-age office, it became the instrument that assisted women's entry into the workplace. Prior to the Civil War, only men held administrative positions. As that conflict emptied offices of their staffs, women stepped in to do the work. But they were immediately displaced after the war when servicemen returned to their civilian jobs.

The proliferation of the typewriter in the decades after its invention in 1876 changed everything. Many male office workers refused to give up longhand and adapt to the new technology. Having formed no attachments to previous practices, women were far more receptive to the transformation. When career schools began to offer typewriting classes, women enrolled in droves. Once trained, they "used their new skill to take over most of the clerical jobs once held by men." *(Source: Association of Independent Colleges and Schools)*

A typical typing lab, circa 1920.

The Confluence: Merging with McLachlan

Restored by the early 1920s into a viable enterprise, Davenport Business Institute was in a position to acquire its chief competitor. Malcolm McLachlan had died in 1918, and within a few years the school he founded was put up for sale by his widow. In 1924, Mr. Davenport merged the two operations to form the Davenport-McLachlan Institute (DMI), then moved his school into the McLachlan facilities on the fourth floor of the Putnam Building on Pearl Street. Davenport had always respected his former rival as a "keen teacher, splendid idealist, and practical businessman," which may have influenced his decision to retain the McLachlan name. Shortly after the consolidation, DMI was granted a state charter to operate as a Class "A" degree-granting institution. It also became fully accredited by the National Association of Accredited Commercial Schools.

The façade of the Putnam Building, home to the McLachlan Business University, can be seen on Pearl Street just east of McKay Tower. It was an era when interurban streetcars traveled city thoroughfares.

BUSINESS SCHOOLS WILL CONSOLIDATE

Union of Davenport Institute and McLachlan University Set for July 1.

WILL EXPAND COURSES

Consolidation of the Davenport Business institute and the McLachlan Business university as the Davenport-McLachlan institute will be effected July 1, it is announced by M. E. Davenport, president of the organization. Capitalization has been increased from $50,000 to $100,000, which puts the institution in class A for colleges with the power to confer degrees. Plans provide for establishment of a college preparatory course Sept. 1, 1924, and courses in public speaking, parliamentary law, accounting, income tax and secretarial work, all leading to college degrees. A course in music will be under the direction of Reese Veatch.

The McLachlan university was acquired by the Davenport Business institute several months ago, the consideration being $35,000. The two schools have been operated separately and, it is stated, will so continue for some time, when it is planned to house the entire institute in a new college building, provided either by enlarging the pres-

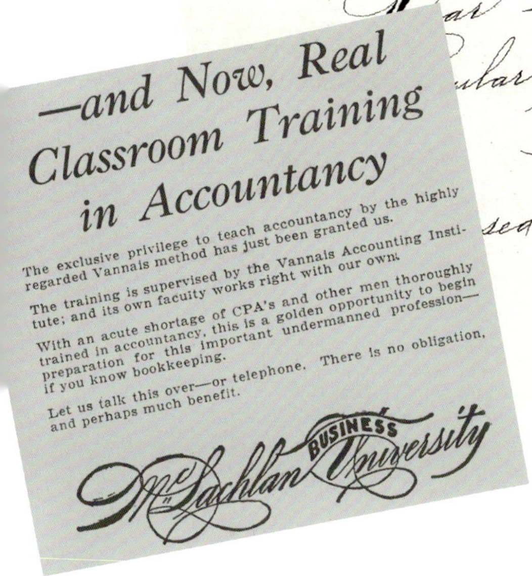

—and Now, Real Classroom Training in Accountancy

The exclusive privilege to teach accountancy by the highly regarded Vannais method has just been granted us.

The training is supervised by the Vannais Accounting Institute; and its own faculty works right with our own.

With an acute shortage of CPA's and other men thoroughly trained in accountancy, this is a golden opportunity to begin preparation for this important undermanned profession—if you know bookkeeping.

Let us talk this over—or telephone. There is no obligation, and perhaps much benefit.

McLachlan Business University

The affiliation with McLachlan—at the time still enjoying a reputation as one of America's leading business schools—was tremendously beneficial to Davenport. In fact, "Macs", as it was called, was so well-regarded that the college maintained the Davenport-McLachlan hyphenation for 25 years.

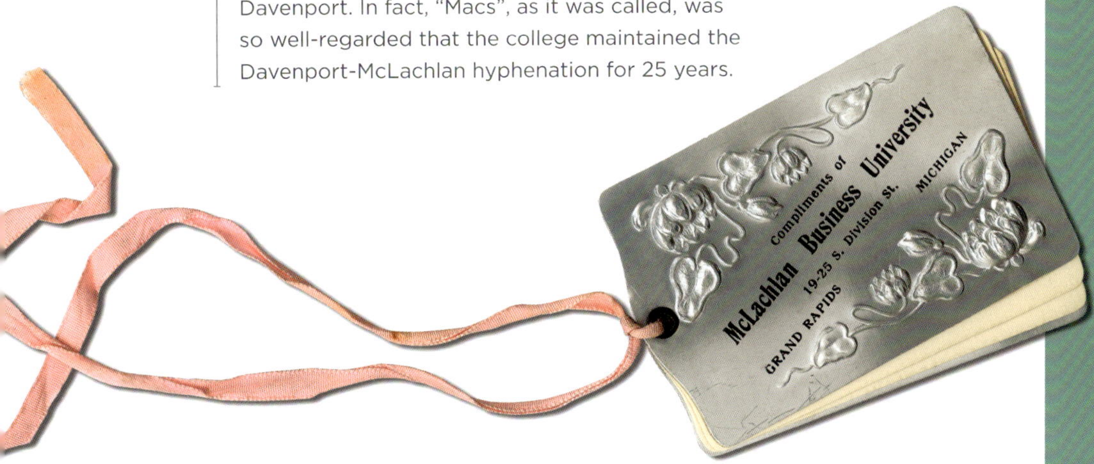

"...keen teacher, splendid idealist, and practical businessman."

– M.E. Davenport referring to Malcolm McLachlan

McLachlan Business University

Enrollment swelled throughout the 1920s, and school social functions like this formal banquet enjoyed large student turnouts.

"We saw why men failed and why they succeeded, and we set out to develop a school that would give to modern business the class of business men and business women it needed."

- M.E. Davenport

An Emerging Educational Mission:
Make a Living, Make a Life, Make a Contribution

With the school stabilized and prospering, M.E. Davenport was free to implement some of his educational visions. The first of the major changes under the merged Davenport-McLachlan organization was a dramatically revised curriculum. Except for languages, business subjects and skills had been taught almost exclusively for nearly 60 years. After the merger, Davenport began supplementing these courses with humanities and electives that more closely resembled a traditional liberal arts education—a move that has remained part of the Davenport educational model ever since.

Davenport sought to fill a niche he saw in the college market: a synthesis of theory and pragmatism. This was not the prevailing orthodoxy of the time; "classical" education was still the norm, with traditional and vocational education operating in distinctly separate spheres. Davenport soon earned a reputation as a groundbreaker, developing programs of "practical education" that combined humanities with studies that prepared the student for specific career opportunities. His objective was to produce graduates with employable skills who also possessed the educational background to grow into positions of responsibility and civic engagement. From this philosophy came the motto that has guided the institution ever since: "Make a Living, Make a Life, Make a Contribution."

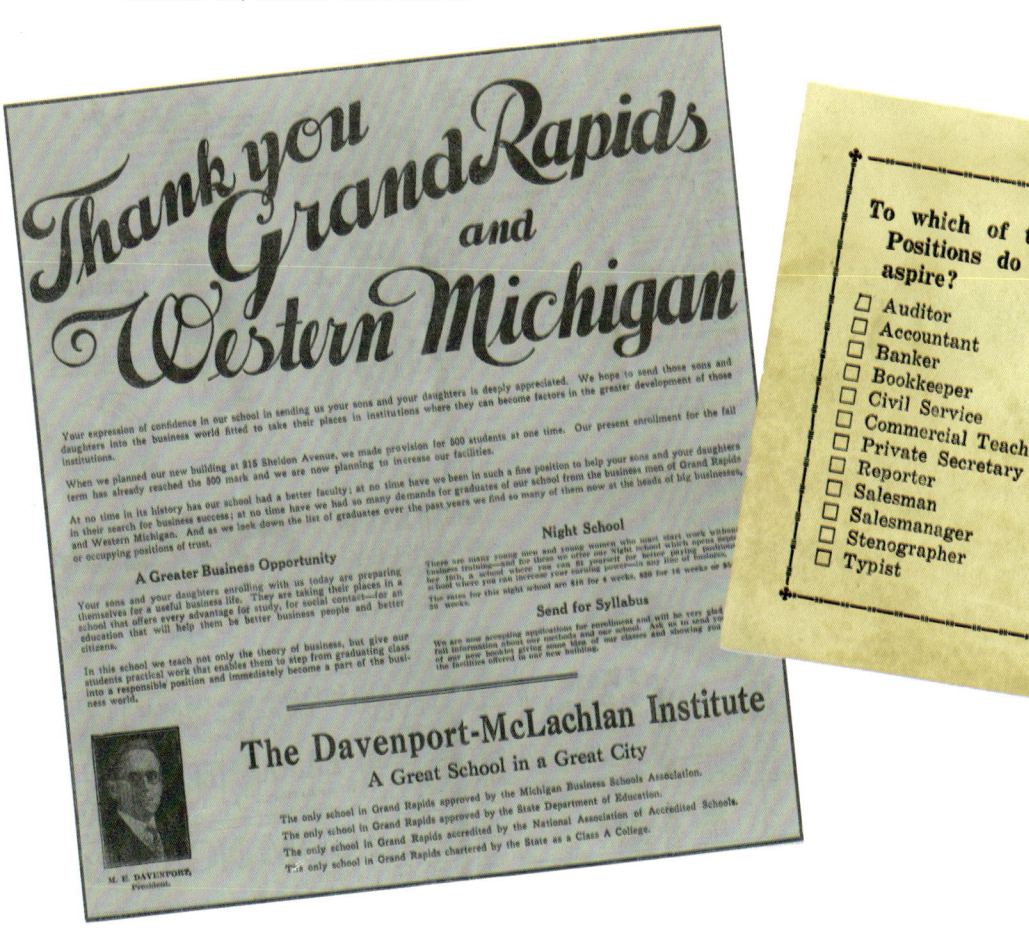

1924
Davenport Business Institute merges with McLachlan Business University to become Davenport-McLachlan Institute. School operates in the Putnam Building on Pearl Street.

1928
DMI moves into its first newly-built facility located at the original site of the Davenport Business Institute at 215 Sheldon.

1928
Kendall Memorial School (later Kendall College of Art & Design) founded.

1929
Stock market crash triggers the Great Depression.

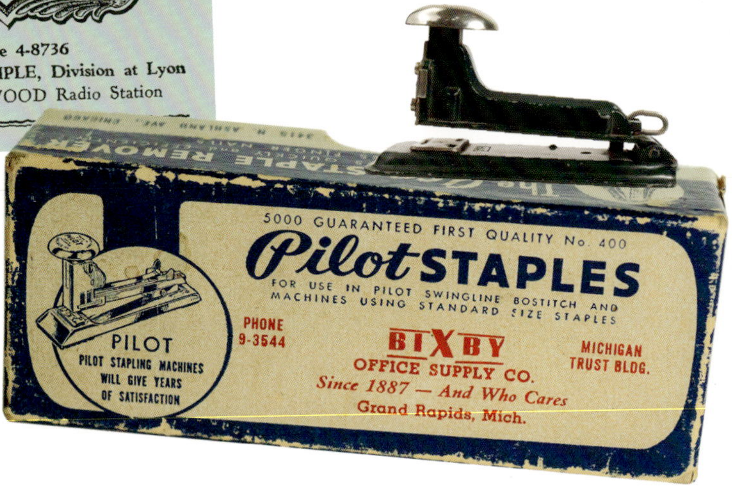

The Emblem of the Efficient School

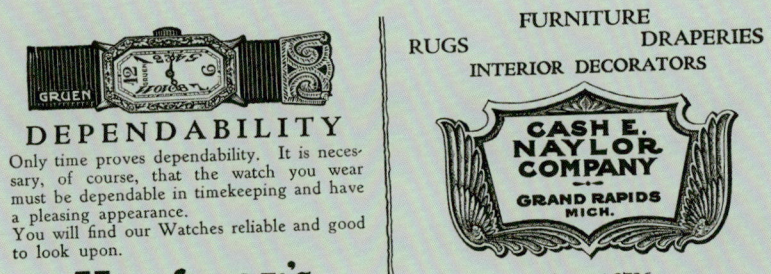

ACCREDITED NATIONAL ASSOCIATION OF COMMERCIAL SCHOOLS

Seal of Approval. Among the first of DMI's institutional endorsements was certification by the National Association of Accredited Commercial Schools (left). NAACS was one of the first national accrediting agencies for higher education and a forerunner of the current Association of Independent Colleges and Schools. (Below) The student body gathers for a group photo. Double desks allowed instructors to work alongside students.

1928

150 ENROLLMENT

10 Faculty/Administration

TUITION $270 One Year $500 Two Years

LOCATION 215 Sheldon Boulevard SE

CLASSES & PROGRAMS
Accountancy and Business Administration, Secretarial Science, General Business and Advertising, Gregg Shorthand and Touch Typewriting, Civil Service, Commercial Teaching, and Music: Vocal and Instrumental

40   Davenport: Educating Across Three Centuries | A New Beginning

The main reception area (above) welcomed students into an elegant atmosphere, while the large gymnasium did double duty as the venue for athletics and student assemblies. Programs were held once a week, typically featuring a speaker, student musical, or performing arts group.

Davenport's First New Building

With the institute growing in popularity, it wasn't long before the Putnam Building was filled to capacity. In 1928, plans were unveiled for the construction of a new building at 215 Sheldon on the site of the college's former headquarters, which had been torn down in the interim.

Beautifully furnished and appointed, the new facility featured some of the most progressive architecture and amenities then found in business schools, including a two-story gymnasium (complete with locker rooms), a library, music room, and sophisticated classroom equipment.

Tradition blended with innovation as DMI anticipated a vigorous new cycle of growth. Instead, the college found itself facing its toughest challenges yet, as back-to-back national crises threatened the school's survival.

Sheldon Reprised. The first facility built exclusively for Davenport-McLachlan, the new building at 215 Sheldon replaced the original building at the same address.

"Those whose ambition and vision do not carry them beyond the average will not appreciate the quality of training given here…nor will they be especially benefited by it." —From DMI marketing brochure

Whether depicting a 'college in the clouds' or students scanning a horizon of opportunity, Davenport-McLachlan brochures depicted a promising future. Language in school brochures stated plainly: "Those whose ambition and vision do not carry them beyond the average will not appreciate the quality of training given here…nor will they be especially benefited by it."

A GROUP OF STUDENTS of the DAVENPORT-McLACHLAN INSTITUTE.
VISITING LEADING BUSINESS OFFICES AND PLANTS

(Above) Exposure to the corporate community through field trips was common even in the early DMI days. (Right) Illustrations by student Virginia Holloway appear inside an invitation to a commencement event.

Annual Commencement Banquet
1930-1931
Davenport-McLachlan Institute
Grand Rapids, Michigan

SUCCESS

Davenport: Educating Across Three Centuries | A New Beginning   43

Student Life

DMI became one of the first institutions of its type to offer its students a full "college experience" that included clubs and organizations, fraternities and sororities, and intramural athletics.

Curriculum electives in music and theatre provided an alternative to the more linear disciplines of business. Men's and women's choral groups enjoyed enthusiastic participation. Instrumentalists performed in the Davenport Orchestra, which gave it own concerts and recitals and provided the score for plays, dances, and other college programs. A derivative, the pep band, played at athletic events through the 1970s.

Greek life began on the Davenport-McLachlan campus in the 1930s, expanded to the University of Grand Rapids (UGR) campus, and thrived for many decades. Along with several scholastic, social, and professional houses, two main business societies—Alpha Iota for women and Phi Theta Pi for men—pledged hundreds of members over the years. Campus activity owed much to the Greeks, who spearheaded many charitable and civic efforts along with social activities. Frequent dances, student mixers, and other functions helped keep DMI calendars full.

Acting Out. In addition to performing on its home stage at 215 Sheldon, the DMI Players theatre company had its own touring company, which traveled throughout Michigan.

Latest Editions. Davenport has had a campus news publication in various formats since the late 1920s. Published originally in booklet form, coverage of school news and events shared space with athletic schedules, social announcements—and some gossip. *Students' Life* went by various titles over the years and earned awards as the best two-year college newspaper in Michigan.

Campus Sports: 1920s

Sustaining a credible athletic program has typically been difficult for specialized colleges, including those with a vocational emphasis like Davenport. With the best talent usually inclined toward large universities and four-year colleges, acquiring teams was a year-by-year affair. Many school sports programs had sporadic existences, sometimes falling into dormancy for periods of time (particularly during the wars), before making comebacks. Despite the limitations, Davenport was well-represented in intercollegiate athletics from the end of the 1920s through the 1970s.

The 1928 basketball team, organized and coached by faculty member Cliff Wonders, introduced organized athletics at Davenport-McLachlan. Initially the team played wherever they could find opponents, in city recreational or church leagues. World War II and the Korean War would force prolonged time-outs for the program.

More challenging competition came in the late 1950s, when Davenport joined the Michigan Business Schools League. Typically Davenport dominated, earning many conference championships. Eventually they adopted "Panthers" as their mascot and scarlet and silver as the school colors.

> The first Davenport basketball team made its debut in 1928 and introduced organized athletics at the school. Although the team had a stop-start existence for the next 50 years, basketball always served as the focal point for campus sports through the 1970s.

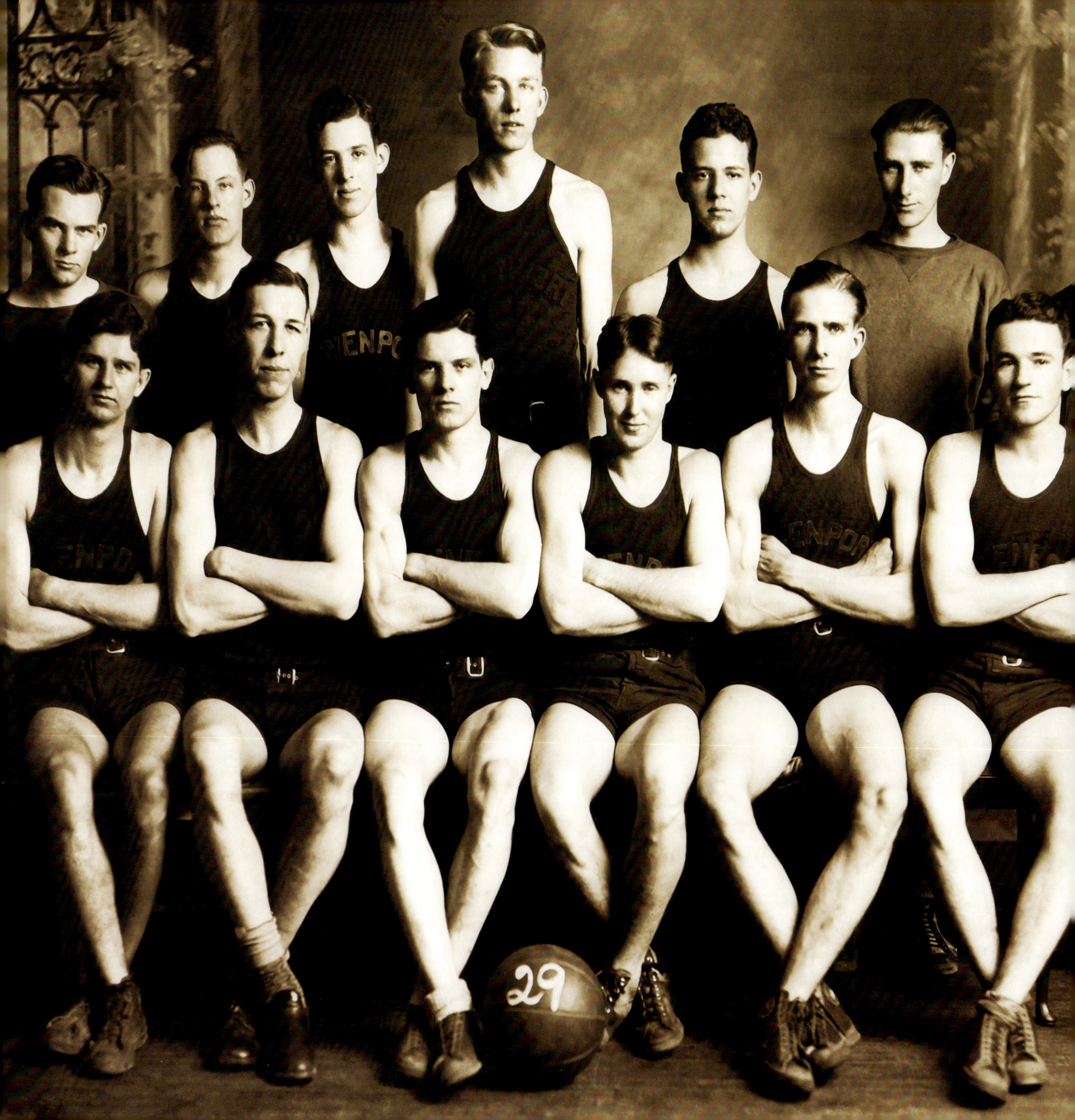
29

DAVENPORT McLACHLAN INSTITUTE

Instrumental in their Education. Long before the days of organized financial aid, Davenport leaders proved adaptive—and creative—in devising their own methods of "tuition assistance." Among the more famous examples is the violin accepted as collateral for classes. In another instance, student Carol Greene's father organized and directed Davenport's first school orchestra in exchange for his daughter's tuition.

Even more unconventional was the bargain struck between the school and a farmer from Luther, Michigan, who offered one of his dairy cows in lieu of payment for his daughter's classes. Mr. Davenport, who ran a farm of his own, considered it a fair deal.

DMI and the Depression

The collapse of Wall Street in October of 1929 launched the nation into unprecedented economic calamity, a hardship multiplied in sectors like higher education. With millions struggling merely to put food on the table, the pursuit of a post-secondary diploma suddenly became a highly discretionary, as well as deferrable, investment.

To be a business training institution when hundreds of enterprises were failing seemed, on the surface at least, the ultimate paradox. Still, Davenport-McLachlan managed to turn harsh irony into advantage. More than ever, "practical education" was demonstrating its utility, since employable skills helped graduates land what few jobs there were. DMI's civil service courses, promoted as "useful even in times of high unemployment," offered concentrated training sessions that prepared graduates for quick entry into government service.

As the social welfare programs of the New Deal expanded, the demand for office skills in newly created federal bureaus escalated: Davenport-McLachlan helped hundreds qualify for these openings. Classes also filled with liberal arts graduates from other colleges, who suddenly found their credentials weren't suited to the barren Depression-era job market.

Davenport staff implemented a variety of financing maneuvers to keep the college open and tuition affordable. Students were allowed to pay what they could on a weekly basis, or "run a tab" and defer their tuition altogether until times improved. Mr. Davenport often had to pool what little tuition they did receive, pay the bills, and use what was left over to pay teachers and staff. More often than not, employees took home as little as ten dollars a week.

"The tuition in 1930 was $25 per month. Because of such an enormous price, I worked day and night and finished a two-year course in seven months. I lived and slept in a single bedroom, rented from a family on Griggs Street. Board and room was $7 dollars per week, and I sent my laundry to my mother in Manistee by parcel post for about 28 cents each way."

—Irving E. White, 1930

The DMI faculty and administration in the 1930s. Some individuals, such as Cliff Wonders (back row, second from right) and Erma Gould (seated, second from left) would serve the school for decades.

As the economy slowly recovered, DMI was one of the few institutions of its kind to survive the devastations of the 1930s. In doing so, the college's methods had merited a second look. Lessons taught by the Depression were making fissures in the bedrock of educational theory and practice. While the academic community hardly rushed to embrace "practical education," no longer could it categorically dismiss its value. But even as others remained circumspect, M.E. Davenport was, characteristically, moving forward.

"We honor this institution because it has inaugurated a new idea in education. We are proud of it because it is fostering in our youth the finest ideals and aspirations of life." —UGR yearbook dedication, 1940

UNIVERSITY OF GRAND RAPIDS
1935–1945

"The New Education"

In retrospect, it seemed an unlikely time to introduce the most ambitious of M.E. Davenport's projects: the city's first nondenominational four-year college. But school leaders saw a niche in the local educational landscape; undeterred by the Great Depression, they set out to fill it.

In 1935 Davenport met with Tyrus R. Wessell and Clifton C. Wonders, his treasurer and vice president. The three had been discussing the need for a four-year institution in Grand Rapids, one that would distinguish itself from others already established in the area. Grand Valley State University was still decades from conception, and all other public bachelor-degree granting colleges were in other cities. The only local school granting bachelor's degrees was Calvin College, which was affiliated with the Christian Reformed Church. Davenport favored a nondenominational operation, with "a more practical kind of education than given in the traditional college." The school Davenport had in mind not only would be independent, but would combine liberal arts instruction with specific professional training through the senior year. At the time such a hybrid was unprecedented: traditional colleges had historically emphasized the liberal arts, while for-profit business and technical schools focused almost exclusively on employment skills.

The new institution was to become a wider forum for Davenport's educational passions, expanding principles that had been operating successfully at Davenport-McLachlan Institute for years. Students would take traditional college courses in the sciences and humanities but would also receive specialized business and career training that would equip them for employment upon graduation. Additionally, Davenport had a higher purpose in mind: "It is the aim of the founders," he said in announcing plans for the Grand Rapids College of Applied Science (later changed to the University of Grand Rapids), "to make the college a civic enterprise which will contribute untold cultural values to the city."

Dr. Paul F. Voelker, former superintendent of public instruction for the state of Michigan and past president of both Battle Creek and Olivet Colleges, was selected to help plan and ultimately lead the University of Grand Rapids.

Chosen to help plan and ultimately lead the new institution was Dr. Paul F. Voelker, former superintendent of public instruction for the state of Michigan and past president of both Battle Creek and Olivet Colleges. Together, Davenport and Voelker designed a progressive but unorthodox prospectus modeled on education philosopher John Dewey's contention that education was not only preparation for life, but was actually life itself. Their "modern methods of education" favored individual abilities and performance standards over a traditional grading system. Teachers were to motivate students intrinsically rather than make "invidious comparisons" of students with each other.

In a later generation these ideas would not be considered radical, but they were clearly out of step with higher education at the time. State regulators and regional accrediting bodies were not favorably inclined toward a small upstart school calling itself a university and operating outside the bounds of academic doctrine. Despite a promising start and growing popularity through its brief lifespan, resistance from the educational establishment—along with mistakes from UGR's own leadership—would contribute to the university's eventual undoing.

"The Liberal Arts School will retain its rightful place in the University of Grand Rapids. Cultural advantages such as better speech, morals, manners, and tastes, tend to result from the pursuit of the liberal arts. Merely making a living doesn't make one a good citizen." —M.E. Davenport

UNIVERSITY OF GRAND RAPIDS

1936
Grand Rapids College of Applied Science (GRCAS) established by M.E. Davenport and Dr. Paul Voelker.

1939
GRCAS acquires the Lowe Estate on Robinson Road for its new campus; changes name to University of Grand Rapids.

1939
Reformed Bible Institute (Kuyper College) established.

1939
World War II begins in Europe.

1941
Pearl Harbor attacked by the Japanese; United States enters World War II.

"The new college will recognize that times and conditions have changed and that the old order, as we have known it, will not return."

—Dr. Paul F. Voelker

MAKE A LIVING — MAKE A LIFE — MAKE A CONTRIBUTION

CARDINAL POINTS IN THE NEW EDUCATION

1. The new education begins with the assumption that every student will require guidance in the discovery of his own capacities and aptitudes, and in the planning of his life.
2. The new education aims to prepare each individual for the specific job for which he is by nature best endowed and qualified.
3. The new education aims to adjust the curriculum to the student, instead of attempting to adjust the student to the curriculum.
4. The new education does not emphasize grades, marks, and honor points, on the theory that true interest in the work the student is doing will furnish the real motivation.
5. The new education includes in the student's program, those activities which serve his needs for personal development.
6. The new education envisions educational opportunity for all the people, and not for a privileged few only.
7. The new education is a process which continues throughout the entire life of the individual, from the cradle to the grave. It will serve the adult as well as the youth.
8. The new education aims to develop in each student the capacity for choosing — choosing his friends, his books, his activities, his college, his church, his philosophy, his mate, his career.

Opening Day

By the summer of 1936, all was prepared for a September opening of the Grand Rapids College of Applied Science (GRCAS)—one of four nonpublic institutions of higher learning to be opened in Michigan during the years immediately preceding World War II.

From facilities shared with Davenport-McLachlan Institute, a faculty of six taught courses in law, accounting, business math, psychology, business English, public speaking, foreign languages, and industrial chemistry. The college planned to grant baccalaureate degrees in pharmacy, law, medical technology, and practical arts, with special attention devoted to two major schools, Business Administration and Pharmacy. The school's charter also permitted post-graduate degrees.

Entrance requirements were comparable to those of other four-year colleges, if somewhat more flexible. High school graduates who had successfully completed twelfth grade were accepted. Others with less formal schooling were sometimes admitted by special permission or by passing entrance exams designed by GRCAS. Advanced abilities as well as special needs were individually accommodated. "Each student is treated as an individual," said a college bulletin, "rather than as a number or a name."

In the media, the Grand Rapids College of Applied Science was skeptically received. While notices of other college openings appeared frequently in the local papers, GRCAS was barely mentioned. What coverage it did receive was generally unfavorable, since prevailing opinion insisted that a college was not "legitimate" unless it offered classical courses. Critics apparently overlooked the fact that the college endorsed absolutely the value of traditional education; but its operating philosophy was designed around a more empirical approach.

Even the school's name became a target for criticism. The institution was originally to be called Grand Rapids City College, but the Grand Rapids Board of Education objected. Board members, perhaps troubled by the prospect of a competing college in their midst, insisted that Grand Rapids Junior College should have first choice of that name should it ever become a four-year institution. Davenport agreed to consider other options.

A chilly reception apparently did not spoil the college's debut nor impede its progress. In 1936, the first full year of operation, 69 students enrolled. By the following fall, that figure had more than doubled to 168.

Nocturne. UGR students serenade the holidays in front of a giant evergreen in Veterans Park.

Learning Lab. Students observe a chemistry experiment in the "Manufacturer's Lab."

UNIVERSITY OF GRAND RAPIDS

UNIVERSITY OF GRAND RAPIDS

Against the Tide

Despite its early popularity, the institution faced challenges from every direction throughout its existence. Accreditation was a chief impasse. When an evaluating committee from the Michigan Association of North Central Colleges (MANCC) paid its first visit to the school in 1936, its members were collectively unimpressed. Among the objections noted in their report: an inadequate library; difficulty in transferring credits; the 40-minute class periods were too brief; course credit seemed exaggerated in comparison to other colleges; and students who hadn't done particularly well in high school were receiving unusually high marks in their college work. They also opposed a "crossover" arrangement between UGR and Davenport-McLachlan that allowed students from one institution to take evening courses at the other at no extra charge. Students participating in this arrangement were counted in the enrollment figures of both schools, a practice MANCC found unacceptable.

The follow-up visit two years later went no better. Included in files from that visit were letters from other colleges regarding their willingness to accept UGR credits in transfer. Of the dozen institutions polled, seven—including the University of Michigan, Wayne State University, Kalamazoo College, Hope College, and Calvin College—refused to recognize UGR coursework. Accreditation was denied.

Undaunted, President Voelker promoted the university as a laboratory for cutting-edge practices. "There have been more changes in colleges in the past few months than in any period in the history of educational institutions," he stated in the college newspaper. "We at the university are proud to say that all those changes have been inaugurated here."

"There have been more changes in colleges in the past few months than in any period in the history of educational institutions, and we at the university are proud to say that all those changes have been inaugurated here."

—Paul F. Voelker

Sharing Voelker's confidence that their ideals would eventually prevail, school officials proceeded with ambitious development plans. In the summer of 1939 they purchased the Edward Lowe estate, a wooded 67-acre property on Robinson Road on the eastern outskirts of the city. Capitulating to the concerns about its name, university leaders announced that the College of Applied Science would henceforth be known as the University of Grand Rapids.

Enrollment continued to climb until registrations topped 400 by 1940. The "Knowledge for Use" concept had tapped into a responsive audience that appreciated the business/liberal arts fusion. The pharmacy department developed rapidly into the best in the state as faculty from Ferris Institute's School of Pharmacology were recruited. The School of Business Administration was similarly successful. By the 1942-43 school year, the university also had professional schools in accounting and finance, engineering, forestry, journalism, industrial chemistry, medical technology, music, secretarial science, and social service. Sororities and fraternities, clubs, and extracurricular activities thrived on campus. Athletic teams, including baseball, tennis, and golf, played a regular intercollegiate circuit. A graduate school specializing in teaching and divinity studies was announced. It appeared that the university would rise above the issues cited by MANCC and others.

"...education is not only preparation for life, but is actually life itself."

—Education Philosopher John Dewey

"Lancers" was chosen as the school mascot, while the UGR colors—scarlet and silver—would be revived years later as the official colors of the Davenport College "Panthers."

U. OF G. R. TO HAVE ITS LARGEST CLASS

Graduation Exercises Take Place on Friday

University of Grand Rapids will graduate the largest class of its history, 47, at commencement exercises of the university and Davenport-McLachlan institute Friday evening at 8 o'clock at 215 Sheldon ave., SE. The public is invited to the commencement; there is no admission charge.

The graduating class includes a class of 24 who will receive a B. S. in pharmacy, 10 who will receive master's degrees, other bachelor's degrees in chemistry, business administration, medical technicians' degrees and liberal arts and one Ph. D., awarded on a thesis written for the school here and credits taken in other universities.

Dr. Paul F. Voelker, president of the University of Grand Rapids, will present the diplomas to the graduates of this institution and M. E. Davenport, president of Davenport-McLachlan institute and vice president of the university, will present the diplomas to the institute graduates, who number 35 from the two-year course and nine in business administration. A number of students in the institute who have completed the two-year course this year have elected to remain two years more, transferring to the four-year secretarial course and so are not graduating at this time.

Dr. Dunning Speaker

Dr. John W. Dunning, president of Alma college, will give the commencement address. The Rev. Edward A. Mohns, pastor of Westminster Presbyterian church, will give the invocation and benediction.

UNIVERSITY OF GRAND RAPIDS

UNIVERSITY OF GRAND RAPIDS

1940

400 ENROLLMENT

20 Faculty/Administration

DEGREES & PROGRAMS
Business Administration
Journalism
Forestry
Pharmacy
Medical Technology
Industrial Chemistry

TUITION $135 Per Semester

LOCATION 1607 Robinson Rd.

Ivy-Covered Halls. Called Holmdene in reference to the stately Holm oaks throughout the property, the Lowe Estate included magnificent gardens and several structures across nearly 70 acres. Centerpiece of the UGR campus was the 22-room main residence, which became an administration and classroom building.

Twist of Fate. In 1935, both Davenport and Catholic Junior College (CJC), later Aquinas College, were interested in the Lowe estate for campus expansion. CJC was uncomfortable with the asking price, but Davenport was able to secure funds for the purchase. According to folklore, CJC academic dean Sister Mildred Hawkins secretly buried religious medals somewhere on campus and asked for prayers of special intention. Perhaps the appeals worked, as UGR later sold the property to Aquinas to establish its four-year divisions.

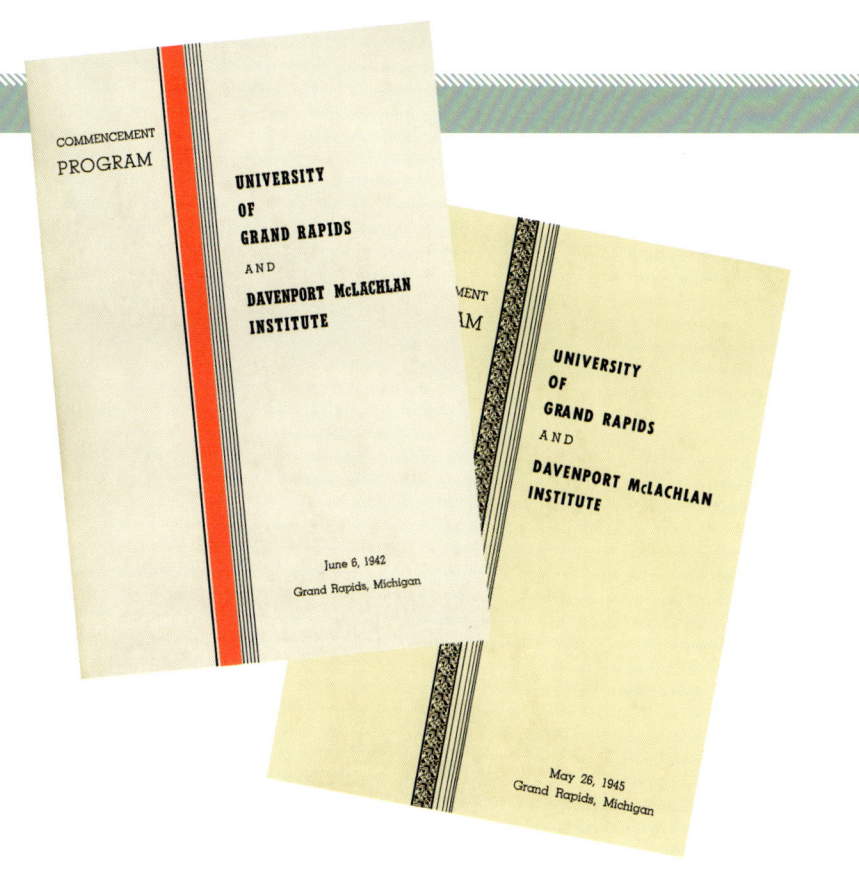

(Above) UGR commencement programs. The school graduated eight classes from 1938 to 1945. (Below) Like the other Davenport schools, UGR was chartered as a proprietary for-profit enterprise. Stock certificates were issued to its principals.

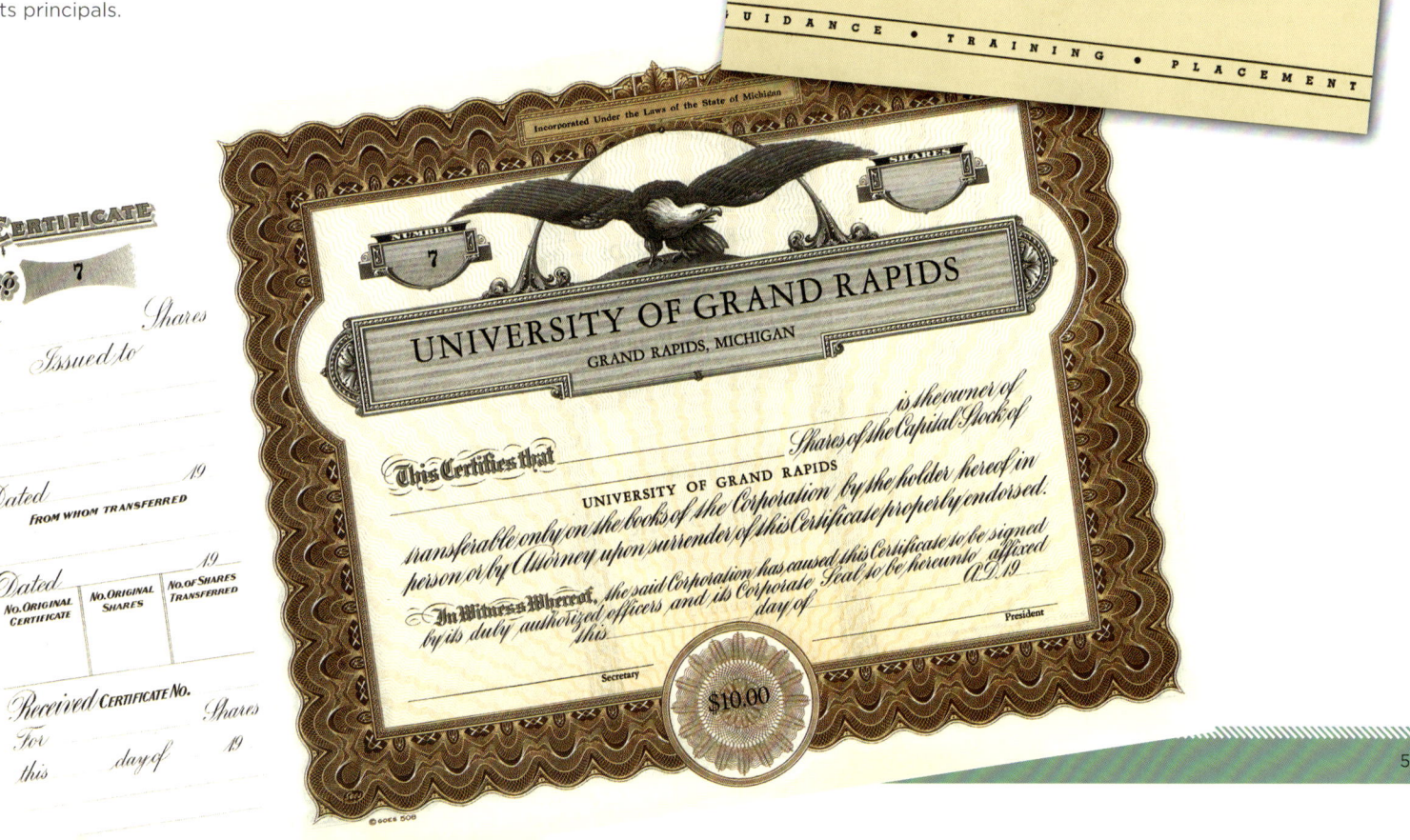

WHAT YOU MAY EXPECT

OCCUPATION	Training Time Required	Approximate Cost of Training	Average Yearly Earnings
Doctor	7 years	$7,000.00	$4,850.00
Lawyer	5 years	4,000.00	4,730.00
Public Accountant	4 years	2,400.00	4,700.00
Engineer	5 years	3,500.00	4,410.00
Sales Manager	4 years	1,800.00	4,250.00
Dentist	5 years	4,000.00	4,170.00
Architect	4 years	2,800.00	3,820.00
Store Manager	4 years	1,800.00	3,600.00
College Teacher	7 years	5,600.00	3,050.00
Advertising Manager	4 years	2,400.00	2,600.00
Industrial Chemist	4 years	2,400.00	2,520.00
Pharmacist	4 years	2,400.00	2,200.00
Journalist	4 years	2,400.00	2,120.00
Personnel Director	5 years	1,800.00	2,100.00
Minister	1½ years	2,500.00	1,980.00
Private Secretary	4 years	750.00	1,800.00
Social Worker	1½ years	2,000.00	1,650.00
Civil Service	2 years	750.00	1,620.00
Medical Technician	4 years	1,000.00	1,550.00
Public School Teacher	4 years	2,000.00	1,350.00
Nurse	1 year	1,500.00	1,310.00
Bookkeeper	1 year	500.00	1,200.00
Stenographer	6 months	500.00	1,160.00
Office Clerk	6 months	200.00	780.00
Sales Clerk		200.00	624.00
Unskilled Laborer			795.00
Farmer			580.00
Farm Labor			485.00

The foregoing statistics are taken, in part, from the following sources: Columbia University Survey, American Bankers Association, and Government Records. The element of training time is fairly well established, but the exact training cost will vary with the educational institution you attend.

GUIDANCE • TRAINING • PLACEMENT

UNIVERSITY OF GRAND RAPIDS

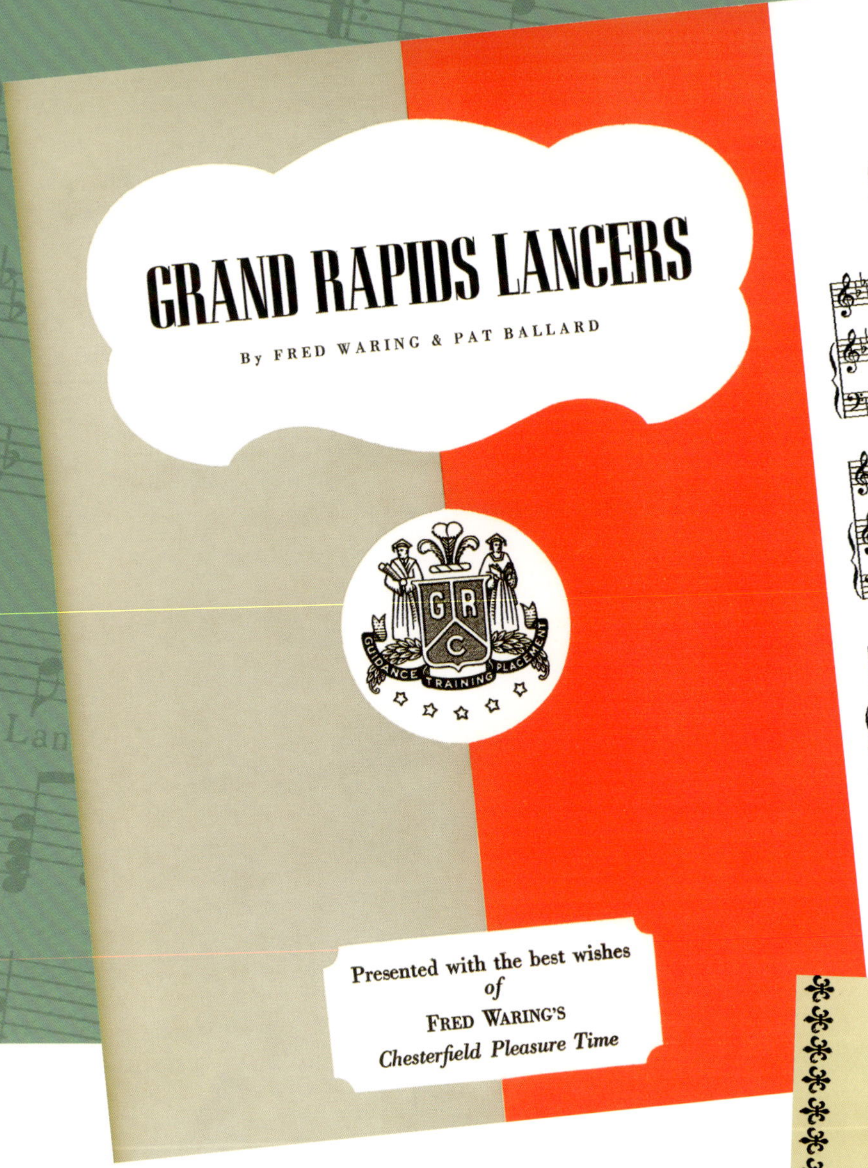

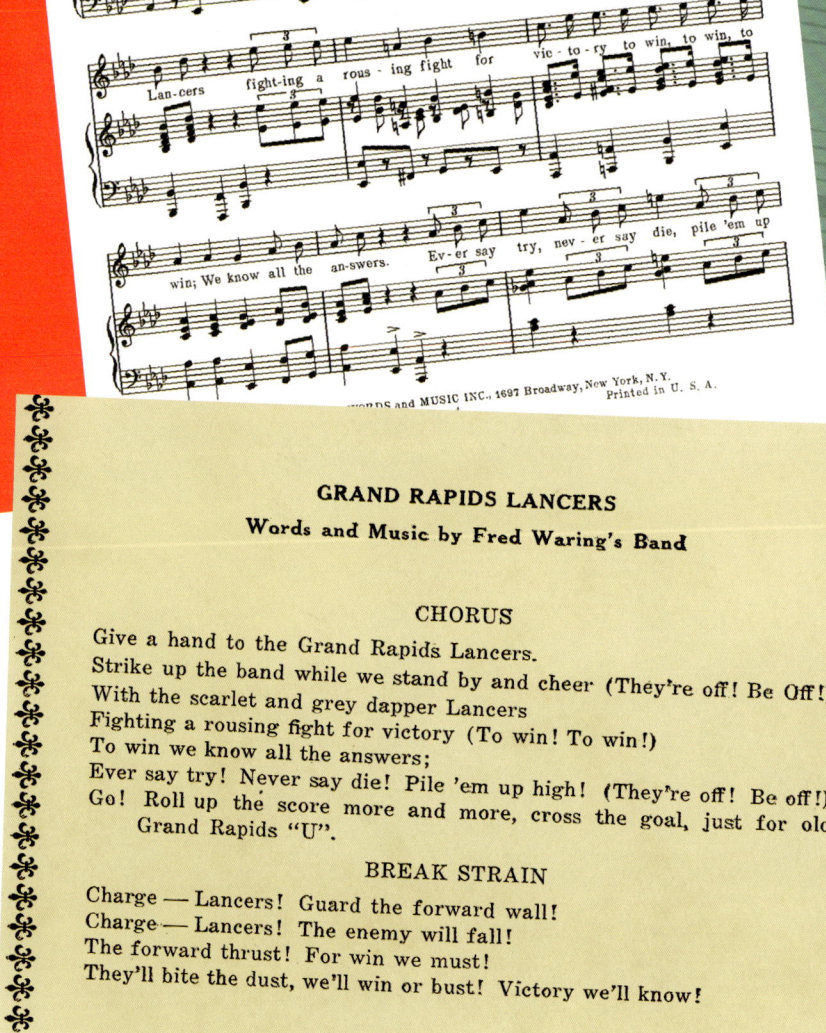

UNIVERSITY OF GRAND RAPIDS

Nationwide Audience. The Grand Rapids Lancers fight song was written by Fred Waring and Pat Ballard in 1939. Waring was a popular band leader of the day, and his NBC radio program, the Chesterfield Pleasure Hour, was heard weekly by as many as 20 million listeners. The anthem to the 'scarlet and gray dapper Lancers' was introduced on the program to coincide with UGR's 1939 homecoming game.

GRAND RAPIDS LANCERS
Words and Music by Fred Waring's Band

CHORUS
Give a hand to the Grand Rapids Lancers.
Strike up the band while we stand by and cheer (They're off! Be Off!)
With the scarlet and grey dapper Lancers
Fighting a rousing fight for victory (To win! To win!)
To win we know all the answers;
Ever say try! Never say die! Pile 'em up high! (They're off! Be off!)
Go! Roll up the score more and more, cross the goal, just for old Grand Rapids "U".

BREAK STRAIN
Charge — Lancers! Guard the forward wall!
Charge — Lancers! The enemy will fall!
The forward thrust! For win we must!
They'll bite the dust, we'll win or bust! Victory we'll know!

Lancer Loyalty. Even in its short history, UGR managed to generate deep attachment from its alumni, who gathered for an all-class reunion in the 1980s. (Below) UGR yearbook, *The Aeonian*.

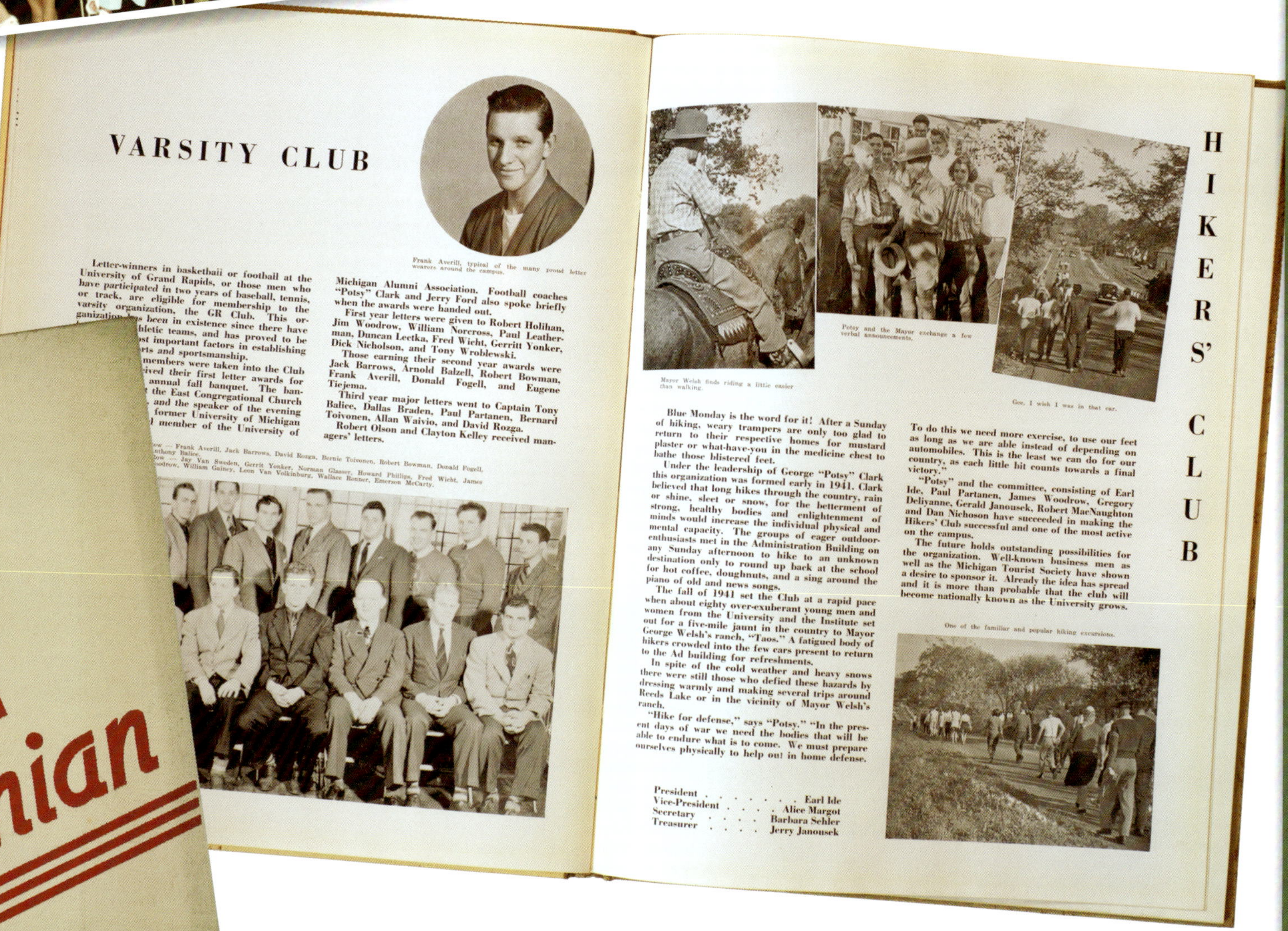

UNIVERSITY OF GRAND RAPIDS

VARSITY CLUB

Frank Averill, typical of the many proud letter wearers around the campus.

Letter-winners in basketball or football at the University of Grand Rapids, or those men who have participated in two years of baseball, tennis, or track, are eligible for membership to the varsity organization, the GR Club. This organization has been in existence since there have been athletic teams, and has proved to be a most important factors in establishing sports and sportsmanship.

New members were taken into the Club and received their first letter awards for the annual fall banquet. The banquet was held at the East Congregational Church and the speaker of the evening was a former University of Michigan and member of the University of Michigan Alumni Association. Football coaches "Potsy" Clark and Jerry Ford also spoke briefly when the awards were handed out.

First year letters were given to Robert Holihan, Jim Woodrow, William Norcross, Paul Leatherman, Duncan Leetka, Fred Wicht, Gerritt Yonker, Dick Nicholson, and Tony Wroblewski.

Those earning their second year awards were Jack Barrows, Arnold Balzell, Robert Bowman, Frank Averill, Donald Fogell, and Eugene Tiejema.

Third year major letters went to Captain Tony Balice, Dallas Braden, Paul Partanen, Bernard Toivonen, Allan Waivio, and David Rozga. Robert Olson and Clayton Kelley received managers' letters.

Row — Frank Averill, Jack Barrows, David Rozga, Anthony Balice, Bernie Toivonen, Robert Bowman, Donald Fogell, Jay Van Sweden, Gerrit Yonker, Norman Glassey, Howard Phillips, Fred Wicht, James Woodrow, William Gainey, Leon Van Volkinborn, Wallace Bonner, Emerson McCarty.

HIKERS' CLUB

Potsy and the Mayor exchange a few verbal announcements.

Mayor Welsh finds riding a little easier than walking.

Gee, I wish I was in that car.

Blue Monday is the word for it! After a Sunday of hiking, weary trampers are only too glad to return to their respective homes for mustard plaster or what-have-you in the medicine chest to bathe those blistered feet.

Under the leadership of George "Potsy" Clark this organization was formed early in 1941. Clark believed that long hikes through the country, rain or shine, sleet or snow, for the betterment of strong, healthy bodies and enlightenment of minds would increase the individual physical and mental capacity. The groups of eager outdoor-enthusiasts met in the Administration Building on any Sunday afternoon to hike to an unknown destination only to round up back at the school for hot coffee, doughnuts, and a sing around the piano of old and news songs.

The fall of 1941 set the Club at a rapid pace when about eighty over-exuberant young men and women from the University and the Institute set out for a five-mile jaunt in the country to Mayor George Welsh's ranch, "Taos." A fatigued body of hikers crowded into the few cars present to return to the Ad building for refreshments.

In spite of the cold weather and heavy snows there were still those who defied these hazards by dressing warmly and making several trips around Reeds Lake or in the vicinity of Mayor Welsh's ranch.

"Hike for defense," says "Potsy." "In the present days of war we need the bodies that will be able to endure what is to come. We must prepare ourselves physically to help out in home defense.

To do this we need more exercise, to use our feet as long as we are able instead of depending on automobiles. This is the least we can do for our country, as each little bit counts towards a final victory."

"Potsy" and the committee, consisting of Earl Ide, Paul Partanen, James Woodrow, Gregory Deliyanne, Gerald Janousek, Robert MacNaughton and Dan Nicboson have succeeded in making the Hikers' Club successful and one of the most active on the campus.

The future holds outstanding possibilities for the organization. Well-known business men as well as the Michigan Tourist Society have shown a desire to sponsor it. Already the idea has spread and it is more than probable that the club will become nationally known as the University grows.

One of the familiar and popular hiking excursions.

President . . . . . . Earl Ide
Vice-President . . . . Alice Margot
Secretary . . . . . Barbara Sehler
Treasurer . . . . . Jerry Janousek

Aeonian 1942

61

UGR Campus Sports: The Gridiron

The promotional and recruiting potential of a big-time sports program, particularly football, was not lost on M.E. Davenport. UGR's inexperienced football team had played to a discouraging 1 and 6 record in its debut 1939-40 season. To galvanize the program, Davenport brought in a ringer who also happened to be a longtime acquaintance. George "Potsy" Clark, creator and first coach of the Detroit Lions, in 1940 accepted the job (and a $20 thousand pay cut) as head football coach of the Lancers. The surprise move made headlines on the sports pages, but although no one knew it at the time, posterity for the team would be secured by the assistant coach: a tenderfoot attorney named Gerry Ford, who taught law at the university and would later go on to become 38th president of the United States.

That M.E. Davenport was able to secure Clark was one of his greatest coups. The arrangement came about informally enough: Davenport had roomed with the Clark family while a young teacher at Illinois' Carthage College in the early 1900s. More than 30 years later he called on the relationship to persuade Clark to salvage UGR's struggling football program.

Clark had been a star quarterback at the University of Illinois, then went on to coach teams at Michigan State (then Michigan Agricultural College), Butler University, and Kansas State. His pro football coaching career began with the Portsmouth (Ohio) Spartans, an early NFL team that was unable to survive the Great Depression. In 1934 Clark relocated the franchise to Michigan as the Detroit Lions, and promptly led the team to a 1935 NFL championship.

Clark left Detroit to spend three years as head coach of the Brooklyn Dodgers, which played in the NFL through 1943. Clark then returned to the Lions. His move to UGR came as a shock to the football world and particularly to Lions management, who were not aware of his plans until the story broke in the papers.

While the Lancers hoped to benefit from Clark's coaching record, the high-pressure style that had made him successful at the professional level would not be transferred to academia. Davenport and Clark had an understanding that the players' grades were more important than their performance on the field. In addition to coaching, Clark would serve as the college's "Industrial Relations" director, functioning as a liaison between the community's business leaders and graduates of the college in order to assist their career placement upon graduation.

George "Potsy" Clark: The University of Illinois star quarterback for two seasons (1914 and 1915) went on to coach the Spartans of Michigan Agricultural College (Michigan State University), and then the Detroit Lions from 1931–36.

The 1941 UGR Lancers. Back row, L-R: Coach George "Potsy" Clark, Bud Norcross, Fred Wicht, Tony Wroblewski, Gerrit Yonker, Jim Woodrow, John Anderson, Dan Nicholson, Wayne Redner, Dick Nicholson, Duncan Leetka, Norm Glasser, George Kobryn, Art Holland, Assistant Coach Gerald (Gerry) Ford. Front row, L-R: David McDowell, Robert Holihan, David Rozga, Frank Averill, Arnold Balzell, Bernie Toivonen, Tony Balice (team captain), Paul Partanem, Dallas Braden, Allan Waivio, Jack Burrows, Gene Tiejema, Don Fogell, Bill Gainey, Hal Edgerton, and Paul Leatherman.

Clark and UGR Athletic Director Jacob Speelman set about renovating the team with a competitive schedule that included both private and public institutions. Opponents included small Midwestern colleges like Bluffton (Ohio), DeSales College (Toledo), Hope, Alma, Indiana State, St. Mary's (Pontiac), Central Michigan, and also Fort Custer, an army base in Battle Creek. Home games were played at Houseman Field in Grand Rapids. In their first season with Coach Clark, the Lancers reversed their previous season's win-loss column to finish with an impressive 6-2 record.

Clark had a three-year contract, with a tacit invitation from Davenport to stay as long as he wished. His tenure, however, lasted just one season. In 1942, he resigned to enlist in the navy, turning his coaching duties over to his assistant, Gerry Ford.

The team rallied for the 1942 season, which was to be its last. Eventually the war siphoned so many young men from the team, including Coach Ford, that college officials were forced to abandon the program.

From Boarder to Boss. While a young teacher in Illinois, Davenport had rented a room from the Clark family. Thirty-five years later he hired Potsy Clark away from the Detroit Lions as UGR's head football coach. Clark's move from the NFL to an obscure start-up college was a sports-world stunner at the time, but Clark was attracted to the university's progressive model. At the contract signing (above) he told reporters "I want to do my bit in building an educational institution that boasts a new trend, one that is unusual, and which definitely appeals to me."

UNIVERSITY OF GRAND RAPIDS

63

UNIVERSITY OF GRAND RAPIDS

GOLF TEAM

TENNIS TEAM

TRACK TEAM

The university had a full sports program that included baseball, basketball (including a women's team), tennis, golf, and track—all governed by a code of ethics (below) that put strong emphasis on "how you play the game."

CODE OF ETHICS

Never quit.

Never alibi.

Never gloat over winning.

Never be a rotten loser.

Never take an unfair advantage.

Always treat players and visitors with respect.

Never jeer officials.

Never under-estimate an opponent or over-estimate yourself.

The Grand Rapids Lancer

VOL. III, NO. II.   GRAND RAPIDS, MICH., OCT. 23, 1941   (ACP)   FIVE CENTS

MEET THE QUEEN

Homecoming Program Opens Friday

BOB KUGEL GENERAL CHAIRMAN; BONFIRE RALLY OPENING EVENT

Parade, Indiana State-Lancer Game at South Field; Homecoming Ball Also on Saturday's Program

A football game and crowning of the queen, a parade, a clean-up party, a torchlight parade and bonfire rally, and a Homecoming Ball are among the scheduled attractions of the Third Annual Homecoming of the University of Grand Rapids, Friday and Saturday, October 24 and 25.

Under the general chairmanship of Robert Kugel, Pharmic Senior and member of the Student Senate, committees have completed plans for the extensive two-day celebration which Kugel predicts will be the "biggest homecoming in the history of the University." A large number of alumni of the University and Davenport-McLachlan Institute are planning to attend one or more of the events,

Bob Kugel

J' accuse

A peculiar and pernicious situation obtains on this campus.

For the past three years the students at the University of Grand Rapids have been voting for, and electing representatives to, what today is known as the "Student Senate." To all intents and purposes, this organization is chosen for the express purpose of administering, in a democratic manner, all affairs on the campus pertaining to the good and welfare of the entire student body.

However, for the past year and more, this Student Senate has been operating without itself being in possession of a written constitution. For it seems that in the process of moving from the Davenport-McLachlan Institute to the campus, the written document was lost, and to date no one has taken the time nor the trouble to locate the lost constitution, nor formulate a new document.

This, certainly, is not according to generally accepted democratic tradition, and perhaps, in part, accounts for the situation which obtains today.

HOMECOMING HI-LIGHTS

FRIDAY, OCTOBER 24

1:00 p.m.—Clean-up party, University campus, Chairman, Michael Olenik.

7:30 p.m.—Freshman-Sophomore torch-light parade, and pep rally, University campus. Chairman, Dave McDowell and Don Fogell.

SATURDAY, OCTOBER 25

1:00 p.m.—A parade through the business section. Chairman, Robert FitzGerald.

2:30 p.m.—Indiana State-University of Grand Rapids foot-

McCarty Asks For 'Closed Session'

At Monday's meeting of this body, Emerson McCarty of-

JEAN HOOK

—Courtesy G. R. Press

At an assembly held last Friday morning, it was announced that Jean K. Hook, daughter of Dr. and Mrs. A. A. Hook of this city, and graduate of Ottawa Hills High School, has been elected by University of Grand Rapids students to reign over Homecoming activities as their Queen.

Jean will be officially crowned between the halves of the Indiana State-UGR game Saturday afternoon. Mayor Collins, of East

UGR Campus Sports: 1940s

UNIVERSITY OF GRAND RAPIDS

BASKETBALL

Grand Rapids College

1938-39

UNIVERSITY OF GRAND RAPIDS

"I remember the day of Pearl Harbor — Sunday, Dec. 7, 1941. We had had a Phi Theta Pi fraternity dance the night previous and we were sort of 'done in' on Dec. 7. On top of that, we had to look at pictures of the Japanese bombing Pearl Harbor and grasping the fact that we probably wouldn't be coming back to UGR until after the war ended. We shook hands, pledged to defend our country and perhaps get together after the war (if we made it). It was a very somber day."

—Donald Campbell, UGR 1941-43

"In 1942 our finance class was advised to volunteer for army duty with the stipulation that we could remain in school to finish our education. However, our time was cut short and we were drafted in April of 1943. Our entire finance class was sent to Fort Custer for physicals and classification. A special graduation was held for this class, ahead of schedule, and they received their Bachelor of Science in Administration degrees."

—Eugene Kozak, UGR class of 1943

"'Education for Use' is Emblazoned on the Skies!" Impassioned war rhetoric in college brochures appealed to patriotism as well as personal ambition in urging students to prepare themselves for both war and peacetime service.

The War Years

Until Pearl Harbor, the war in Europe was still a distant bell for the United States. But with America's full entry into the conflict late in 1941, the draft called tens of thousands of college students from across the country into the military. As the nation ramped up its war effort, UGR also tried to position itself 'defensively.'

Students in several divisions qualified for deferment—pharmacy, engineering, mathematics, physics, and chemistry were designated critical fields. Following a directive from the federal government, the school amended its curriculum to include short, training-intensive pre-enlistment courses, for both men and women, which emphasized instruction in other high-demand fields such as meteorology, drafting, surveying, medical technology, and civil engineering, among others.

Despite the fact that demand for employees in civil service positions was higher than ever, the university suffered from simple lack of supply as the draft siphoned students, particularly men. Between 1941 and 1945, the school lost three-quarters of its student body, along with many key members of its faculty and administration. With Davenport-McLachlan's enrollment similarly decimated, Mr. Davenport sold the Sheldon Avenue building and moved the handful of remaining students (fewer than 50) to the UGR campus. Before the war ended, enrollments at DMI dwindled even further.

Other colleges across Michigan and the nation were likewise struggling. Even Grand Rapids Junior College was threatened; support from the University of Michigan helped save JC from bankruptcy.

The UGR Roll Call honored students who left school to enter the military during World War II.

President Voelker recognizes student military recruits as they prepare for deployment.

UNIVERSITY OF GRAND RAPIDS

Down for the Count

UGR was never able to recover from the damage of these difficult years. Already weakened from its depleted student body, the university became especially susceptible to the accreditation challenges that had troubled it from the beginning.

Additionally, UGR found itself caught in the crossfire of a sensitive political issue. State educators were increasingly alarmed by the paucity of laws governing the incorporation of educational institutions, which had given rise to a spate of legally chartered "degree mills." MANCC pressured lawmakers to toughen Michigan's educational regulations. The resulting legislation mandated that only institutions ranked as B-1 (capital assets of $1,000,000 or more) could be authorized to establish and operate colleges and universities of a graduate rank. UGR's assets fell below that requirement.

Three previous attempts at establishing a public institution of higher education in Grand Rapids failed—in 1833, 1837, and 1903. To this day, the city does not have its own nondenominational four-year college.

Band of Brothers. Fraternity brothers from Phi Theta Pi ready to roll before a football game.

Even the acclaimed School of Pharmacy underwent its own accreditation travails. Tentatively approved by the Michigan Board of Pharmacy, but not the National Council of Pharmaceutical Education, the department toppled when the former refused to license the university's pharmacy graduates unless the program had national certification.

The final blow landed in 1944, when certification under the Veterans Readjustment Act was denied the university. Commonly known as the G.I. Bill of Rights, the federal program offered educational benefits to all service men and women. Most colleges were banking on the returning tide of veterans to restore their campuses to normalcy.

To determine UGR's eligibility as a veterans training institution, an ad hoc evaluation committee consisting of officials from the University of Michigan, Western State Teachers' College (Western Michigan University), the University of Detroit, and Hope College was sent to appraise the UGR campus. Here, politics of a different sort may have contributed to the university's demise. All of the members of the committee represented institutions that stood to compete for students with an emerging rival—the area's first independent four-year college. Half of the committee members were from the University of Michigan, "which supported an active extension program in Grand Rapids and relied heavily on transfer enrollments from GRJC," according to an article written for the *Grand River Valley Review* in 1988. Western, also heavily represented on the committee, at the time was immersed in its own expansion plans and had always relied heavily on the Grand Rapids area for recruitment. "It was obvious that any new programs developed by Western would be in direct competition for students with the University of Grand Rapids," noted the article.

"I was in charge of a hayride for our fraternity. Somehow not many members were interested and it appeared we might lose some money on the project. An inspiration hit me; I called the hayride people and explained we had a flu epidemic going around UGR and would like to cancel. Meanwhile I passed the telephone around to our brothers and each coughed loudly into the phone. The ride was cancelled and we were financially excused. Shame on me!"

"One of the members had a slot machine in the frat house. (I won't mention his name because he became a successful businessman.) I don't think the slot paid off much; but I understand he used some of the proceeds for his tuition."

- Donald Campbell

UNIVERSITY OF GRAND RAPIDS

Committee members unanimously vetoed UGR as a candidate for veteran training. A fusillade of criticisms echoed the MANCC appraisals: inadequate library, laboratory facilities, personnel, and course work. In November 1944 the Michigan Department of Education notified Davenport that his school was denied Veterans Administration approval.

At this same time, personal tragedy struck the Davenport family with the death of M.E. and Mabel's only son, Warren, killed in action when his B-17 crashed during training exercises in Italy. His loss also ended M.E.'s hopes for succession: Davenport had imagined that the nineteen-year-old—who'd left Michigan State University as a sophomore to enlist in the U.S. Army Air Corps—would return from the war to resume his education and then help lead the schools. The combination of personal grief and professional barriers was too great to overcome.

There seemed little point in continuing. Without V.A. sanction, the university was almost certain to be bypassed by the biggest student boom of the century. It did not have North Central accreditation, and its application to become a college of commerce was granted instead to Davenport-McLachlan. Finally, the city refused to accept UGR into its educational system as a gift from its founders, as was originally intended.

On April 27, 1945, the Lowe Estate, along with all UGR assets and equipment, was sold to Aquinas College. UGR finished out the school year and graduated 14 seniors—the smallest class in its history—bringing M.E. Davenport's progressive experiment to an end.

Heroism and Heartbreak: Warren Davenport

The probable next-in-line to succeed his father, Warren Davenport had just begun his studies at Michigan State University as America's involvement in World War II was escalating.

As the primary support for a family farm, Warren qualified for an occupational deferment from the military draft. Choosing instead service to his country, he forfeited his exemption to enlist in the Army Air Corps.

Trained as a B-17 tail gunner and stationed in Foggia, Italy, Staff Sergeant Davenport and his crew flew many successful missions over Axis targets. In October 1944, during a training exercise, the aircraft experienced engine failure and crashed while attempting an emergency landing. Warren was among the fatalities.

The telegram announcing the terrible news was delivered just one day after M.E. and Mabel Davenport had received their last letter from their 19-year-old son.

Posthumously, he was awarded the Purple Heart. Fifteen years later, Warren Hall, one of the first residence halls at Davenport, was named in his honor.

Pitching In. Warren was doing his share of farm work when the pitchfork was twice his height.

Warren (kneeling, third from left) with the crew of the B-17 "Lassie and Her Lads."

The demise of the University of Grand Rapids was to some extent attributable to factors beyond its control. Also apparent is that university leaders uncharacteristically misread or minimized important signals. While many recommended improvements were made—including a tripling of volumes in the library and an extension of class periods—other steps that might have removed barriers to peer acceptance were never taken. Recommendations that UGR narrow the curriculum's wide focus or jettison the graduate school, for example, went unheeded.

And yet it had been an exercise not entirely in vain. Selling to Aquinas assured that much of UGR's groundwork could be implemented in Aquinas' new senior level. Additionally, by bringing Davenport-McLachlan under its auspices during the war, UGR had literally saved that school from extinction. Extending the UGR model, the postwar Davenport Institute carved out a niche in higher education that merged the academic with the practical, preparing graduates to live enriched lives while performing meaningful work.

Left to conjecture is whether the institution might have prospered in a later era, when the higher education landscape became much more pluralistic. Ironically, the concept of "relevance"—so summarily dismissed in the late 1930s—was to become the foundation of college curricula development a generation later.

UNIVERSITY OF GRAND RAPIDS

The Progressive — Dr. Paul F. Voelker

By the time he was chosen to lead the University of Grand Rapids as its first and only president, Paul F. Voelker had had an extensive educational career in Michigan. He had already served as president of two private colleges and had just completed a two-year term as state superintendant of public instruction.

Born in Evart, Michigan, in 1875, Voelker was the oldest of several children. He earned his bachelor's and master's degrees from Drake University in Des Moines before beginning his career in higher education with administrative posts at the University of Wisconsin and Drake University. Compelled by the idea of helping students and society through personal guidance, he entered Columbia University—at the age of 40—to obtain his doctorate in education. Eventually he returned to Michigan to become president of Battle Creek College and later Olivet College.

Throughout his long career in education, Voelker had hoped for an opportunity that would allow him to fully implement his progressive theories in education—ideally, at an institution he could build from the ground up. The development of the University of Grand Rapids was exactly what he sought.

"It's one of my dreams come true, to be head of a school based on sound educational principles," Voelker said. "The artistic beauty, our type of students, and community cooperation will make this one of the outstanding educational institutions of the country."

While the new university was intended as the expanded arena for the "empirical-theoretical" academic hybrid, President Voelker was its voice and champion. It was his educational philosophy that shaped the university in all its facets, from its curricula to its operating principles.

Dr. Voelker's convictions about academic and career goal-setting—combined with his background and training in psychology and human behavior—led him to develop what he called "personality diagnosis" surveys for students unsure of their professional direction. "Any person who cannot make up his mind about the important question of what he should do in the next few years" said Voelker, "should be evaluated in relation to intelligence quotient, social interests, and personal characteristics." Incubating methods that anticipated aptitude tests of later decades, he trained 12 of his psychology students to assist others in planning both their college and post-college futures. It was academic advising and personal counseling in its earliest forms.

Dr. Paul F. Voelker

A dormitory at Battle Creek College was named for President Voelker. BCC was founded by Dr. John Harvey Kellogg and operated from 1923 to 1938. It was one of two private colleges Voelker headed before coming to the University of Grand Rapids. The other was Olivet College.

Called "Doc" by many who knew him, Voelker ardently advocated the synthesis of idealism and realism. He defended the university's unique—and controversial—curriculum as essential for a post-war society. His background as a social psychologist and a minister (he was ordained in 1944 by the Grand Rapids Association of Congregational Churches) informed strong positions about the evolution of the individual in the 20th century.

"After the war we shall have to prepare ourselves for citizenship in a new type of world," he predicted, "because civilization has reached a point where it cannot maintain itself without the improvement of peoples' characters."

"Kindness must replace hatred, cooperation must replace competition, justice must be put in the place of force, and war must be done away with in favor of peace. Only by the regeneration of humanity on a large scale can we accomplish this."

A "regeneration" of the sort Voelker envisioned required a platform of delivery available through higher education. In the aftermath of depression and war, he was committed to the notion that society's purposes must be not only served by education, but elevated by it.

"Economic problems have absorbed the civilized world's moral and material energies," he stated. "But if, through education, sufficient good will and thought can be brought to bear, the day need not be far off when the economic problem will take a back seat where it belongs, and the arena of the heart and head will be occupied by our real problems—the problems of life and of human relations, of creation, and behavior."

After the closing of UGR, Dr. Voelker spent the rest of his career as a minister in Centreville, Michigan.

The world-renowned Battle Creek Sanitarium (popularized in the novel and movie *The Road to Wellville*) was established and operated by Dr. John Harvey Kellogg in 1903. Dr. Kellogg later established Battle Creek College* (BCC) as its founder and first president. Originally an all-women's college, BCC combined existing training academies in nursing and home economics.

Dr. Kellogg persuaded Paul Voelker to leave his presidency at Olivet College and succeed him as president of BCC. Voelker immediately made the college coeducational and expanded the curriculum beyond its sanitarium precedents to include full departments in the sciences and humanities, including chemistry and physics, mathematics, psychology, and sociology, history, English, and philosophy. Voelker served as BCC's president until the mid-1930s, when he was appointed Michigan's state superintendant of education. Battle Creek College closed in 1938.

*A Seventh-day Adventist college originally known by the same name became the present-day Andrews University.

Postwar Recovery

As the war ended, Davenport-McLachlan Institute moved back downtown to a temporary location at 14 Fountain Street, site of the former Klingman Furniture Building. The postwar years were ones of convalescence, during which the school healed from the wounds of the Great Depression, war, and the closing of the University of Grand Rapids.

The Davenport family also had much personal trauma to endure. The loss of their son was a blow from which M.E. Davenport would never completely recover. Close friends thought Warren's death may have influenced Davenport's decision not to salvage UGR.

But there were signs of promise as well. By acquiring Heaney Commercial College in 1944 and the Lucid Secretarial School the following year (both launched by former Davenport executives), Davenport-McLachlan took sole possession of the business college market in Grand Rapids. Fortified by that status, college officials felt secure enough to drop the "McLachlan" name and proceed as Davenport Institute.

Peace on the Doorstep. Crowds gather to celebrate the long-awaited good news of the Allied victory.

Regaining Momentum

Finally, the school could reap some reward for its years of austerity, sacrifice, and risk. With peace came prosperity, along with developments both federally and locally that accelerated Davenport's progress. Repeal of wartime taxes, and the reduction of others, freed up billions in capital for business expansion. Government subsidies helped facilitate the transition to a peacetime economy, while consumer appetites, long suppressed by years of scarcity and rationing, revived.

As manufacturers geared up to meet the backlog of demand, the "office industry" fell into step. Growing service sectors like finance, insurance, and construction clamored for personnel. In Grand Rapids, the transformation of furniture manufacturing from residential to office production reflected the nation's booming commerce; it also attracted more business graduates to that industry's administrative and executive ranks.

In 1945 there were fewer than 100 students enrolled at Davenport; within two years that number had quadrupled and would continue to multiply on the strength of programs that included the G.I. Bill, an ambitious expansion strategy that established branch campuses around lower Michigan, and curricula that attracted an increasingly career-oriented student body.

During this period, M.E. Davenport also added a new faculty member. Son-in-law Robert W. Sneden, a Davenport graduate and returning war veteran, was hired to teach salesmanship and public speaking. Eventually he would transfer into administration, working his way up to vice president and eventually president.

With its student body reduced to a fraction, DMI returned downtown to establish temporary quarters at 14 Fountain in the former Klingman Furniture exposition building.

1945
World War II ends; University of Grand Rapids dissolved and assets sold to Aquinas College. Davenport-McLachlan moves to temporary quarters on Fountain Street in downtown Grand Rapids.

1946
Robert W. Sneden joins the Institute as a faculty member.

1949
Davenport Institute moves to a new building at the corner of Fulton Street and Division Avenue and becomes Davenport Institute.

1949
Greenville grocer Hendrik Meijer and son Frederik open the first Meijer supermarket at 28th Street and Kalamazoo Avenue in Grand Rapids.

Preparing for a New Era

In the immediate postwar years, Davenport administrators began considering ways to reduce the college's dependence on tuition receipts for revenue. M.E. Davenport had witnessed enough enrollment fluctuations in his career to desire a funded cash reserve that would cushion the school through lean periods. Many alternatives were considered; two were implemented.

In 1947, M.E. Davenport commissioned designs for a new classroom building at the corner of Fulton Street and Division Avenue. The former site of the Livingston Hotel had been vacant for more than twenty years after the building was destroyed by fire. Architectural plans called for a dual-purpose building where the school could hold classes and also generate cash flow by leasing commercial office space. Adaptability was built-in: during times of reduced enrollments, extra classroom space would become available for rent.

The building became one of the first in Grand Rapids to embrace the "modular" concept. Walls were made of movable steel and could be quickly rearranged to create different configurations of commercial or classroom space.

Several retail tenants accepted street-level occupancy, including Ehinger Shoes and the Juvenile Shop, a children's clothing store. The second floor accommodated ten classrooms and administrative offices for the college. A 500-seat auditorium and club rooms for students occupied the below-street level.

A Streamlined Statement. Davenport Institute's new location was built in Art Moderne style, with sleek elongated lines meant to symbolize mid-century momentum and progress. Movable steel partitions allowed modular space configuration, a new concept in office planning. The original architect's vision called for six floors, topped with a roof garden.

Mid-Century Modern. The modern minimalism of 2 Fulton was displayed both outside and in with its austere styling and emphasis on no-nonsense function.

Succession in the Making. M.E. Davenport dictates to his assistant while Robert Sneden, at desk in foreground, appears at the ready. Sneden had recently been appointed Davenport Institute's vice president and worked closely with his father-in-law for years.

During the hot summer of 1949, the school once again headed for a new home. Staff and students pitched in to help with the move, making countless trips along the blocks between Fountain and Fulton Streets. On foot, they carried cartons loaded with books and office supplies.

The mixed-use strategy fulfilled itself as planned during the Korean War. When the military draft again reduced college enrollments, empty classrooms were quickly leased as commercial office space. In this manner Davenport Institute was able to remain solvent for the war's duration while many other private colleges were forced to close their doors.

The second major step toward financial sovereignty was one that significantly altered the school's corporate structure—and greatly advanced its opportunities for future growth.

Classes in the popular salesmanship program quickly filled to capacity, where students drilled in the fundamentals of becoming account representatives.

Vitae: Erma Gould

By the early 1940s, World War II was creating massive labor shortages in offices, and the college was getting more requests than it could fill from area employers needing qualified personnel. M.E. Davenport asked Erma Gould, head of the college's secretarial division, to establish an employment referral service.

Gould developed Davenport's first employment placement office, a unit that went on to generate an incredible record of career placement for Davenport graduates, a ratio consistently near 100 percent. Gould's efforts helped establish the school's reputation as a primary source of workplace talent, and in the ensuing decades companies throughout the region learned to place their first calls for qualified employees to the Davenport placement service.

Erma Gould matched graduating students to positions with area employers.

The Thoroughly Modern Office. International Business Machine Corporation's booth at a Michigan Educator's Association Convention in Grand Rapids, shows time clocks and the new IBM electric typewriter, introduced in 1949.

The original "think pad"—a pocket memo book—was standard issue for all IBM employees.

A group of admirers surrounds leadership guru Dale Carnegie at a seminar in the 1950s. Among the fans is a young Robert Sneden, who subtly displays Carnegie's classic text —which was second only to the Bible in nonfiction popularity.

Dale Carnegie classes were considered the industry standard for executives looking to sharpen their managerial and presentation skills on their way up the corporate ladder. Introduced in 1912, the program was enormously popular worldwide and significantly influenced 20th century business. At Davenport alone, thousands graduated from the Carnegie Course, which focused on effective communication, persuasive public speaking, and other principles of business success.

79

Happy Feet. Dances held a prominent spot on the college social agenda and went by names like "The Stable Stomp," the "Cupid Swingeroo," and the "Tinsel Ball." (Top) Homecoming at the Rowe Hotel, 1948.

(Top left): A faculty talent show entertains students. (Top right): A training skit for salesmanship students demonstrates some on-the-job 'don'ts.' (Right): Preparation underway for the annual Davenport prom.

81

Campus Sports: 1950s

From the Court to the Course. Davenport athletics gained momentum through the 1950s. After a hiatus of many years, basketball would make a return, along with other sports including golf, tennis, bowling, and softball.

Davenport squads played in the Wolverine League, a Grand Rapids recreational league that included corporate teams from around the city, such as American Seating and Grand Rapids Motor Coach.

The business/academic sorority Alpha Iota was chartered at Davenport in 1937 and was active for decades. (Opposite page) AI sisters gather for their formal initiation in 1951. "Initiation was a really big occasion," recalled Mildred Dean Blett. "We all wore long dresses and had a fancy meal."

Lillian Myners, head of the secretarial division, demonstrates a four-reel tape deck used for Dictaphone playback. "I laugh about it now," said Myners when recalling the experience years later. "We thought we had really stepped into the age of technology!" Myners was an instructor for more than 30 years and had a residence hall on the Heritage Hill campus named in her honor. (Far left) An advertisement promotes a career credential that could be earned quickly.

1950

700 ENROLLMENT

COURSES & PROGRAMS
Executive Accounting and Management, Business Administration, Executive Secretarial, Special Secretarial, Stenographic, General Business, Office Machines, Salesmanship, Dale Carnegie

16 Faculty/Administration

TUITION $360 Per Academic Year

LOCATION 12 S. Division Ave.

Setting National Precedent: From Proprietary to Nonprofit

While a new facility changed Davenport Institute's outward appearance, the other major initiative of the time was internal, and also far more transformational: a complete conversion of the school's operating and governance model.

Like nearly all independent business schools, Davenport had operated since its inception as a proprietary, for-profit enterprise. While this was viable during years of prosperity, it was perilous in times of low enrollment, particularly with long-range commitments to students and faculty. Although the school had been under the stewardship of the Davenport family since 1910, the owners were shareholders in name only; after covering expenses, operating surpluses were invested in the institution. But without a legal reorganization, it was difficult to create funding reserves because of federal taxes on for-profit revenue.

In 1952, M.E. Davenport arranged to convert the school's corporate charter to nonprofit 501(c)(3) status, including in the new corporation all the family's private equity and assets invested in the school since 1910. Davenport became the first school of its type in the country to undertake this transformation. "With this recognition," Mr. Davenport explained, "we now will be able to use any surplus to improve and expand the educational facilities and to set up a fund with which to ensure its permanence." In 1954, the Internal Revenue Service approved the charter.

> Along with business administration and accounting, a salesmanship course was offered as part of Davenport's business department. The Sales Executive Club (opposite) augmented their studies with seminars and events on the aspects of their profession. An appliance demonstration to the group by a representative from Michigan Consolidated Gas Company (far right) explains concepts of product knowledge.

Davenport Institute had made a notable identity shift from business enterprise to educational institution, with all the cultural commitments this implied. Besides alleviating the corporate tax burden, this measure opened the door for accreditation; allowed the institution to solicit contributions from the private sector; and created opportunities that would stimulate growth and development for years to come. In certain respects the decision was also one of clairvoyance, since it secured Davenport's eligibility for an array of state and federal educational programs that wouldn't begin to appear until the 1960s.

With these opportunities also came new responsibilities. Because the reclassification implied a closer identification with the educational mainstream and a stronger institutional image, it also accelerated Davenport's commitment to a deeper academic agenda. Prepared to execute these new directions was Davenport vice president Robert Sneden. A faculty member since 1946, he served as the college's second-in-command from 1952 to 1959. Working alongside his father-in-law, his influence made possible many of the ambitious projects the institute embraced during this important era, including its expansion into most major cities in Michigan's lower peninsula.

In Grand Rapids, meanwhile, the home campus was growing exponentially. Enrollment swelled to 1,000 day and evening students. In 1957, for the first time in its history, the school was forced to suspend registration of new students to avoid overcrowding.

Well into his later years, M.E. Davenport remained an astute leader who never lost his affinity for his students.

A Founder Passes

With its record of achievement the highest in its history, the college suffered the loss of its leader. M.E. Davenport, who had been seriously ill for many months, died in January of 1959.

"The passing of our president has a significance that goes beyond the loss of a head of an institution," said Robert Sneden in his first address as president to students and staff. "If ever an enterprise was the product of the dedication, the devotion, the creativity of one individual—this institution is."

It is impossible to overstate Davenport's half-century of leadership. Not only did his steady hand and inexhaustible resourcefulness keep Davenport intact through the major events and upheavals of his time, his landmark contributions to business education had earned for Davenport Institute nationwide acclaim.

M.E. Davenport, who never formally retired, delivers one of his last commencement speeches, ca. 1958.

Succession. Groomed for leadership, Robert Sneden (opposite) prepares for his role as Davenport's next president.

86 | Davenport: Educating Across Three Centuries | A New Beginning

1951-53
Korean War

1952
Davenport Institute converts from proprietary to nonprofit status.

1958
Two homes in Heritage Hill—the Sligh and White estates—purchased for use as student residence halls.

1959
M.E. Davenport passes; Robert Sneden becomes president of Davenport Institute.

The Education Pioneer M.E. Davenport

From the moment M.E. Davenport agreed to stay at the Valley City Commercial College and help the students finish their courses, he put their interests ahead of all else.

"He was like no other person relative to young people," said Tyrus Wessell, Mr. Davenport's student, colleague, and friend for nearly 30 years. "All he had to do was talk to that young person for awhile, and that young person thought he or she was the most important person around." So precisely were Davenport's senses tuned to his students that even when enrollment was in the hundreds, he knew virtually every one of them by name. He was just as committed after-hours: often, after finishing a long day at his school, he could be seen bicycling through city neighborhoods to visit with current or prospective students.

Associates and colleagues were accorded the same regard. Described as a "subliminal" manager, Davenport had a knack for achieving his own objectives by eliciting ideas—and by extension results—from those around him. Rarely did he give a direct order; the contributions of others were always accorded the highest respect and credibility. In return he evoked intense loyalties. During the Great Depression, when staff and faculty were obliged to settle for whatever salary the school could afford, they remained faithful to the institution and its founder. "We believed so much in the institution that money was a secondary consideration," said Wessell.

Recognizing talent was a key attribute of his management style, and he made a policy of putting "new blood" on his staff. Other business school proprietors, reluctant to delegate responsibility, hired only peers or played their authority close to the vest. As their leadership aged, the schools were left without a succession plan, eventually forcing many to either merge with other institutions or languish and expire.

Adaptability and creative resiliency were also his signature skills. Long before the days of financial aid packages, Davenport would go to any lengths to accommodate students who couldn't afford tuition. Typically he offered custodial, maintenance, or other tasks around campus to allow them to earn their class credits; other times he needed to get more imaginative, once accepting a student's violin in lieu of payment. To Davenport, an earnest commitment often proved as valuable as cash.

"If you are discussing…the buildings, grounds, equipment of the college, you will have his courteous attention. If you swing the subject to the careers of his former students, you have his complete interest; for the true motivation of his work is his deep desire to train young men and women for life." —Davenport Institute *Students' Life*

"In the office of Mr. Davenport you meet dignity but not a dignitary; reserve without coldness, caution without suspicion, acumen without greed, pride without conceit."

—*Students' Life*

Piloting an acclaimed business school was a far cry from Davenport's upbringing in the farmlands of Montcalm County. Born in Crystal, Michigan, on December 28, 1884, M.E. Davenport was the second of Warren and Sarah Davenport's six children. Sarah, a devout Catholic, named their son after the archangel Michael; but as he grew up the boy preferred being called by his middle name, Edward.

Besides a younger sister, "Ed" Davenport was the only family member to attend college, entering Ferris Institute at Big Rapids in 1903. He began teaching while still a student in his junior and senior years. After graduation he helped establish a business department at Carthage College in Illinois, then returned to Michigan and the struggling Valley City Commercial College.

It was while salvaging the school that Davenport met and married Mabel Engle, an elementary teacher in the Kent County School System. Together they nurtured the school back to health and raised their own family of three: daughters Margaret and Marian (called "Mame"), and a son, Warren.

M.E. Davenport

Dedication to Davenport did not preclude a busy schedule of professional and civic activities. Affiliations included the National Business Teachers Association, Michigan Business Educators Association, the Grand Rapids Chamber of Commerce, and the Civil Service board. He even ran for mayor of Grand Rapids in 1934, campaigning on a platform of Jeffersonian principles. The effort was unsuccessful, but didn't discourage the man's convictions.

Davenport's grass roots politics found their way into his personal ethos, even his daily routines. He shaved with an old-fashioned straight-edge razor, claiming it was better than any safety razor made. He was also obsessively punctual. Missing appointments, said an observer, "disturbs, slightly, an otherwise perfect poise." So unblemished were his integrity and judgment, one newspaper biographer remarked, "Even his enemies are a credit to him."

Devoted as he was to the college, Davenport reserved time for recreation. His love for the outdoors nurtured a lifelong passion for hunting. Excursions throughout northern Michigan were augmented by trips to Wyoming and Montana. Approaching 70 years old, he was still riding horseback into the Wyoming wilderness to hunt antelope and elk. Weekends were devoted to his many other interests. Saturdays were for hunting, fishing retreats at his Manistee County cabin, or tending the "working farm" the Davenport family maintained in Crystal for 25 years.

The loss of his only son, Warren, who was killed in action in World War II in 1944, dealt Davenport his most devastating life blow. Crushed in spirit and energy, he never fully regained his previous vigor.

And yet his natural resilience prevailed. Despite another personal loss in 1949 of wife, Mabel, Davenport continued to build his college into an eminent business training institution. He never formally retired; illness finally incapacitated him, but he continued to act as a consultant to college administrators until his death in 1959.

Gentleman Farmer. Like Davenport Institute, the Davenport ancestral farm was a family enterprise where M.E. Davenport's grown children—daughters Margaret and Marian, and son Warren—worked alongside their father.

The Outdoorsman. Hunting and fishing were lifelong passions, and M.E. devoted much time to both. One newspaper profile described him as belonging to the "past generation of rugged individualists."

THEY'RE ALL NEAR 70

Montana Mountain Hunt Was by Foot, Horseback

A 50-year-old man who sits on a stump in Michigan may think he's a pretty rugged outdoorsman and, for sure, he's no pantywaist.

But take a look at the three youngsters in the picture. They're just back from Montana, where they rode horseback on narrow rocky trails — often without trails — on the steep sides of mountains.

They scrambled around in the rocks and brush on foot, lived in a seven-by-seven tent on open-fire cowboy cooking and did some shooting that would make a sniper envious.

What's more, they did all this at the respective ages of 68, 70 and "almost" 71, an aggregate for the party of 208 years.

George W. Ashby of 2223 Buchanan is the boy of the group at 68. "They made me do most of the work just because they're old men," grumbled Ashby.

M. E. Davenport of 1702 Hiawatha, SE, who figures on being 71 in December, reported seeing several mountain goats every day on a rocky point near their "spike camp" in the valley.

"But they didn't interest me. Had more old goats right in camp than we could use."

THEIR THIRD

He and Ashby have made three western hunting trips but it was the first for Arthur E. Dunn of 1056 Calvin, SE.

"I wouldn't be crazy enough to go again," he snorted. "At least, not on horseback. Why those horses scrambled up mountains like goats and me hanging on for dear life, afraid to look down. By truck, sure. I had a great time between horses. One day we spent 12 hours in the saddle and I'm cured."

The three have hunted together in Michigan for 15 years, own a cabin in the Upper Peninsula for the purpose.

How did these durable sportsmen make out in Montana?

One moose, three mule deer and six antelope — all running shots at the antelope — that's how.

"We didn't get any elk although we sure tried," reported Ashby. "But golly, time we got all that we just didn't want any more game."

They're looking forward to going again.

are M. E. Davenport, George W. Ashby and Arthur E. Dunn. At left, Davenport and Dunn exult over Ashby's moose while Ashby mans the camera. They hunted elk on the distant mountain, without success.

Duck Stamp

The Candidate. In 1934, M.E. Davenport threw his political hat into the Grand Rapids mayoral campaign. His candidacy vigorously advocated nonpartisan public policy over what he described as 'machine' politics left over from the city's alderman days. "Elections cannot be manipulated by self-serving politicians if the intelligent voters will shake off their indifference and vote their convictions" said his campaign literature. In a crowded field, Davenport did not advance beyond the primaries. The election ultimately went to William Timmers, who served a two-year term as Grand Rapids mayor from 1934 to 1936.

M.E. Davenport

In education, commitment to posterity, foresight, and dedication are expected of the profession. But Davenport went far beyond the mandatory. In his ideas and educational initiatives, he was inventor, academic, and entrepreneur combined, whose experiments broke new ground. He was possessed of a rare gift—the ability to apply insight to the future while vanquishing immediate problems with pragmatism and confident, competent optimism.

"Mr. Davenport proved that there was a significant place for private enterprise in education," said the *Grand Rapids Press* following his death. "He proved that specialized schools of wide appeal could be established and maintained on a self-sustaining basis. And he proved that if standards were high enough, great numbers of students would enroll in these schools in preference to seeking a more general education in a public institution.

Grand Rapids can consider itself fortunate that a man of his vision lived and worked here."

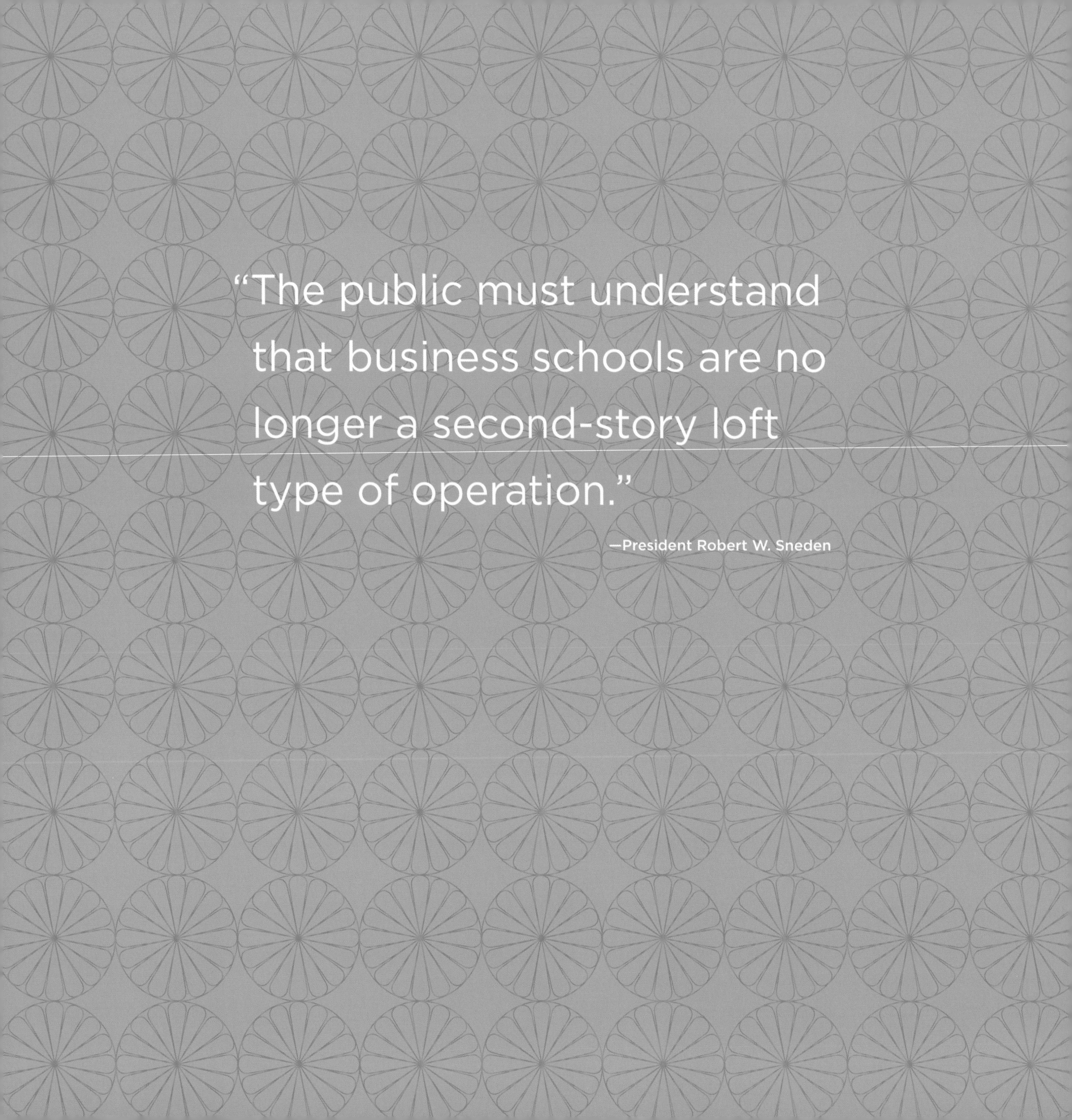

"The public must understand that business schools are no longer a second-story loft type of operation."

—President Robert W. Sneden

FROM INSTITUTE TO COLLEGE
1959–1977

Rites of Passage

VIEWED BOTH SYMBOLICALLY AND STRUCTURALLY, Davenport's 1959 presidential succession was an event of considerable meaning. The school was saying farewell not merely to a leader, but to its namesake and guiding presence for a half-century. At the time it was not unusual for independent schools with long proprietary histories to be closely identified with a singular figure. Leadership transitions could be difficult and sometimes even terminal. Davenport Institute, however, had planned well in advance.

M.E. Davenport's successor, son-in-law Robert W. Sneden, brought to the presidency an established history with the school as student, teacher, and administrator. He had enrolled at Davenport-McLachlan Institute in 1937 and from there entered the University of Grand Rapids. While pursuing his degree he worked for the Burroughs Adding Machine Company as a salesman before enlisting in the army in 1940. Like so many students, he had developed a close relationship with M.E. Davenport and frequently visited the college during his leaves and furloughs. The ties became filial with Sneden's 1944 marriage to Davenport's daughter Margaret. When the war ended, Davenport asked Sneden to consider working for the school instead of returning to Burroughs as he had planned. Sneden accepted.

He began his career at Davenport in 1946, first as a faculty member and later as director of admissions and manager of Lansing Business University. From 1952 until 1959 Sneden served at Davenport's side as executive vice president. Groomed for leadership by his father-in-law, Sneden was prepared to accelerate the momentum of Davenport Institute.

"It is not easy to step into the shoes of M.E. Davenport. As long as Mr. Davenport was the head of the institution it was his institution. Now it takes on a new character; the character of a public trust. No one recognizes the responsibility of the future more than I do."
- Robert Sneden

Higher Education's "Golden Age"

In addition to economic prosperity, the postwar years had introduced a "Golden Age" for higher education that would continue into the late 1970s. Two powerful trends propelled major growth at college campuses around the country. The first was demographic; the Baby Boom generation was growing up. Students graduating from high school during the 1960s and '70s were filling college classrooms faster than ever before—and from there entering the job market.

Simultaneously, higher education itself was becoming a matter of national policy. Powerful, high-visibility legislative measures directed huge amounts of government support into public colleges and universities, most notably through the Higher Education Act of 1965. Not only did this enable growth at the facilities level, it made a college degree increasingly more accessible and mainstream.

"This legislation...will swing open a new door for the young people of America. It is the most important door that will ever open—the door to education. This act means the path of knowledge is open to all that have the determination to walk it."

—President Lyndon Johnson, upon signing the Higher Education Act of 1965

More than 600 colleges were developed in the United States from 1945 to 1975.

1959
Robert W. Sneden succeeds M.E. Davenport as president of Davenport Institute.

1959
Amway Corporation, founded in Ada, Michigan, by Richard DeVos and Jay Van Andel.

1962
Telstar satellite launched, creating first global telecommunications network.

1963
Grand Valley State College opens in Allendale, Michigan.

1963
President John F. Kennedy assassinated in Dallas, Texas.

1964
Davenport Institute changes name to Davenport College of Business.

1965
Higher Education Act of 1965

For Davenport Institute, this era represented not just growth, but maturation. Determined to dispel notions of Davenport as a "shorthand college," President Sneden galvanized the school in all its spheres of operation—first and foremost academically, but also by fortifying ties to local business leadership and the community at large. He made sure all organizational efforts, and his own energies as a leader, were focused on a redefined institutional image.

The new administration immediately began reinforcing Davenport's "practical education" traditions with an expanded curriculum that included stronger courses in business administration, accounting, and secretarial training, deeper liberal arts studies, and an honors program. Sneden also made it a priority to expedite credit transfer arrangements with senior colleges and universities, so that students could apply all their Davenport work at the baccalaureate level.

(Above) Manual typewriters in classrooms would soon be replaced by the IBM Selectric, introduced in 1962. At left, vice presidents Robert Schmiedicke and Ty Wessell try out the new machine. Its debut in Davenport classrooms was the first educational use in the state. (Opposite) Davenport staff members welcome students through the Division Avenue main entrance of the school's downtown location.

"Get Your Toe In The Door"
by J. P. McEvoy

An Open Letter to Young Men and Young Women

College Character. Features of a traditional college environment emerged during the 1960s: a college annual—*RetroSpectus*—along with a school mascot, the "Panthers," accompanied by the vivid scarlet that would become the school's signature color. (Below) Students gather on the porch of Warren Hall, one of the first student dormitories on the developing Heritage Hill campus. (Above right) Members of Phi Theta Pi business fraternity organized many campus activities.

Fraternity Officers planning something!!

1960

1,000 ENROLLMENT

DIPLOMAS and PROGRAMS
Secretarial (Executive/Legal/Medical),
Sales and Marketing,
Retail Management,
Transportation and Distribution,
Real Estate and Insurance

40 Faculty/Administration

TUITION $1,500 Per Academic Year

LOCATION 12 South Division

Living on Campus. On the top floor of Warren Hall, standing wardrobes served as room dividers. (Above left) Co-op living included shared kitchens in both the men's and women's dorms, where residents took turns preparing group meals. (Above) On move-in day, an arriving student unloads belongings from his father's car. (Left) A jam session in the men's residence.

Davenport: Educating Across Three Centuries | From Institute to College

Legacies Tyrus R. Wessell

Like most Michiganders in the summer of 1912, Carl Wessell was closely following the career of Detroit Tiger outfielder Ty Cobb. Cobb had earned the American League batting title for the 1911 season and appeared to be well on his way to a repeat. So avid was Wessell's admiration for the baseball hero, that when his first son was born during that same summer, Carl had a name already picked out.

As it would turn out, Tyrus Raymond Wessell went on to become as valuable to the Davenport organization as Tyrus Raymond Cobb was to the Tigers. Wessell devoted nearly a lifetime of service to the college, actually spending more years with the school than M.E. Davenport himself.

Ty graduated from Grand Rapids Central High School in 1930, then enrolled at Davenport-McLachlan Institute. But with only a year's worth of tuition money, Wessell told M.E. Davenport he wouldn't be returning for his second year. Mr. Davenport gave him a job doing maintenance work around the college, which kept him in school until he completed the two-year accounting course.

Ty Wessell was among three vice presidents on the original "leadership team" formed by President Sneden. Seated L-R: Charles Anderson, Ray Null, Cliff Wonders, Robert Sneden (center), Ty Wessell, Robert Schmiedicke, and James Stauffer.

After graduation Ty was hired as a cost accountant for Swift and Company meat processors, but kept in touch with M.E. Davenport through the years. When Davenport offered him a bookkeeping position in 1935, Wessell began a career with the school that would span the next six decades.

Like most staff members during the cash-strapped years of the Great Depression and World War II, Ty alternated administrative duties with teaching. Soon he was appointed treasurer, a position he would retain for 35 years except for a hiatus during World War II. Wessell was also instrumental in the development of the University of Grand Rapids.

Ty Wessel

"There are very few people that we meet during the course of our lives whose advice and reassurance are able to show us the way to achieve our goals. Among these outstanding people there is one who is the symbol of the qualities we all admire and seek to attain: honesty, generosity, congeniality, kindness, and most of all the genuine friend of every student at Davenport."

—1963 yearbook dedication to Ty Wessell

After a brief period of service in the army (he was honorably discharged due to poor eyesight), Ty returned to Grand Rapids, hoping to again work for Davenport. It was 1943, and with at least half the student population serving overseas, there wasn't much to do on the quiescent campus. Ty had married and needed steady employment, so he accepted an accounting position at Dexter Lock Company. Again, his eyesight interfered: unable to sustain prolonged close-up work with figures, Wessell was forced to give up his job.

After the war, Wessell was asked to return to DMI and resume his treasurer post. He never left again.

In the early 1960s Wessell was appointed one of three original Davenport vice presidents by President Robert Sneden. When the corporate structure of the college was changed in 1971, Wessell retired from administration and returned to the classroom as an accounting instructor. His ties to the executive offices remained close, and he contributed to some of Davenport College's most important advancements, including accreditation.

With the presidential transition from Sneden to Maine in 1977, Wessell "retired" once again (his incremental "retirements" became a fond anecdote at Davenport). He assisted the Maine administration with special projects and remained an officer on the boards of the M.E. Davenport Foundation and Davenport Schools, Inc. It was not until DSI was dissolved in 1996 that he stopped working entirely.

By then he had committed 60 years to the university.

In his career, Wessell elicited sincere affection from students and colleagues alike. Praised one faculty member: "You've been a model in demonstrating the Davenport-style commitment of teacher to student."

Wessell's legacy was honored at both the Heritage Hill campus with a dormitory and later at the W.A. Lettinga campus with the Tyrus R. Wessell Bookstore. An endowed scholarship and the annual Tyrus R. Wessell Award for Distinguished Employee Service are given annually in his name. (Far right) The Wessell household of five children included daughter Kim, adopted from Korea.

In the years leading up to the 'women's lib' movement and the proposed Equal Rights Amendment, traditional gender roles still held firm. Early 1960s brochures for professional training showed the divergence of career directions, with men depicted in managerial positions. At right, a 'Secretary of the Year' was honored in the 1964 Davenport College yearbook, while an article from the *Student Life* college newsletter labels a student by her hair color.

BLONDE OF THE MONTH

Vicki Williams, graduate of Lake Odessa High School and one year at Western Michigan University, is enrolled in her first term of the stenography course.

In High School Vicki participated in many activities. She was a member of the Student Council, Glee Club, Mixed chorus, captain of the pep club, in both Junior and Senior Plays, on the Prom Committee and on the School Paper.

Vicki enjoys such hobbies as swimming, golf, water skiing, music, reading, and art.

When asked what she thought of Davenport, Vicki replied, "I like the way the teachers take interest in the students, and I think it is a very friendly school."

Poised and Proper. Young women received guidance in workplace appearance and comportment through instruction developed at the Chicago-based Nancy Taylor Secretarial School program. Modeling, makeup and wardrobing, and even a weigh-in, were all part of Nancy Taylor training.

Davenport: Educating Across Three Centuries | From Institute to College

Starved for Space. With enrollments growing rapidly, Davenport squeezes a class into the main floor living room of Warren Hall.

Launching the Accreditation Drive: The Associate Degree

Upon completion of their programs, Davenport graduates prior to 1960 earned not degrees, but diplomas. The two-year equivalent courses of study differed little from those of traditional associate degrees, but formal certification from an accrediting authority was required for a school to become a degree-granting institution. In order for Davenport Institute to compete at comparable levels with other colleges, accreditation became a necessity and a priority.

Accreditation requires compliance with rigorous standards in facilities, programs, curricula, and every aspect of educational delivery. Davenport leaders dedicated years of effort and financial resources toward meeting these requirements.

This was a precedent-setting decision. No independent specialized post-secondary school had received—or even attempted—approval from a regional accrediting commission. No criteria even existed for measurement of their programs. The journey to place Davenport on the same level as other higher educational institutions would take more than 15 years.

In 1961, the first step was taken when Davenport was approved as a junior college of business by the Accrediting Commission for Business Schools (ACBS), a predecessor of today's Association of Independent Colleges and Schools. The evaluating committee took special notice of the "excellent residence halls for women, high morale of students and faculty, commendable curricula, and excellence of educational leadership." Davenport became the first independent business school in Michigan to achieve collegiate status, the highest scholastic ranking available to institutions in its field. With this designation, Davenport became authorized to confer associate degrees, a significant step in raising its academic profile.

The new classification began paying dividends almost immediately in record enrollments and increased recognition. At the suggestion of local employers, specialized courses were developed to accommodate the growing need for dedicated skills, since advancements in office technology required employees trained expressly for certain tasks like data or word processing. Addressing incoming freshmen in 1962, President Sneden said, "In the years immediately ahead, automation and an increasing labor market will create competition for employment that only those with higher education and specialized training will be able to meet with any degree of success."

Not long after its approval from ACBS, Davenport leaders began planning for accreditation by the North Central Association of Colleges and Schools (NCA), the largest regional accrediting agency in the country. It was a highly ambitious goal, and in the private business school sector, virtually unheard of. At the time Davenport set its sights on this distant prize, no other school of its type in Michigan—and few in the country—possessed this level of certification.

106   Davenport: Educating Across Three Centuries | From Institute to College

Accreditation: Critical Impact

Accreditation solidifies the academic image of any school by verifying that its educational delivery meets or exceeds recognized standards, both regionally and nationally. For schools with origins in an independent or specialized model, the impact cannot be overstated: accreditation signifies nothing less than peerage within the higher education sector.

Regional accrediting agencies began to develop in the late 1800s. Ultimately, six associations were established throughout the United States, gaining influence as the century progressed. Eventually the agencies themselves sought formal recognition from the U.S. Department of Education. By the 1970s, proper credentialing from a recognized accrediting body was mandatory for federal student aid.

Accreditation is a rigorous process, typically demanding years of preparation and self-study by applicants. Evaluation teams scrutinize candidates according to curriculum and academic performance, administrative policy, financial stability, institutional resources, and physical facilities. Support systems are examined as well, including student services, recruitment, financial aid, and records. After initial accreditation, member institutions must pass follow-up inspections, typically every 10 years.

Membership in a regional accrediting body conveys powerful messages, raising the school's profile in the eyes of the community, donors, students, and educators themselves. Employers also view accreditation as assurance that the graduates they hire have received a quality education.

Davenport was years ahead of other institutions of its type when it began pursuing North Central Association accreditation in the 1960s. In this endeavor, school leaders anticipated a future where such endorsement would be essential to a school's reputation—and even its survival.

Davenport College Gears for Regional Accreditation — The Grand Rapids Press, Sunday, August 3, 1969

ACCREDITED

An institution's highest credentials are conferred by a regional accreditation agency approved by the U.S. Department of Education. During much of the 20th Century, this authority for schools in the Midwest and South was the North Central Association of Colleges and Schools (NCA), a nongovernmental league of educational institutions. Founded in 1895, the NCA was the largest of the country's six accrediting bodies, serving 6,000 member schools, colleges, and universities from Arizona to West Virginia. Since 2001, they have been known as the Higher Learning Commission.

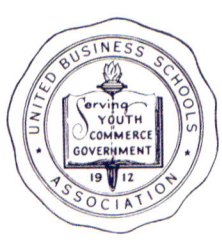

In the field of office career training, formalized accreditation began in 1912 with the National Association of Accredited Commercial Schools (NAACS). Its mission was to "advance the quality of education and the standards of excellence at private career schools and colleges."

Through a series of mergers over 50 years, this entity became the United Business Schools Association. UBSA had its own accreditation subcommittee, known today as the Accrediting Council for Independent Colleges and Schools (ACICS). For many years Davenport held dual accreditations through ACICS and NCA, until rules changes introduced complexities with that status. Davenport eventually discontinued its affiliation with ACICS.

Charter board of advisors, created in 1963, was composed of Albert Schrotenboer, L.V. Eberhard, Wallace Chamberlain, Philip DeJourno, and Donald Porter.

"The Character of the Institution:" Davenport College of Business

Other important changes marked the school's maturation. More formality was introduced to overall planning and governance with the organization of the first outside board of advisors in 1963. Composed of business and professional leaders, the group served as a policy-making and advisory body in matters of educational standards, programs, and future development. (Several years later, with the dissolution of family control, this group was reconfigured to become the college's first independent governing board of directors.)

In formalizing affiliations with area CEOs, this move also placed Davenport closer than ever to the heart of the business community.

A more visible sign of transformation occurred in 1964 when the school's name was changed from Davenport Institute to Davenport College of Business, a name which "more closely reflects the character of the institution," said President Sneden.

The emphasis on creating graduates not only trained, but educated, remained as strong as ever. The college continued to increase its range of liberal arts offerings and deepened its business courses with more theory—without diluting the effectiveness of the "employer-ready graduate" model.

GRAND RAPIDS PRESS, Thursday, Nov. 14, 1963

GUIDE BUSINESS SCHOOL—The new board of trustees of Davenport Institute holds its first formal meeting Wednesday night in the Peninsular Club. Left to right are Albert Schrotenboer; Robert W. Sneden, president of Davenport; L. V. Eberhard; Wallace M. Chamberlain; J. Philip DeJourno and Donald J. Porter. Sixth member is Joseph A. Hager, absent when the picture was taken. He later was elected chairman.

Local Business Leaders Form 1st Davenport Board

Appointment of Davenport Institute's first board of trustees was announced Thursday by Robert W. Sneden, president of the Grand Rapids college.

Trustees are Wallace M. Chamberlain, general manager of Michigan Consolidated Gas Co., Grand Rapids district; Joseph A. Hager, president of Guardsman Chemical Coatings, Inc.; Donald J. Porter, president of Porter-Hadley Co.; Albert Schrotenboer, president of Sackner Products, Inc., and a graduate of Davenport; J. Philip DeJourno, president and general manager of Wurzburg's, and L. V. Eberhard, president and treasurer of Eberhard Foods, Inc.

Hager Is Chairman

All have long records of community service and high offices in civic organizations. Hager was elected chairman and Schrotenboer secretary.

"We are grateful that you men of high business and civic caliber accept our invitation to serve on our first board of trustees," Sneden said. "Your wisdom, experience and knowledge of Grand Rapids' business needs will be of great value to Davenport Institute as it grows

credited junior college for business with 600 full-time students, a nonprofit educational institution so recognized by the concerned state and federal agencies, with a broad curriculum including general education subjects as well as a full schedule of business courses from professional accounting to stenography."

"Appointment of this board looks ahead to the day when Davenport will be operated as a community institution by a constituted permanent board of trustees," he said.

Sneden explained that the other five schools of the Davenport system — in Kalamazoo, Saginaw, Bay City, Lansing and Detroit—are not affected by the

Checks GV Study Plan

"We believe Davenport makes a very real contribution to this area's cultural and educational environment, with the self-supporting free-enterprise independence we endorse."

—Chairman Joseph Hager

The first lay board of advisors established the precedent for the first governing board of 1970. Both were chaired by Joseph Hager (right), president of Guardsman Chemical Coatings, Inc. With the new board came accreditation as a junior college of business, and most visibly, a new name: Davenport College of Business.

THE GRAND RAPIDS PRESS, Wednesday, Sept. 2, 1964

Davenport Institute Is Now College of Business

Davenport Institute, a Grand Rapids business education institution for nearly 100 years, officially became Davenport College of Business Tuesday.

The name change was voted unanimously by the school's new Board of Trustees and has been officially approved by the State Department of Public Instruction and the Michigan Cor-

beral arts subjects leading to degrees in business education. Its credits are accepted by transfer to several state colleges and universities," Hager said.

Four prominent educators in the business field have headed the Davenport College through several changes of name since it was established in 1866 as Grand Rapids Business College

and in 1899 Malcolm McLachlan established McLachlan Business University which soon became one of the largest in the Middle West.

In 1910, the late M. E. Davenport, a graduate and faculty member of Ferris Institute in Big Rapids, joined the faculty of the Grand Rapids Business College and later became president and owner.

When Mr. McLachlan died in

Several small secretarial schools were added through the years and two new buildings, including the present quarters at 12 S. Division Ave., were erected in Mr. Davenport's regime.

Robert W Sneden was elected to president of the college in 1959. Under his leadership, the enrollment has risen to 600 full-time day college students last spring and 400 evening students. The college has won its accredi-

Schools. Four student residence buildings were purchased on Fulton Street hill in the last few years, including the former Sligh Mansion and the Grand Rapids Furniture Museum buildings.

Sneden is president of the United Business Schools Association and former president of the National Association and Council of Business Schools. He has testified in Washington at several congressional committee hearings on higher education.

tional Business Teachers Association and president of the Michigan Business Education Association.

Last January, to expand the leadership of Davenport College, a board of trustees was formed of local business leaders. In addition to Hager, the members are Wesley Aves, Wallace Chamberlain, Philip deJourn, L. V. Eberhard, Harold Hartger, Donald J Porter and Albert Schrotenboer, secretary. This board will continue to gu the college and the policy-mak

Davenport Inside the Beltway

In Washington D.C., as well as in Lansing, President Sneden was highly visible as both advocate and emissary for causes important to independent and career education.

He was a delegate at the White House Conference on Youth called by President Eisenhower in 1960. That same year, he testified before the House of Representatives Veterans Affairs Committee to urge G.I. educational benefits for peacetime veterans, which led to an important extension of the original G.I. Bill.

At home in Michigan, he advised the state panel that administered the Vocational Education Act of 1965 and was a founding member of the Goal Four Committee of Higher Education—an effort that culminated in the issuing of the Michigan Tuition Grant to private college students.

Fast Forward. By the mid-2000s, enrollment at Michigan's independent colleges and universities exceeded 25 percent of the state's four-year college population—nearly 112,000 students. More than a third of these were paying for a portion of their education with a Michigan Tuition Grant. More than 30 Michigan colleges can offer financial support through the MTG.

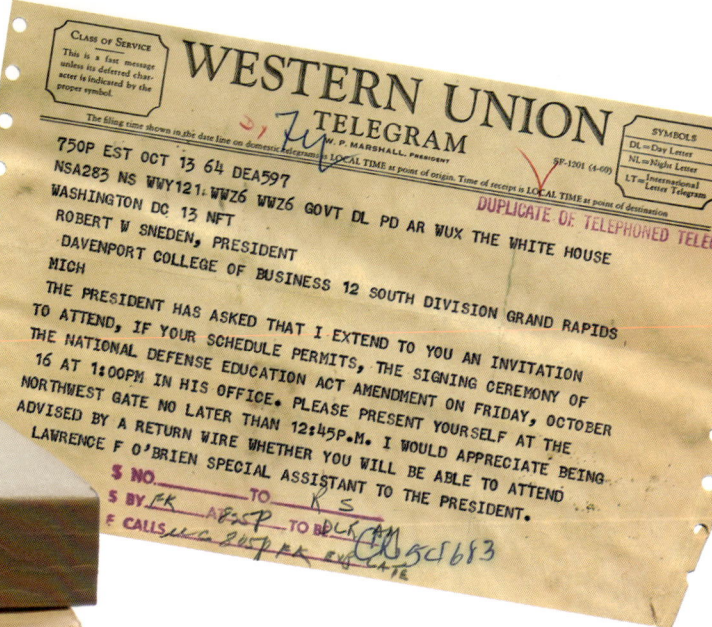

Artifacts of Advocacy: Objects reflecting Davenport influence on important federal education and employment measures include a pen used by President Lyndon Johnson to sign the Manpower Training act; bound copies of legislative bills, and the telegram inviting Robert Sneden to the Oval Office signing ceremony for the bill extending educational benefits to all military veterans.

Fair Share: Establishing the Michigan Tuition Grant

One of Sneden's most diligent efforts began during his vice presidency at Davenport and continued throughout his presidential career and beyond: the drive for state scholarship support for Davenport and other private colleges in Michigan.

While private institutions could not receive support directly from public tax dollars, Sneden argued that the students themselves deserved a share of state tuition assistance. The substantial contributions of private institutions to the economy, the labor market, and their individual communities, Sneden maintained, merited an allocation of the state's educational resources.

He helped organize Goal Four, a coalition of private school executives that worked with the Michigan State Board of Education and the state legislature to make financial aid available to students at private colleges. Their efforts culminated in the Michigan Tuition Grant of 1966, which created a line item in the state education budget for this purpose. Davenport College became the first private school to receive money under this new legislation.

Sneden would remain a committed advocate of the MTG for the remainder of his presidency, most notably as a member of the executive council of the Association of Independent College and Universities in Michigan (now Michigan Independent Colleges and Universities). The chief public policy advocacy organization for private, nonprofit colleges, the association continues to ensure the Michigan Tuition Grant remains part of the annual education appropriations process.

Roses and Royalty. President Sneden congratulates the homecoming queen and her court, circa 1965.

A Capitol Relationship: The Davenport–Ford Connection

During World War II, Ford served on the aircraft carrier Monterey in the Pacific, but kept in touch with his University of Grand Rapids friends, including Margaret Davenport. During his early years in Congress, Ford used a mobile office (left) to travel throughout his home district.

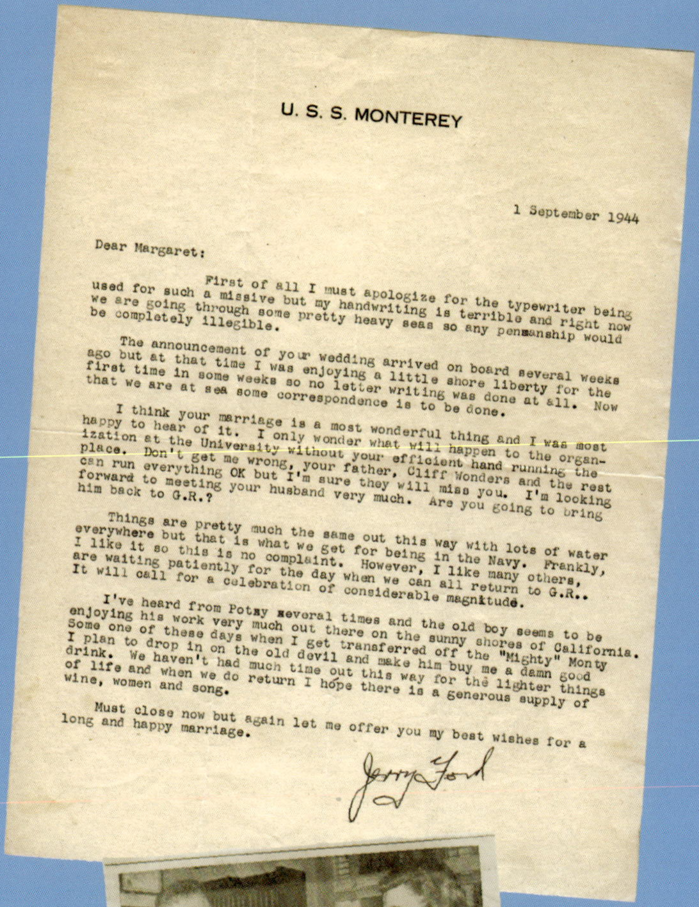

U.S.S. MONTEREY

1 September 1944

Dear Margaret:

First of all I must apologize for the typewriter being used for such a missive but my handwriting is terrible and right now we are going through some pretty heavy seas so any penmanship would be completely illegible.

The announcement of your wedding arrived on board several weeks ago but at that time I was enjoying a little shore liberty for the first time in some weeks so no letter writing was done at all. Now that we are at sea some correspondence is to be done.

I think your marriage is a most wonderful thing and I was most happy to hear of it. I only wonder what will happen to the organization at the University without your efficient hand running the place. Don't get me wrong, your father, Cliff Wonders and the rest can run everything OK but I'm sure they will miss you. I'm looking forward to meeting your husband very much. Are you going to bring him back to G.R.?

Things are pretty much the same out this way with lots of water everywhere but that is what we get for being in the Navy. Frankly, I like it so this is no complaint. However, I like many others, are waiting patiently for the day when we can all return to G.R.. It will call for a celebration of considerable magnitude.

I've heard from Potmy several times and the old boy seems to be enjoying his work very much out there on the sunny shores of California. Some one of these days when I get transferred off the "Mighty" Monty I plan to drop in on the old devil and make him buy me a damn good drink. We haven't had much time out this way for the lighter things of life and when we do return I hope there is a generous supply of wine, women and song.

Must close now but again let me offer you my best wishes for a long and happy marriage.

Jerry Ford

Ford stayed connected to Davenport throughout his political career, as a speaker at school functions, an advocate on Capitol Hill, and an employer of Davenport graduates. (Above) Congressman Ford works in his Washington, D.C., office with his Davenport-trained assistant.

Gerald R. Ford represented Michigan's fifth congressional district in the House of Representatives for a dozen consecutive terms before becoming the nation's 38th president. The relationship between Ford and Davenport University, however, preceded Ford's career in politics, lasted throughout his path from Capitol Hill to the Oval Office, and continued long afterward.

In 1941, several years before his first campaign for Congress, Ford was hired by President Paul Voelker, M.E. Davenport, and George "Potsy" Clark at the University of Grand Rapids. Fresh out of Yale Law School, Ford taught courses in law at UGR while serving alongside Clark as assistant football coach of the "Lancers."

Ford left Grand Rapids in 1942 to enlist in the U.S. Navy. Returning to West Michigan after World War II, he practiced law with partner Philip Buchen and became active in Republican politics. He was elected to the House in 1948, a seat he would hold for the next quarter century.

(Top) Congressman Ford joins Robert Sneden in congratulating William Milliken after being elected to his first term as Michigan's governor in 1970. (Center) As House Minority Leader, Ford was instrumental in securing federal support for the Inner City Education Project, an initiative aimed at recruiting more minority students to area colleges. In 1970 Ford visited Davenport to discuss the program with student Dennis Devlin, president Robert Sneden, and program director Robert Stokes. Standing is John Hunting, president of Dyer-Ives Foundation, which matched a private grant with Davenport-raised funds to support the program. (Right) President and First Lady Betty Ford circa 1975. Ford never aspired to the White House; after eight years as Republican Minority Leader, he was contemplating retirement when history made other plans. Amid the Watergate scandal, Ford succeeded resigning Vice President Spiro Agnew in 1973, then President Richard Nixon in 1974.

College Chiefs Back Library Drive

The Public Library was the prime topic of discussion as heads of five area colleges met with Edsko Hekman, left, chairman of the Public Library's Fund Campaign.

Pledging their support for the $200,000 drive to help fund the Ryerson Library expansion were, from left, Robert Sneden, Davenport College president; John Vandenberg, Calvin College dean; Msgr. Arthur Bukowski, Aquinas College president; Dr. James Zumberge, president of Grand Valley State College and Francis McCarthy, dean of Grand Rapids Junior College.

Although each college has its own library, its students depend on the Public Library for reference and research material in depth.

The library fund drive starts Feb. 21 with library officials hoping for an early April ground-breaking. Remainder of the cost of the expansion is $3.2 million, with $1.6 million coming from a municipal bond issue and the rest from the federal government.

(Left) The era of transformation for Davenport was an era of renewal for Grand Rapids as well. While Monroe Avenue remained intact as the city's main retail thoroughfare, just blocks away a massive reconstruction project created the government complex known as Vandenberg Plaza. (Top left) The Grand Rapids Public Library also received a major structural addition, thanks in part to collaborative support from local college presidents, including Davenport's R.W. Sneden.

- *1968*
  Davenport relocates its campus to Heritage Hill.

- *1968*
  First classes held at the new Academic Center.

- *1969*
  Neil Armstrong becomes first man to set foot on surface of the Moon.

- *1969*
  Davenport launched its first annual public fund drive and far surpassed its goal of $125,000.

- *1969*
  Old City Hall demolished.

Famous Firsts. The modernization of Grand Rapids included a new Kent County Airport, which relocated in 1963 to Cascade Township from its original location at Madison Avenue and 36th Street. That airfield, built in 1912, had established the country's first scheduled passenger service, between Grand Rapids and Detroit. Among the passengers on that first route in 1926 were M.E. Davenport and his family (top). Standing third from left are Mr. and Mrs. Davenport with their daughters Margaret and Marian.

Installed next to the new city hall in 1969, Alexander Calder's abstract stabile *La Grande Vitesse* became the first work of public art in the nation funded by the National Endowment for the Arts. The $45,000 NEA grant was combined with private donations, making it the first civic sculpture financed through a public-private partnership.

Girl Golfer on DI Link Squad

"There was a certain amount of shock," smiled Cynthia Claus, "when I walked out on the course with the Davenport Institute golf team members to face other college groups."

This sports oddity, at least first in this part of the state, where a woman competes in the almost exclusive men's sports world, doesn't seem to bother Cynthia.

Called Cy, she just steps up to the tee and bangs them down 220 yards or so like most of the other good golfers.

Playing No. 2 on the team, Cy, who has an engaging personality, found herself on the winning side with some of her opponents. "They took the woman beating man," laughed Cy, "quite graciously."

A Medical Secretarial student, Cy is as excited about her career as winning in golf. "I think it is tremendous," she said, "and I know that this is just what I've wanted to do."

An East Grand Rapids graduate, she attended the University of Miami for a year before coming to Davenport.

Cy is also a member of the Alpha Iota and Sigma Iota Chi sororities. Afternoons she can be seen out at Cascade banging away at golf balls. She doesn't particularly relish this practice. She says, "There are a lot of other things I would rather do, but if you are going to win, you have to practice."

Since the age of 7, about 15 years ago, Cy has been living with the game of golf. She likes all sports but has found it necessary to give them all up to concentrate on golf.

A mid-70 shooter, Cy thinks a new golfer should try to hit the ball hard as he can while first learning. "Extra yardage is important," she said, "and this will also help develop the shoulders and arms."

She is already looking forward to next year's DI team. "The team should be much stronger," Cy

GAME FUN

A new load of sports and ... ment has found its wa... ... ... itories.

(Cont'd from Page ...) as follows: Worthy Matron, Pat Yoak; Worthy Protectoress, Jill Toler; Worthy Scribe, Tracey Perry; Worthy Keeper of the Treasury, Lorna Bjorkman; Worthy Directoress, Barbara Eerdmans. Committee Heads are Carol Burton, Pin Committee; Dona Van Singel and Joyce Newland, Parchment; Mary Pat Reilly, Reporter.

In The Parchment, national publication of the sorority, the following words were written:

... chapters extend con... ... ... to our

Some of the ... selling used ... sorority are and cleaning Margaret Hall in order to get it ready for the fall.

Other plans are to rush the new students and to send the President with several members to the convention in St. Louis, Mo., the end of August.

Main purpose of the sorority is to do all they can to be professional women and to help other girls to reach this status.

All of these young women are striving to be on the Dean's List each ... ... very term.

The 1964 Golf team includes Tom Cook, Cy Claus and Fred Sparks, Jr., all from East Grand Rapids; Morrie Fongers, Creston, Bob Kunnen, G. R. Christian, and Tom Collins, Stockbridge. A story on Miss Claus appears elsewhere on this page.

Teeing Up. Davenport's golf team dominated on the course and outlasted all other sports at the college. By 1971 the team was rated #1 in the Midwest region and #14 in the nation. Except for intramural competition, women's athletics did not exist at Davenport because the college's athletic budget could not support separate programs. But one talented co-ed, Cynthia "Cy" Clause, found her way to the number two position on the men's golf team. The opponents she outshot accepted their defeats, according to Ms. Clause, "quite graciously."

Campus Sports: Panthers in Their Prime

Athletics gained momentum through the 1960s and '70s, led by a strong basketball program. Coached by Dexter Rohm, the team compiled an impressive record in its first season with the Michigan Business School League (1960-61), going 10-0 in the MBSL and 12-3 overall. Later, led by Al Wooten and Roger VanderLaan, the Panthers continued to repeat as conference champions for the next several years, posting only 1 losing season in 12.

For the first time, the college also had a cheerleading squad to provide team spirit for the Panthers' growing fan base.

A tennis team was organized in 1962 under Coach Larry Elkins, followed in 1964 by golf, under the leadership of Karl Killman.

Men's softball played several seasons, bowling was added as a minor sport in 1967, and cross-country in 1971.

The Centennial Year: 1966

Davenport had much to celebrate at its century mark. What had begun with a handful of students taking penmanship courses in a single classroom had developed into a thriving educational enterprise with over 2,000 students and branches in five other Michigan cities. Scanning the horizon from 1966, the college's future looked brighter still.

In that year, expansion plans several years in the making began to ripen. Under provisions of the Higher Education Act, Davenport now qualified for federal grants and loans to assist with the development of its first multi-building campus.

Establishing a new site resonated powerfully as tangible validation of Davenport's progress. It had been 20 years since the University of Grand Rapids relinquished its campus on Robinson Road. While the downtown location offered high visibility and an architecturally unique imprint, it could not compare to the distinguished Lowe estate for collegiate atmosphere. A signature priority on President Sneden's agenda was building Davenport into the institution once envisioned for UGR.

With that objective in mind, the college made preparations to move to a seven-acre campus in an historic residential district just a quarter mile east on Fulton Street—an area that would later become known as Heritage Hill.

Davenport had already established a presence on the block between College and Prospect Avenues several years earlier. In order to accommodate the growing number of out-of-town students, M.E. Davenport had purchased four homes for conversion to dormitories, beginning in 1958 with the Charles Sligh estate on East Fulton Street. Three adjacent homes were later obtained, including the distinguished T. Stewart White residence, which had functioned as the Grand Rapids Furniture Museum during the 1930s and 40s. The building was renovated to include a library, two classrooms, dorm rooms for men, and quarters for the Phi Theta Pi fraternity.

College leaders study plans for a new academic building to ease the shortage of classroom space. The homes behind the group, both in poor condition, were demolished to make room for the new structure.

118 Davenport: Educating Across Three Centuries | From Institute to College

> "In the years immediately ahead, automation and an increasing labor market will create competition for employment that only those with higher education and specialized training will be able to meet with any degree of success."
>
> —President Robert Sneden

In 1966, Davenport is recognized by the state of Michigan for 100 years of education. Even as it celebrated its centennial, the college was planning for major advancements in the years ahead.

Vitae: Jim Stauffer

When Academic Vice President James Stauffer joined Davenport in 1962, the school was just starting its ascent of the accreditation ladder. As the architect of Davenport's college-level program, Stauffer helped build the curricula toward North Central Association levels and served as the chief liaison in preparing the college for its final NCA certification. He also developed the popular associate degree in restaurant and lodging management, whose graduates were much in demand at top resorts nationally. Later he administered the bachelor's degree program while it was affiliated with Detroit College of Business.

Much of the move between downtown and Heritage Hill was done on foot. Faculty, staff, and students pitched in to haul armloads of books, supplies, and even typewriters the entire four-block distance—uphill—from 2 Fulton to 415 Fulton.

In 1967, Davenport officials acquired the former headquarters of the Packaging Corporation of America, a handsome Georgian colonial at the northeast corner of Prospect and Fulton, for the college library and administrative offices. That same year, groundbreaking began for the new $1.1 million academic building that would accommodate 1,200 students, 24 classrooms, a student center, and the college bookstore. A prestigious new campus—Davenport's first under its own name—was taking shape.

The Academic Center held its first classes in February of 1968, with a three-day celebration to mark the event. With the move to Heritage Hill completed, the dream of a distinguished campus was finally realized, giving the college a defined collegiate environment and greater stature. Its structures, both new and restored, gracefully blended the character of the neighborhood with academe.

DAVENPORT COLLEGE OF BUSINESS

An Expanding Campus Profile

Signature buildings of the Heritage Hill campus were the new Academic Center (left) and the Administration Building (below), former headquarters of the Packaging Corporation of America. Built in 1957, it stood on the previous home sites of Henry Widdicomb, president of Widdicomb Furniture Company, and Delos A. Blodgett, president of Blodgett Homes for Children.

Two properties in advanced states of decline could not be salvaged for long-term occupancy. The Gorham and Howard residences (top right) were demolished to create space for the new Academic Center.

The Heritage Hill Campus A History of its Own

The decision to transform a deteriorating city block into a college campus was not only inspired, but well ahead of its time. The flight from urban cores was draining vitality from cities around the country, and Grand Rapids was no exception. But even as the wrecking ball demolished venerable downtown buildings, Davenport Institute committed itself to the city, leading the way in the restoration of a prestigious residential district well before preservation became a trend.

By 1958—the year Davenport Institute began investing in the 400 block of East Fulton Street—the area known as the "Hill District" had already become a tarnished shadow of its former elegance. Many of the homes—once the estates of some of the city's most prominent families—had been converted to apartments and were often poorly maintained by landlords. It would be a dozen years before the Heritage Hill Neighborhood Association was formally organized and the district was placed on the National Register of Historic Places.

In the neglected mansions Davenport leaders saw not blight, but opportunity. The development of its first campus began with the acquisition of several historic residences, each with its own impressive legacy, which were renovated and converted to residence halls and administrative offices.

Campus expansion and development accelerated through the 1960s. Work began in the winter of 1967 on a new 44,000-square-foot classroom building, which would open to students the following year. Not long after construction on the Academic Center began, Davenport learned that the Packaging Corporation of America would soon be vacating its headquarters at the corner of Fulton and Prospect. The stately Georgian colonial, built just ten years earlier, was perfectly suited to become the college's Administration Building.

Eventually two more apartment buildings were added—the Regency Apartments on Prospect Avenue, and the Fountain Hill Apartments at 301 Fountain, bringing Davenport's total investment in the neighborhood to nearly $2 million.

During its 40 years in Heritage Hill, Davenport made many adaptations to the campus to accommodate growth and student demographics. An addition to the

Mabel Engle Hall. Named for M.E. Davenport's wife, the home was built in 1890 by Charles Sligh, owner of one of the city's largest furniture manufacturers.

Warren Hall. Lumber scion T. Stewart White built the Tudor-style residence in 1908. Named for Davenport's son.

Tyrus Wessell Hall. Originally called Margaret Hall, the house at 401 Fountain was renamed for Wessell in 1985. Previously owned by the Griswold family, also furniture manufacturers.

Academic Center (renamed for Robert Sneden in 1980) gave the college another 10,000 square feet of classroom space, and in 1988 the college obtained the former Sherman home next to Mabel Engle Hall. Here the college established the Lettinga Entrepreneurial Center, which offered programs and services supporting small businesses. Altogether the college owned more than a dozen properties.

As Davenport evolved toward a commuter campus, it converted some buildings to administrative offices while selling noncontiguous properties. By the early 2000s, with Davenport's conversion to a university, it became evident that much more space would be needed to accommodate the school's future. A new campus on the city's outskirts was developed and named the W.A. Lettinga Campus for longtime board chair, Davenport alumnus, and Grand Rapids businessman Wilbur Lettinga. While both campuses operated for a time, eventually the decision was made to transfer all of Davenport's operations to the new location. Grand Rapids Community College purchased the property to expand its downtown campus.

Davenport had played a vital role in restoring and galvanizing an auspicious part of the city's heritage at a time when prevailing winds blew in the opposite direction. With its early commitment to the neighborhood, Davenport became a bellwether—even a catalyst—of the Hill's eventual return to distinction. Its ongoing presence anchored an important city block with stability, vitality, and "educational character."

> "Davenport Business College is serving this community admirably in more ways than one. Not the least of them is the way [Davenport] has moved to help establish an educational character of the Near East Side."
> —*Grand Rapids Press Editorial*

Lillian Myners Hall. An annex behind the Sligh estate.

Heritage Hall. Formerly the Regency Apartments.

Florence Woods Hall. Built as Fountain Hill Apartments and named for long-time faculty member Florence Woods.

Warren Hall   A Grand Rapids Landmark

The acquisition of the former T. Stewart White residence brought an important page of Grand Rapids history—and one of its most colorful families—into Davenport's own narrative.

Thomas White was born in Grand Haven in 1840 and moved to Grand Rapids in 1866 (coincidentally the founding year of Grand Rapids Business College) where he established, with partner Thomas Friant, the White and Friant Lumber Company. For the next 20 years the enterprise was the exclusive broker of every log that traveled down the Grand River from Grand Rapids to Grand Haven. These were the boom years for the city's furniture industry, and White made a fortune.

In 1908, he moved his wife, Mary, and their five sons into the new mansion built in the city's most fashionable neighborhood. The Whites resided at 427 East Fulton for the next 30 years.

The White sons inherited their father's genius for success, although they showed a propensity for the arts rather than business. The eldest, Stewart Edward, became an author of more than 70 adventure-genre books. Gilbert became a popular artist who painted the murals on the walls of his father's library. Son Roderick became a concert violinist, while Harwood became a tennis pro and coach. Middle-born Ruggee often joked that he was the only family member with no talent.

In 1939, the White sons donated their parents' home to the city of Grand Rapids for use as a furniture museum, the first of its kind in the nation. During its 20-year existence, the museum attracted more than 356,000 visitors.

Flex space: Built as a private home, the White residence went on to become a city museum, residence hall for Davenport students, and finally college offices.

Completed in 1908 at a cost of $250,000, the Tudor revival featured some of the most splendid craftsmanship of its time, and Davenport took care to preserve the finest details during the restoration process. In addition to the intricate woodcarving throughout the home, also preserved were a 300-year-old imported wall clock and the 24-karat gold leaf Tiffany ceilings.

President Sneden (center), with vice presidents Charles Anderson and Wessell, admire the distinctive wall fresco in the White mansion's library. Gilbert White painted the murals depicting his family as characters in King Arthur's court. After it was converted to a women's residence hall, the room would remain a library and study area.

(Bottom inset) The carved staircase in the entry foyer led to second- and third-floor living suites.

IT CAN BE DONE!

TRUSTEES	AND	TEAMS		TEAM GOALS	PLEDGED	PERCE. OF GO.
CHAMBERLAIN $5000.				$5,000.		
DE BOER $1000.	PRINS $2000.	LLOYD $2,500.	MYAARD $1000.	$6,500.		
EBERHARD $4000.	MILLER $1,500.	MARTINDILL $2,500.	HOOKER $5,500.	$13,500.		
HAGER $4000.	VANDERWALL $3,500.	DE JOURNO $4,000.	BYINGTON $1,500.	$13,000.		
HARTGER $1000.	LITSON $2,000.	WHITTIER $2,000.	FORD $2500.	$7,500.		
MCBAIN $1000.	MELLEMA $1,500.	LATHROP $3,500.		$6,000.		
PORTER $14,000.	TAMMINGA $2,500.	STREETER $2,000.	BONFIELD $3,500.	$22,000.		
SCHROTENBOER $4000.	BULT $4000.	BYLENGA $5,500.	VANDER VEEN $2,000.	$15,500.		
SNEDEN $5000.	TANZER $2,000.	BYTWERK $2,000.	BERMAN $2,000.	$11,000.		
				$100,000		

Sustainability for the Future: Creating an Endowment

Administrators realized that Davenport's revenues, still derived primarily from tuition, could not continue to meet future expenses if the college wanted to maintain its pace of growth. Additional income was needed to keep up with the escalating demands for equipment, facilities, scholarships, and improvements. There was a limit to the frequency and amount of tuition hikes that could meet operating expenses and still fall within the average student's budget.

There was another consideration; indigenous support for a college—as reflected by the gifts, contributions and bequests it receives—elevates its image not only in the eyes of the community, but also with the North Central Association accrediting commission, where reduced tuition dependence is an explicit requirement. Most private colleges received anywhere from 20 to 35 percent of their operating revenue from sources other than tuition; at Davenport, this proportion was less than five percent, a ratio college officials were determined to change.

In 1969, Davenport launched its first public fundraising drive and far surpassed its goal of $125,000. The fund drive became an annual affair, building a solid donor base of corporate and individual supporters, growing toward what would later become a permanent endowment.

(Opposite) The college held its first public fund drive in 1969, with a goal to raise $125,000. Intended originally to demonstrate public support to the North Central Association accrediting commission, the effort became an annual campaign eventually leading to the establishment of the college's endowment fund in 1982.

(Above) A view of Grand Rapids facing south depicting development north of the downtown core.

Vitae: Charles "Andy" Anderson

Instructor Andy Anderson generated more than his share of fond memories among students. An outstanding English teacher recalled for his droll wit, Anderson was a dynamic presence on the college faculty for 35 years. He served also as a college vice president and, along with B. Margaret Vos, established the offices of dean of men and dean of women. In the Robert Sneden Academic Center on the Heritage Hill campus, the student center was named in his honor.

Anderson was first and foremost a teacher, maintaining a full class load until his retirement in 1986.

Pavement Protest. While it did not experience the student protests or sit-ins of larger colleges, the Davenport campus during the Vietnam War years did see expressions of opposition. At left, a student makes his statement as a human peace symbol.

Classes underway at the new Academic Center, circa 1969.

Decades of dedication. Davenport's first alumni association, its first basketball team, and early student retention initiatives can all be attributed to Clifton C. Wonders. Beginning his Davenport career in the 1920s, he was also among the triumvirate—along with M.E. Davenport and Tyrus Wessell—that established the University of Grand Rapids. Later he became an original member of the Executive Cabinet created by President Sneden to manage the rapidly growing school.

A practicing CPA, Robert Schmiedicke joined Davenport as a full-time accounting instructor in 1958 and continued to teach while serving in key administrative positions through the administrations of presidents Robert Sneden and Donald Maine. Also an author, current editions of his original text *Principles of Cost Accounting* continue to be standard reference in colleges and universities.

PROMOTED AT DAVENPORT—Clifton C. Wonders, left, director of college relations at Davenport Institute, and Robert E. Schmiedicke, director of the evening college and dean of Davenport's account department, have been named vice presidents of the business school.

Davenport Names 2 Vice Presidents

Establishment of two new vice presidencies to bolster the administrative leadership of Davenport Institute in view of growing enrollment was announced Friday by Robert W. Sneden, president of the Grand Rapids business college.

Clifton C. Wonders...

a textbook, "Principles of Cost Accounting." He was a private and public accountant for 10 years, and a part time instructor at Davenport for several years before joining the faculty full time in 1958. He was made dean of the...

1971

876 ENROLLMENT

44 Faculty/Administration

DIPLOMAS and ASSOCIATE DEGREES
Business Management, Accounting, Marketing, Computer Programming

TUITION $17 Per Credit Hour

LOCATION 415 East Fulton

Divesting the Family Interest

Another requisite of accreditation would also prove one of the most bittersweet—that Davenport relinquish family management to a governing board broadly representative of public interest. The prospect would have been unthinkable to M.E. Davenport and for many years was similarly unpalatable to Sneden. But times were changing, along with criteria and expectations for education; Davenport College had to adapt if it wanted a prosperous future.

On New Year's Day 1971 a new charter of incorporation became effective. An independent, public board of trustees assumed oversight of the total administration of the college, which included hiring the president, approving the budget, and contributing to major strategic directions. Joseph Hager was appointed chair, and five members of the existing advisory committee—Schrotenboer, Chamberlain, Eberhard, Hartger, and Porter—were elected trustees. The family board of control, which had been the school's compass for six decades, was dissolved. North Central Association rules permitted family representation at an approved ratio, allowing Robert W. and Margaret Sneden and Marian Davenport Wynalda to continue in their previous governance roles. Joining as new members were the college's CPA Robert McBain and attorney James DeBoer, who went on to become the longest serving trustee in the college's history. This group became the first official governing body of Davenport College.

A separate corporation, Davenport Schools, Inc., was created for the affiliate schools in Lansing, Kalamazoo, Bay City, and Saginaw. This entity retained family oversight.

One giant step. Davenport's first governing board of trustees was elected in 1971. Five original members of the original advisory board continued to serve, along with Robert and Margaret Sneden. (Right) The new academic building included a multi-purpose room used for lectures, school functions, and the popular Davenport dances.

Pursuing the Prize

The year 1971 became a watershed for two other important accelerators into a new era. First, an Executive Council was established as a president's cabinet. Made up of leaders in key positions, this structure created a management template for future administrations. Secondly, a Faculty Senate was convened. An informal committee had already been in place for several years, and the new coalition strengthened the relationship between instructional and institutional policy.

But nothing had greater impact on the college's overall trajectory than the announcement that came in the middle of the year: in July Davenport was notified that it had been awarded correspondent status from North Central Association, the first threshold in the three-level process toward final accreditation. The event was a crucial affirmation of the academic status Davenport had committed to for years, and the response from four-year universities around the state was immediate. Western Michigan University agreed to rank credits transferred from Davenport College on an equal basis with those from public community colleges. The University of Michigan—which had previously declined Davenport transfer credits—now accepted them on a provisional basis.

Acceptance from its public peers was pivotal and gratifying, but the college also took the opportunity to reaffirm its identity as an independent specialty educator. "We've no intentions of modifying or changing Davenport College's most fundamental purpose of preparing students for careers in business," said President Sneden. "Our new identification with North Central Association is simply an indication of our successful and continuous efforts to provide an education appropriate to a constantly changing and complex society."

Five more years of diligent effort followed, with the college achieving high ratings from the Higher Learning Commission at each level of candidacy. In addition to the behind-the-scenes effort, the college was gaining steadily in the public eye as well, with its prominent campus and cutting-edge programs. When in 1976 Davenport attained North Central accreditation, it had the distinction of becoming one of the first "special purpose" two-year schools in the nation to do so.

Membership in NCA conveyed a wealth of important messages, primarily ones of quality, status, and willingness to meet the demanding educational standards upheld by other member colleges and universities. On an even deeper level, accreditation represented the culmination of a 70-year effort, to which scores of people had devoted their life's work. Officially, Davenport had entered the big leagues. From this point on, little could block the college from attaining its most ambitious goals.

A Defining Moment

In an interview with the college newspaper, President Sneden acknowledged the prodigious effort and its meaning for Davenport. "The process was a long journey," he told the *Davenport Digest*. "The battles and struggles were not few. Approval and acceptance by other institutions came slowly."

Dr. Therese Tomaszek, Davenport's longest-serving faculty member, recalled accreditation as a game-changer, altering outside perceptions of Davenport inestimably. "Becoming regionally accredited was huge for the college. It represented the first time the institution was no longer exclusively recognized as a vocational school."

Betty LaCroix, who served as President Sneden's executive assistant, and later as a college trustee, also witnessed firsthand the impact of accreditation on Davenport's internal culture. "The requirements for accreditation changed the thinking of Davenport's leaders and employees and forced the college to always be working to become better. Regional accreditation was the key to all subsequent changes."

Accreditation was also an important personal culmination for President Sneden. Occurring in the year he announced his retirement, North Central certification presented an opportunity for him to complete his administration "on top." During his presidency enrollment had increased tenfold; Davenport had become a degree-granting institution; its campus was the envy of comparable colleges. He had secured for his successors a dynamic organization, one enjoying growing prestige not only regionally but around the United States. Conditions were in place for the college to enter its next major era of progress.

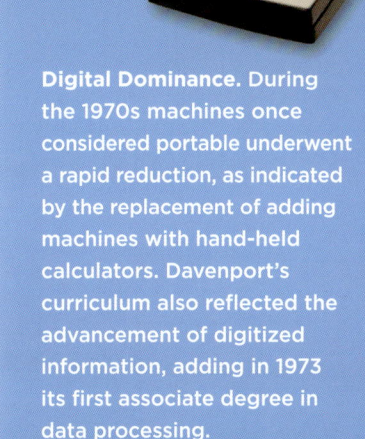

Digital Dominance. During the 1970s machines once considered portable underwent a rapid reduction, as indicated by the replacement of adding machines with hand-held calculators. Davenport's curriculum also reflected the advancement of digitized information, adding in 1973 its first associate degree in data processing.

Vitae: Betty LaCroix

Twenty-year-old Betty Saur completed the coursework for her executive secretarial diploma from Davenport Institute on a Friday in the spring of 1960. The following Monday, she returned to school—not to the classrooms where she had studied, but to the executive offices, where she spent the next 15 years as assistant to President Robert Sneden. During her career, her attachments to Davenport deepened as she became director and patroness for the Grand Rapids chapter of Alpha Iota business sorority and also one of the first woman trustees to join the college governing board. The 1985 Distinguished Alumni Award recipient remains active in the alumni association.

In an era when female pilots were the exception, Betty Saur LaCroix was licensed to fly single-engine airplanes. Above right, she maps a route with passenger B. Margaret Vos, Davenport's first dean of women.

Scenarios for Succession

With four grown daughters already pursuing careers and educational paths of their own, it became apparent with Sneden's approaching retirement that the presidency—for the first time in nearly seven decades—would no longer be in family hands. The board was faced with divergent choices: selecting a nonfamily president (as Sneden himself had suggested) or affiliating with another institution. Either direction felt daunting to an organization with so strong a legacy.

One opportunity existed at Grand Valley State College (now University) in Allendale, where officials from both institutions began exploring the feasibility of a potential merger. Davenport insisted that if an affiliation occurred, it would retain both its city campus and the authority to grant associate degrees.

The entire prospect contained mixed emotions. Although it would secure Davenport's name and posterity as an ongoing business division of Grand Valley, assimilation into a much larger school meant that Davenport's unique identity—upheld even in the most uncertain conditions for more than a century—could not remain fully intact. Even more incongruous to some was the prospect that Davenport would no longer be private, nor independent.

The greatest resistance came from Grand Rapids Junior College (now Grand Rapids Community College), at that time still a unit of Grand Rapids Public Schools. As negotiations advanced, it became apparent that the district opposed any agreement that would establish a second public two-year degree option in such close proximity to GRJC. Ultimately, the idea was abandoned.

In the meantime, a candidate search had begun for Sneden's successor. Among the field of applicants was a young local college executive who would soon put to rest any uneasiness about the transition to a nonfamily leader.

Davenport, GVSC Talk Of Affiliation

Representatives of Grand Valley State Colleges and Davenport College of Business are discussing a possible affiliation of academic programs.

Officials stress that the proposal is still in the infant stages, and that no definite outline has been discussed, but the affiliation apparently will center on coordinating the two schools' business programs.

"Inflation and higher educational costs have made colleges tend to cooperate with each other in the past," said Bruce Loessin, vice-president of the colleges at GVSC. "Affiliation is just a continuation of the is concept."

Loessin said affiliation would benefit both colleges through a pooling of resources, such as classes, faculty, and library and mechanical facilities.

Eliminating duplications of services would be one result of this, he said.

Loessin added that affiliation would mean the state would not have to pump more revenue into educational and building expansion: "That way we can utilize each other's better facilities."

JC Blocks GVSC-Davenport Linkup

By Paul Chaffee

A merger agreement between Grand Valley State Colleges and Davenport College of Business has died of a lethal dose of opposition from Grand Rapids Junior College.

"We couldn't keep chewing on it forever, so negotiations ended," Davenport President Robert Sneden said Monday of clashing stands by his Board of Directors and Grand Rapids school officials, who operate JC.

JC refused to allow another public, two-year, associate-degree-granting school like itself in its own back yard. Davenport insisted a condition of merger be the college's retention of power to award the two-year certificate.

Sneden and GVSC President Arend D. Lubbers had hoped the downtown private college would become one of Grand Valley's cluster colleges, maintaining much the same faculty, the same community contacts and its character as the business school the Davenport president's father-in-law rescued from oblivion in 1914.

Grand Valley and Davenport had reached tentative agreement according to Sneden, who said the arrangement perished because JC viewed it as a threat.

"Not a threat," commented Grand Rapids Schools Supt. Phillip Runkel. "We see it as an invasion of our geographical territory."

He said a second downtown public junior college would be an unjustifiable duplication of facilities and services JC provides at less cost. "A ripoff of the taxpayers' money," Runkel added.

A school system study indicated JC for $1,367 per student does essentially the same job Davenport has been doing for $2,332 per student, according to Runkel. He said JC is willing to continue negotiations that would bring a "second" two years of business training downtown so students could work on bachelor degrees and a third two-year program for master diplomas.

"There's no acrimony between JC and Davenport," Sneden said, "We want to continue in the same direction we have historically and Junior College couldn't agree to it."

Sneden said little danger exists of relations between the two operations slipping to the conditions of prior to three years ago, when the colleges were barely speaking to each other.

"No animosity," echoed Runkel. Without the backing of the Grand Rapids Board of Education, no GVSC-Davenport merger agreement is practical. Unless the local colleges face the Legislature united for the funds such a consolidation would require, approval chances would be remote.

Even with unanimity, JC Dean Francis J. McCarthy noted, the proposal might have faced a cool reception. He said public colleges recently received state Budget Bureau inquiries on what effect appropriation cuts would have.

Despite termination of merger talks, GVSC and Davenport are to continue discussions this week on how the two can "cooperate" better, said GVSC Vice President Arthur C. Hills.

Grand Valley, which had hoped to establish a "toehold" campus in downtown Grand Rapids, likely will discuss cooperative use of Davenport facilities for bachelor degree courses during slow hours. Most Davenport activity takes place in the morning and the evening.

Sneden said JC and Davenport also will continue discussion on cooperative projects, notably one in which the public junior college would subcontract to its neighbor some Manpower vocational training programs.

Nevertheless, both he and Runkel acknowledge that brisk competition between the pair of colleges continues; business offerings are nearly identical. Though JC tuition is about $350 a year and Davenport's is $1,440, Sneden claims an edge in business education experience, reputation and contacts in the business community, which translate into jobs. Davenport is helped by the fact that less affluent students can get $1,200 tuition grants from the state and, Sneden adds, JC is unlikely to catch up to the school on its strong points.

But Davenport's leaders, while operating well in the black, reportedly foresee difficult financial times for colleges of its type and had hoped to gain from the merger the security of state appropriations.

- *1971*

  First public board of trustees installed at Davenport College.

- *1971*

  First commercially available personal computer (KENBAK-1).

- *1973*

  First cellular phone call made.

- *1974*

  President Richard Nixon resigns; Vice President Gerald R. Ford becomes 38th president of the United States.

- *1976*

  Davenport College regionally accredited by North Central Association of Colleges and Schools.

- *1977*

  Robert Sneden retires and is succeeded by Donald Maine, Davenport's first nonfamily president.

Visionary Leadership

Although Sneden's departure closed the era of family leadership, continuity at Davenport was assured by the proactive measures taken during his years of service. The conversion to nonprofit (which occurred during his vice presidency), establishing a public governing board, and securing accreditation all anticipated future developments in career-based education. Schools like Davenport that had avoided similar preparations either went out of business or were acquired and transformed by large for-profit corporations.

As a member of the Davenport College board of trustees, and as president of Davenport Schools, Inc., Sneden maintained a significant voice in the direction and development of the Davenport educational presence.

> At the Heritage Hill campus, Davenport for the first time had space to develop a full library, a requisite for accreditation. (Right) Donald Maine introduces himself to Davenport students as the college's next president. Maine was actually returning to Davenport, having worked for the college in 1971–72 as director of special programs.

Presidential Profile Robert W. Sneden

With four generations of farming in his lineage, Robert Sneden seemed destined for a career in agriculture. Raised on the Jamestown, Michigan, farm settled by his great-great grandfather just after the Civil War, Sneden had a typical rural youth: chores before and after classes in a one-room schoolhouse, dawn-to-dusk farming in the summer. But by the time he graduated from Hudsonville High School in 1936, he was ready for something different.

Sneden found a job with McInerney Spring & Wire Company, a major supplier of seat frames to the automotive industry. He worked 12 hour days, for 30 cents an hour, as a "hogringer" fastening staples into automobile seats with heavy pliers. It was a physically exhausting job; but more importantly it was a learning experience. "I learned fast what I didn't want to do with the rest of my life," Sneden recalled.

He enrolled in Davenport-McLachlan Institute, initially working his way through college as a short-order cook. As he accumulated business training he was able to get a position as a salesman for the Burroughs Adding Machine Company. Upon M.E. Davenport's recommendation, Sneden entered the University of Grand Rapids and also took extension courses at the University of Michigan.

Sneden joined the army in January of 1941, hoping to complete his compulsory year of service and return to his education. But as that year drew to a close, the bombing of Pearl Harbor on December 7 rerouted his civilian plans. Conscripted for the duration of the war, Sneden was accepted into officer's candidate school, assigned stateside, and promoted to the rank of captain.

Sneden had returned home on several leaves during his years of active duty. One of these visits took him back to Davenport-McLachlan Institute to visit its president. Instead, he found himself chatting with the president's daughter Margaret, who had finished her degree at UGR and was working in the college administrative offices. A courtship developed, and the couple married in 1944, just before Sneden's unit, the 76th Infantry Division, was deployed in Europe.

While overseas, Sneden began receiving letters from his new father-in-law, asking about the possibility of working for the school after the war. "I always was polite but never entertained the proposal too seriously," Sneden recalled. He'd planned to return to Burroughs

Robert W. Sneden

"Bob Sneden was the best listener I've ever known. He always knew everything that was happening around him."
—Betty LaCroix, executive assistant to President Sneden, 1960–1975

after his discharge; but when the company offered him less money than his army salary, he decided to accept Davenport's offer.

Discharged in early 1946 with the rank of major, Sneden became a Davenport faculty member. He was also accepted into the graduate business school at the University of Chicago. "But there was no time, then," Sneden said, to pursue an advanced degree. In addition to his new career he was also a new father to the first of four daughters.

Sneden spent the next several years returning Davenport Institute to its prewar vigor. He taught math, speech, salesmanship, and the local Dale Carnegie course, and took a lead role in developing the college's new headquarters at Fulton and Division. He also served as M.E. Davenport's administrative aide-de-camp and in 1952 was made executive vice president of the institute. These were dynamic years for Davenport as it mobilized the expansion efforts that added campuses in Saginaw, Bay City, Kalamazoo, Lansing, and Detroit.

An agenda packed with professional and civic activities filled Sneden's "other" life. There wasn't a business school organization Sneden didn't serve. In 1955 he presided simultaneously over the Michigan Business Schools Association (with 15 member business colleges), and the Michigan Business Education Association, comprised of 1,000 secondary and post-secondary business teachers from around the state. He served also as director of the 4,000-member National Business Teachers Association. He held several executive positions as a lifetime member of Phi Theta Pi, the international commerce fraternity.

(Top) Sneden at one time contemplated a career in the ministry: occasionally he stood in as "guest pastor" at his family church in Jamestown. On the Hudsonville High School football squad, Sneden (wearing #21) was one of the smallest members of the team.

Presidential Profile Robert W. Sneden

National assignments poured in later. He devoted years of service to the National Association and Council of Business Schools, as a director, vice president, and president. When that group later became the United Business Schools Association, members elected Sneden as their president.

In that role he became one of the most visible emissaries for independent colleges, making several trips to Washington on behalf of legislative measures supporting the private education sector. Having experienced tuition hardships firsthand, he worked tirelessly on efforts to extend student assistance programs to others in need—most notably the Michigan Tuition Grant initiated in 1966.

All this he pursued while propelling his own school higher on the academic ladder. His ubiquity was instrumental in securing Davenport's status in the top ranks of independent business education. Davenport College achieved major goals in rapid succession: the move to Heritage Hill in 1968, North Central Correspondent Status in 1970, and finally full North Central Association accreditation—the college's long-pursued goal—in 1976. "My all-consuming objective," he told a reporter, "is the perpetuation of this institution."

Locally he was just as involved, as president of Blodgett Homes for Children (now D.A. Blodgett /St. John's), as an active Rotary Club member, and on numerous civic development committees, including the capital campaign to expand the downtown Ryerson Library in 1963.

Sneden retired from the presidency in 1977 with several impressive awards, including the Distinguished Service Award from the Association of Independent Colleges and Schools, that organization's highest honor. Davenport College also honored him with its top tributes: the Distinguished Alumni Award in 1980, and an honorary doctorate—the college's first—in 1985. The Academic Center was renamed in his honor in 1980.

President Emeritus Robert Sneden receives an honorary doctorate from President Donald Maine, the first awarded by the university. (Below) The Robert W. Sneden Center, completed in 2010, contains classrooms, executive offices, and a 232-seat auditorium.

He continued to work, serving simultaneously as president of Davenport Schools, Inc., which operated Great Lakes Junior College in Saginaw, and as president of the M.E. Davenport Foundation, which he and wife, Margaret, established in 1986. He remained a member of the Davenport College Board of Trustees until his death in 1992.

In addition to a passion for education, Sneden shared M.E. Davenport's love of fishing, hunting, and the outdoors. At home in Grand Rapids he kept busy with golf and his four children.

Because of Sneden's leadership, Davenport did much more than grow—it crossed critical thresholds as a higher education institution. He began his presidency in a single building with 400 students; he left his successors a fully accredited college with a distinguished historical campus, an enrollment of 2,000 and growing, and a vanguard position in the field of business and career preparation. He had also inspired greater expectations for Davenport, which would continue to be fulfilled by new leaders in new eras.

In 2010, on Davenport University's new Lettinga campus, the Robert W. Sneden Center was dedicated to his legacy.

"Ever since its beginning in 1866, Davenport College has built upon its uniqueness. The institution has projected a spirit of restlessness, of adapting its educational mission to the ever-changing needs of business and industry." —President Donald Maine

COMING OF AGE:
GROWING TOWARD A UNIVERSITY
1977–2000

Ongoing Heritage, New Directions

EVEN AS IT RECOGNIZED GREAT POTENTIAL IN Donald Maine, the search committee vetting President Sneden's successor held some concerns about the transition. "We took a risk hiring Don because of his inexperience," said Fred Vandenberg, a search committee member who would later chair Davenport's governing board. "But it quickly became clear we had made a good decision."

Maine himself approached his new position with some trepidation; he was both acutely aware and respectful of the heritage preceding him. Moreover, he was about to become—at age 35—the youngest college president in Michigan.

Maine took office just as several major socioeconomic trends were converging. The baby boom, with its enormous supply of new students, was on the descending side of its curve. On the horizon a severe economic recession was forming, where a sharp escalation in energy prices would collide with an even greater upheaval: the end of America's great Manufacturing Age. Profound shifts in the global economy were challenging the country's industrial and commercial dominance. International competition, automated assembly, and digitization would all compel America's corporate culture to reexamine its core assumptions.

One thing was obvious: the old boundaries were beginning to blur.

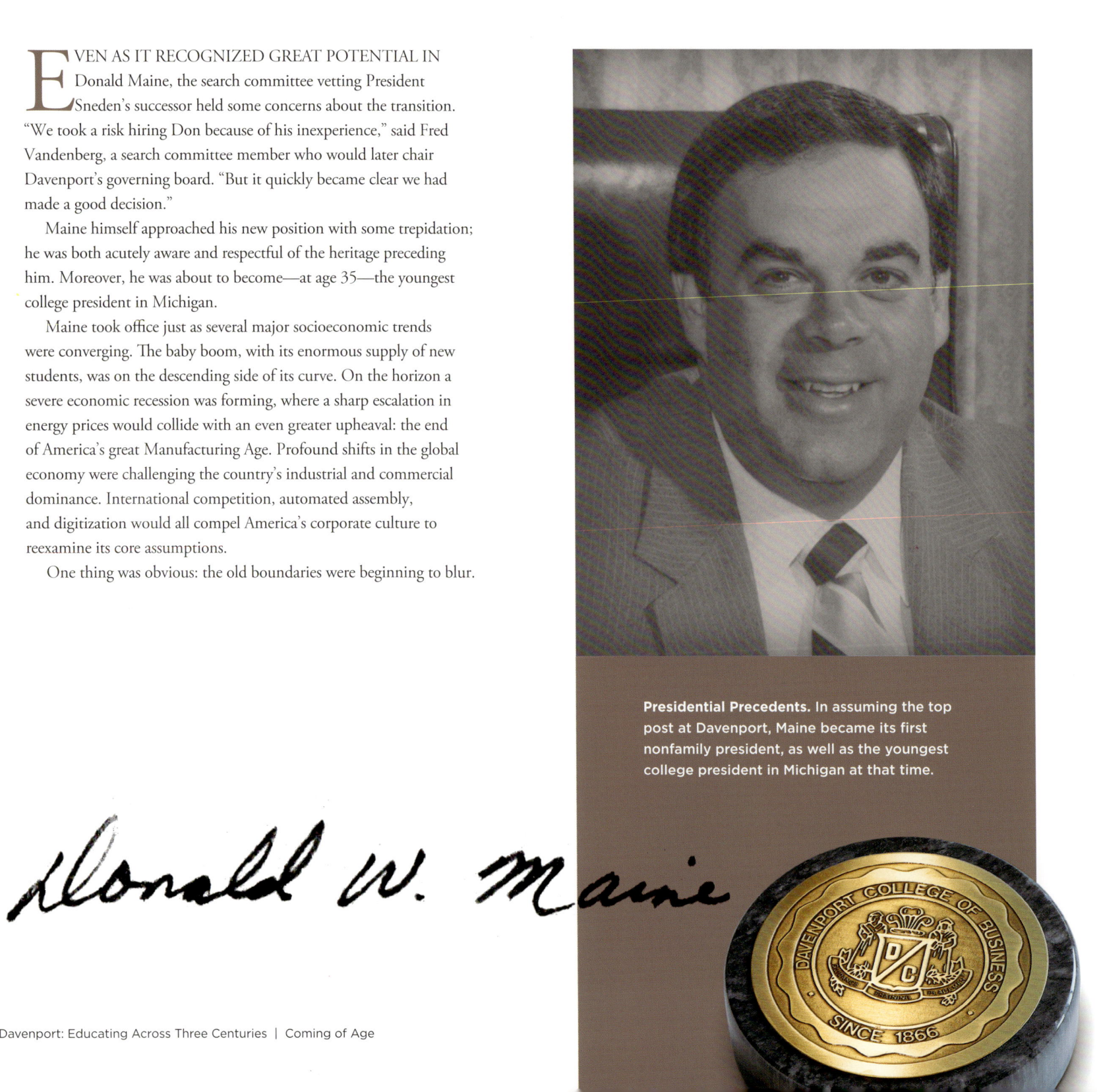

Presidential Precedents. In assuming the top post at Davenport, Maine became its first nonfamily president, as well as the youngest college president in Michigan at that time.

142 Davenport: Educating Across Three Centuries | Coming of Age

Pointing the Way. Retiring President Robert Sneden and incoming President Donald Maine prepare for the change of administrations.

1979
Lansing Business University acquired.

1980
Davenport begins offering baccalaureate programs in Grand Rapids through Detroit College.

1979
First cellular telephone network developed in Japan.

1981
Emergency Medical Services program acquired from Grand Valley State University.

Kalamazoo branch opens with the acquisition of Parsons Business School.

1982
During a severe economic recession, unemployment rate hits 10.8%, the highest in the U.S. since 1940. At 14.5%, Michigan's jobless rate is the worst in the nation.

1982
Davenport College Foundation established.

Taking the Helm

Maine wasted no time embracing both the opportunities and the challenges that awaited. The day he was notified of his selection, he composed an ambitious to-do list. Among its 25 objectives: a baccalaureate program, expansion of off-campus and continuing education initiatives, acquisition of branch campuses, and the continuing elevation of Davenport's image and visibility.

In his 23 years as president—the longest presidential term outside that of M.E. Davenport himself—Maine would end up accomplishing all this and more. The new leader understood that the school's formula for success was based on collaborative, anticipatory leadership, and patterned his own administration on that precedent. Recognizing Davenport College as a "constantly changing and growing institution," he initiated a long-range planning model that combined executive and support positions into task forces. This basic template remained in place throughout Maine's tenure.

Vol. 8 No. 4

Davenport Digest

September 1977

Davenport College of Busi[ness]
415 East Fulton Grand Rapids, Mich[igan]

Donald Maine Assumes Davenport College President

* * *
"Excited about Challenges of the Future" — Maine

President—Davenport College.

That's the distinguished title of Donald Maine, who, on the first day of August, assumed the leadership position created by the retirement of Dr. Robert W. Sneden.

In expressing his feelings, Maine said: "I'm delighted! I'm very pleased to succeed Dr. Sneden. He has played such a vital role in developing the institution's educational programs, its fine relationship with business and industry and, of course, the beautiful campus facilities."

Maine will complete his Doctoral Program in Higher Education at the University of Michigan next spring. He also holds a Bachelor's and a Master's Degree in Education from Michigan State University.

He is very familiar with the campus, having served Davenport College as Director of Special Programs from 1971-75. In that capacity, he was responsible for such projects as the College Achievement and Transition Program, Inner City Education Project, CETA Employment Training Programs, Work Incentive Program, Special Services Consortium and the Model Cities Higher Education Project.

Even before coming to Davenport, Maine had proven himself to be an educational innovator. For his achievements in the educational field, including instructorship with the Kenowa Hills Public School System, he was honored by the Jaycees in 1969 as the Outstanding Young Educator of the Year.

Maine also reviews, gratefully, the past two years with Grand Rapids Junior College from 1975-1977, where his titles included Director of Public Information and Fund Development, Dean of [...]

Viewing the campus from the President's Office are retiring President Robert Sneden and Donald Maine, who assume[s] the leadership post on August 1.

Education activities to make these opportunities more available for our community. An example is our new arrangement with the Wyoming Public School System's Community Education Division where we are now offering business courses within the City of Wyoming."

"We'll even be assessing the possibilities of offering classes on Friday evenings, Saturday or Sunday afternoons."

"Similarly," added Maine, "we'll continue to respond to the needs of industry by offering special seminars. As we face the future of declining K through 12 enrollments nationally, it seems that the role of

[Continued on page 2]

Next Issue: Dr. Sneden Ret[...]

Davenport College

Demographic Shift. (Right) As the last of the baby boom generation entered college, the population of traditional-age students would begin to level off. The gap would be filled by adult students enrolling in greater numbers.

Desk Job. During a role-swapping event (inset), President Maine becomes a "student for a day."

A New Educational Compass

As the 1970s drew to a close, the population of 18- to 24-year-olds began a steady decline. The dissipating pool of traditional college-age students, coupled with an inverse rise in tuitions, closed many colleges and imperiled others. Many institutions, which had expanded to meet the demands of the previous two decades, discovered themselves overbuilt. Independent schools suffered disproportionately: by 1978, nearly 130 independent colleges and universities nationwide had closed their doors.

That Davenport did not become one of these casualties testified to its resilience. Measures taken in previous eras—the conversion from proprietary to nonprofit, establishing a public governing board, regional accreditation—had contributed greatly to the school's image and competitive edge. Curricula continued to evolve with classes that reflected the more sophisticated skill sets that employers demanded. Prevailing trends in business education pointed toward the increasing need for deeper levels of classroom preparation. Before long, Davenport College would be compelled to make one of the biggest changes in its history.

By his second year in office, Maine had increased the number of governing board trustees from 14 to 22. The expansion included the board's first black member—Dr. Ralph Mathis—and doubled the number of women trustees. Board leadership changed as well. Wilbur A. Lettinga was named chairman in 1978, replacing Joseph A. Hager, who had served as President Sneden's board chair for 15 years. Mr. Hager and trustee Donald Porter, both of whom were founding board members, were awarded emeritus status.

Head of the Table. During four consecutive terms as chair, Mr. Lettinga (seated at far end of table next to President Maine) helped guide the college through major advancements.

1970s Sports: The Panthers in Hibernation

Davenport Claims Lack of Student Interest in Sports Shutdown

3-1-79

By Vern Plagenhoef

Davenport College President Don Maine today announced the termination of the school's two-sport intercollegiate athletic program, effective at the conclusion of the coming spring term.

Maine, acting on a vote taken Wednesday by Davenport's Board of Trustees, cited a lack of student interest as the principal reason for phasing out men's basketball and men's golf.

Estimates for student attendance at basketball games begin at 25 and drop. Maine attributes the scant turnout to the fact that nearly 90 percent of Davenport's students commute to classes and then go to work in one of the many job placement programs sponsored by the college.

The struggle for identity also has been hindered by a lack of college-owned facilities on campus. Davenport has played its home basketball games at Kenowa Hills High School for the past several years.

Maine stated that any discussion of the possible construction of a college-owned facility was merely "superficial."

Davenport is a private business college with an enrollment of 2,300 students. This year's athletic budget of roughly $15,000 served a very small percentage of those students.

"We want to focus our attention to service student needs, and it's obvious they don't want to go and watch anyone play basketball," Maine said. "There has been a growing phenomenon here to which we haven't properly addressed ourselves and we believe if we spend even a small percentage of this (athletic) sum it will be money better spent."

Maine specified the increased growth and popularity of academic and social clubs such as skiing, cross country-hiking, hospitality, association of legal students and a vets club.

"These clubs have been operating at their own expense, and we now see the merit they hold," Maine explained. "We are interested in promoting current and future academic and social pursuits as well as others suggested by faculty or students."

Maine said a "substantial" amount of the $15,000 which had been budgeted for athletics now will be earmarked to assist the campus club concept.

Maine also stressed that athletic scholarships extended to current freshmen, of which there are four, will be honored through their sophomore year provided they remain in school and meet academic requirements.

Golf coach Karl Killman and athletic director-basketball coach Al Wooton both will remain on the faculty.

Killman served as golf coach for six years and his squads showed a 126-39 record. Killman's academic duties have expanded greatly in the past few months, and that has reduced time he could devote to coaching.

Wooton's basketball teams endured only one losing season in 12 and finished 14-13 this year. Wooton will continue as a full-time instructor in the secretarial science division and also will receive selected special assignments from Maine's office.

Pressures inherent in the incorporation of Title IX did not greatly influence Davenport's decision to leave the intercollegiate athletic arena, according to Maine.

"The litigation at Michigan State and the implications involved in Title IX were on the back of everyone's mind," Maine admitted. "But if that had become an issue we would have had to terminate for the same reasons — lack of facilities, need for coaches, operating expenses and the level of spectator interest."

Davenport's intercollegiate program at one time counted four men's sports — tennis, cross country, basketball and golf. The program was reduced to basketball and golf six years ago when tennis was dropped for lack of participant interest.

Maine does not foresee resurrection of an intercollegiate athletic program in the near future.

"We have spent the better part of a year making a detailed analysis of the needs of this school, and we arrived at this decision," Maine said. "I don't see any change on the board."

Despite the success and popularity of athletics at Davenport, by the mid-1970s issues emerged that required reevaluation of a formal athletic program.

The college had always lacked athletic facilities of its own; gymnasiums and courts for the basketball and tennis teams were rented from area high schools. Scheduling grew increasingly complicated, and attendance at sports events suffered as a result.

At the same time Davenport was experiencing an increase in its commuter student population while on-campus residency was diminishing. School officials were challenged to maintain both student and spectator interest in Panthers athletics at a level that justified the growing expense.

Federal legislation known as Title IX, passed in the mid-1970s, also had a peripheral influence. Title IX contained provisions requiring educational institutions receiving any federal funds (including Pell grants) to provide comparable access and resources to women's athletics as well as men's. Davenport lacked the budget to maintain two full sports programs. All factors combined, the college was obligated to phase out athletics altogether by 1979.

Some 25 years later, Davenport University was able to restore and expand its intercollegiate sports commitment. A new campus provided both the space and facilities to support a full athletic roster that included more than 20 sports for both men and women.

Final Golf Team Competes for National Championship

They finished in grand style, those golfers from Davenport College.

In the final chapter of the school's intercollegiate sports history book, five young men went all the way to Odessa, Texas and the National Junior College Athletic Association Golf Championship.

Guided by Coach Karl Killman, whose seven season record features 153 wins and only 24 losses, the Panthers scorecarded an unprecedented 27-5 season including the top spot in the Region 12 competition with 32 junior colleges in Michigan, Ohio and Indiana.

In Odessa, Texas, the fivesome chipped and putted in 95-100 degree temperatures and 45 mile-per-hour winds to an 18th place position. Fairwayman Doug Snoap finished 30th out of 220 golfers, with scores of 74-81-76-78. Jim Foguth also scored in the top third of all those who "teed it up" for the 72-hole tournament.

Others who made the Texas trip were Ed Wesseldyk, Bob Stuewe and Jim Mohrig, whose 18-hole averages during the year were 78, 79 and 80, respectively.

"The kids were shooting for Texas right from the start of the season," smiled Killman. "They were determined to go all the way in our last season. I'm proud of them. It was a lot of fun."

"Show me a business college that does away with golf...and I'll show you a business college that defeats its purpose."

—Mark Russell, political pundit, speaking at an "Executive 100" Lecture Series event

Last Team Standing.
The 1979 golf team, coached by Karl Killman, retired the sports program at Davenport.

Davenport to Initiate Four-Day Class Week

By Joan Verdon

Most people complain that there aren't enough days in the week, but administrators at Davenport College of Business have decided they can get by with one less.

They've come up with an unusual plan they believe will increase opportunities for faculty and students and save a lot of gasoline.

Starting this fall, the college will go to a four-day course schedule and no classes will meet on Fridays.

"It's taken us just about a year to do it, but we've been able to fit all of our courses into four days instead of five," said President Donald Maine.

He estimates the change will cut student gas consumption by about 20 percent.

He said he doesn't know of any other colleges in West Michigan that have adopted a four-day plan.

The college still will require the faculty to work five days a week. But Fridays the school will hold educational sessions for the faculty, committee meetings and special programs, Maine said.

All of the college's facilities, such as the library and administration offices, will remain open Fridays.

Most of Davenport's classes currently meet four days a week, but the "off" day varies. A student might have one class that meets every weekday except Tuesday, another that meets every day except Thursday and another that meets every day but Monday.

"About 24 percent of our students drive in from places like Holland and Zeeland," Maine said. "They might have only two classes on Tuesday and come all the way in for half a (class) load."

The four-day class schedule should result in "considerable gas savings for the students and, at $1.40 a gallon, that's something," he said.

About 800 of the colleges 1,000 day students attend classes on Fridays.

Another advantage of the change is that it will help working students. Most of Davenport's students work while attending college "and they will now have a full day off when they can work," Maine said.

The faculty knows about the new schedule and is "delighted with it," he said.

"We haven't had a chance to react. We have a special meeting coming up early next week, that's when the reaction will come," said communications instructor Terri Tomaszek, a faculty senate officer.

But, she added, several faculty members have lobbied for four-day weeks for more than a year.

"The faculty has, for the most part promoted the idea of four-day weeks. It's worked at other places. And, with the gas situation, some people have wanted to try it here," she said.

The college will assemble the faculty for Friday meetings and workshops without having to work around class periods, the school's president said.

Fridays also will become a good day for scheduling conferences for the noncollege community, he said.

The college will announce the new schedule to students Monday, Maine said.

The 1970s oil embargo by OPEC (Organization of the Petroleum Exporting Countries) introduced an energy crisis that greatly impacted America's fossil fuel consumption habits. One of Davenport's own conservation policies was to shorten its class week. This not only saved gas for commuting students, but lowered campus utility costs.

Davenport Buys Lansing School

By Marianne Rzepka

Davenport College of Business officials will acquire the Lansing Business Institute as an extension of its main campus in Grand Rapids.

Davenport will rename the 200-student Lansing school Davenport College, Lansing Branch, when paperwork completes a purchase decision made last week by the local college's Board of Control.

Davenport president Donald Maine told The Press that eventually his school will offer only accounting and secretarial skills associate degrees in the capital city school.

Maine said students enrolled in other programs offered by Lansing Institute may have to take the remainder of their courses in Grand Rapids.

Another alternative Davenport is considering, the president said, is phasing out those other programs, keeping them going only as long as already-signed-up students are taking courses.

Maine said Davenport will not release terms of the acquisition.

Davenport will gain students and said LBI covered the same recruiting area as Davenport.

Students will benefit too, Maine said, because the Lansing campus will start offering associate degrees and financial aid will be available.

They also will be able to transfer to the Grand Rapids campus, if they wish to go on for a four-year degree through Davenport's new co-op program with the Detroit College of Business.

The four-year program was announced in March. It permits students to receive two-year associate degrees through Davenport and go on to four-year degrees through the Detroit College of Business, while remaining on the Grand Rapids campus.

Davenport used to be part of Davenport Schools, a group of institutes which also included programs in Saginaw, Detroit, Kalamazoo and Bay City. At one time, Lansing was part of the chain.

Davenport became a nonprofit school in 1960, formed a Board of Control in 1971 and received accreditation from the North Central Association of Colleges and Schools in 1975.

Robert Sneden, son-in-law of founder M.E. Davenport, cut ties completely between Davenport and Davenport Schools in 1976, when he retired as president of the business college.

Sneden gradually is retiring from his positions at the head of the other schools. After transfer of the Lansing school, he will serve on as chairman of the board for schools in Detroit and Saginaw.

Roger VanderLaan, Davenport director of admissions, said he broached the transfer subject with Sneden last year.

"He's retiring, he doesn't need any more problems," said VanderLaan. "I asked him about it, let him think about it and came back with more information and he said all right."

Maine said Davenport leases the three-year-old building which houses the institute. "We don't think it'll be big enough for our needs," he said. "It's kind of at a maximum now."

Maine said he believed the Davenport program will catch on fast in Lansing, where LBI graduates have been able to get jobs easily.

Vitae: Donald Colizzi and C. Dexter Rohm

Donald Colizzi devoted his entire professional life to Davenport-affiliated institutions. When Davenport College acquired the Lansing Business Institute in 1979, Colizzi—LBI's director of admissions for the previous 12 years—was appointed associate dean. Enrollments doubled in his first year of leadership and steadily increased thereafter, making it one of Davenport's best-performing sites. After the 1985 Davenport/Detroit merger, Colizzi became a senior vice president in the expanded organization, while continuing as dean in Lansing. Promoted again in Davenport's 1996 acquisition of Great Lakes Junior College, he supervised the GLJC main campus in Midland. He spent the rest of his career developing and leading enrollment strategies before retiring in 2000.

Donald Colizzi

Dexter Rohm's career with Davenport began in 1958 when the Davenport Institute freshman was hired to revive the dormant basketball program. "Dex" left just long enough to earn a bachelor's degree from Aquinas College, then returned to Davenport as an instructor and admissions representative. Soon he was put in charge of the Parsons Business School in Kalamazoo, which he later purchased. Under his leadership, Parsons grew into a new location on West Main Street. After Parsons was acquired by Davenport College in 1981, Rohm continued as dean of the Kalamazoo branch. In 1994 he became a senior vice president with the Davenport Educational System, serving until his death from cancer in 1997. A memorial scholarship was established in his honor.

C. Dexter Rohm

Re-expanding Across Michigan

As the median college age began tracking upward, adult learners represented a greater proportion of college enrollments. Educators everywhere began to reframe not only their curricula, but its delivery. Considerations like site proximity and schedule flexibility gained traction.

Assessing these factors, Davenport College began to reaffiliate with schools that had existed under its previous corporate structure, but had since gone on to operate independently. Lansing Business Institute (which decades earlier had been Davenport's first satellite location) was the first to be reacquired in 1979. Donald Colizzi was named associate dean to replace retiring owner Martin Wynalda. The Lansing merger was the first step in what would become a remarkable period of growth.

Two years later, in 1981, Davenport acquired the Parsons Business School of Kalamazoo, appointing C. Dexter Rohm as dean. Both Wynalda and Rohm had managed their respective schools for many years, originally as operating units of Davenport Schools, Inc., then as independent owner/directors after DSI downsized in the early 1970s. When reconnected with the Grand Rapids campus, the names of both LBI and Parsons were changed to Davenport College to reflect their status as branch campuses.

Along with these main hubs, Davenport increased its regional penetration through a network of attendance centers in communities throughout western and central Michigan. By the end of 1983, there were 28 of these sites in operation, where students could take business courses leading to a Davenport degree.

Parsons School of Business is Davenport College's second acquisition within two years.

Reagan brings new mood to Washington

By Randall Vande Water
Sentinel managing editor

GRAND RAPIDS — A different mood permeates Washington today, a mood of optimism, hope and change in anticipation of Ronald Reagan's administration, Hugh Sidey, Time magazine author of the weekly column "The Presidency" told members of the Executive 100 Club at Davenport College Tuesday.

He doesn't believe the new president will make many changes but does believe Reagan "will make the nation feel proud again and could help to bring inflation down. Reagan may not be the most popular but he will give direction.

"It's a time to exaggerate and feel good as we enter a new period of national life."

He noted something has changed in the nation's capital. He was "fascinated that a broken down, aging actor could get a chance to make the change."

For 40 years the same ideas reassembled in Washington. President Jimmy Carter made thrusts but no changes and the city sees the administration trying to changes, Sidey indicated.

Last week Reagan was in and Carter was across the White House and there were troops in the streets. Sidey of this happening only in phasizing Communist lead

no successful way to succeed themselves. Sidey said he had never seen a president drop out of sight as fast as Carter in the 25 years covering chief executives. Even though Carter faces policy decisions, threatened vetoes and still has certain authority, he has been pushed aside and few stories are generated about him. "Washington is kind of sick of him and this is the reflection of the voters throughout the country."

Comparing Reagan and Carter, Sidey said the president had great, high purpose but didn't know what to do. He talked too much, resulting in contradiction and became a bore. He had no idea who he was or where he was going. He made 625 promises and then choked on them. Reagan may find "less may be better" and may get a few things accomplished. But he knows where he stands and he will restore dignity to the office.

Sidey felt Carter used the hostage crisis in Iran for political advantages and it backfired because people got sick of it, the weekend before the election

his talents. Johnson was the most skilled legislator but passed too many bills and didn't understand the Vietnam war.

"Nixon was a brilliant strategist on foreign affairs who destroyed himself because he forgot the oath of office. Ford knew who he was and will get a good shake from history. He returned force and direction to the office. Carter was a part of the age of permanent campaigning, an expert on election but no good at running the government. Sidey sees Ford and vice president George Bush playing major roles in the next administration.

Commenting on Ford and Reagan, Sidey said Ford had the toughest job in history but returned decency to the office. Reagan will be more dogmatic but won't be as sure-footed. He doesn't know Washington as well as Ford and will have to rely on others, including Ford, to help him. He has the advantage of Senate control and a conservative mood in the House.

Sidey felt the U.S. will be more predictable under Reagan and he would welcome

Reinventing Itself. Like many other urban centers facing business and retail exodus, Grand Rapids fought to maintain viability. To compete with shopping malls, the southern portion of Monroe Avenue was closed off to create a pedestrian mall. The concept proved unsuccessful, and eventually downtown Grand Rapids would lose all three of its iconic department stores: Wurzburg's, Herpolsheimer's, and finally Steketee's. All had been in business for over a century. (Monroe Avenue would be reopened to automobile traffic in the late 1990s.)

Grand Rapids would struggle for years reinventing its downtown core. Eventually, the convergence of economic improvement, private capital, and civic leadership—which included Davenport President Donald Maine—would establish a range of projects that would help the city establish a new and vibrant identity.

Always inclusive by tradition and practice, Davenport has had an established minority student union on campus since the late 1960s. During the 1980s diversity grew more organized with an annual celebration of Black History Month, which featured an impressive roster of keynote speakers. Among the VIPs who visited were civil rights activist and Georgia state congressman Julian Bond and Alex Haley (pictured at right with President Maine), the Pulitzer Prize-winning author of *Roots: The Saga of an American Family*.

The first person of color elected to Davenport's board of trustees, Dr. Ralph Mathis, M.D., was instrumental in developing Davenport's medical programs, including the Emergency Medical Services curriculum. He served on the board for nearly 20 years.

The Grand Rapids Press, Saturday, January 7, 1978

Davenport College Board Joined by First Black

Davenport College's Board of Trustees has elected four new members, including its first black man and a former teacher at the school.

The new trustees are Dr. Ralph E. Mathis, Marvin R. Brummel, Robert L. Bytwerk and Emerson G. McCarty.

Mathis, a local obstetrician, is the school's first black trustee, according to Davenport President Donald Maine.

Mathis is a graduate of Aquinas College and the University of Michigan School of Medicine. He is an associate professor of obstetrics at Michigan State University, a director of the Kentwood Savings & Loan Association and a member of the local NAACP chapter.

Once a teacher of advertising and economics at Davenport, Bytwerk now heads Manpower, Inc., of Grand Rapids, is a director of the Lansing Business Institute and a past president of the Grand Rapids Advertising Club.

Brummel is president of Boulder Bluff

Hardware, Inc. He is part owner of the Candlestone Inn Motel in Belding and of the Riverview Racquet and Tennis Club in Grand Rapids.

Besides serving as a director of the Michigan National Bank-Wyoming and the Grand Rapids Home Builders Association, Brummel is a past president of the Godwin Christian School board.

McCarty is president of McCarty Communication, Saranac. He also is president of PrintCraft Company and AdCraft Advertising Agency of Fort Myers, Fla., and a director of the Lansing Business Institute, the Independent Bank Corporation and First Security Bank. He serves as treasurer for Manpower, Inc., and chairs the Ionia County Board of Canvassers.

The other 14 board memb Peter C. Cook, James N. Robert J. DenHerder, Jos Walter F. Johnso Wilbur A. Letti Donald J.

○ **1983**
Davenport College is approved by the North Central Association to begin offering baccalaureate degrees.

○ **1983**
South Bend Career Center opened.

○ **1983**
Davenport begins management of Candlestone Inn Recreational Complex in Greenville, Michigan.

○ **1984**
Compact discs (CDs) allow digitized information storage.

○ **1984**
Apple Computer introduces the MacIntosh, the first portable desktop PC.

○ **1984**
Grand Rapids Career Center opened.

Groundbreaking Programs and Educational Outreach

Important career training initiatives accompanied the proliferation of physical sites. In 1980 Davenport College acquired the Center for the Study of Emergency Medical Services from Grand Valley State College (now University). The program trained students in first-response medical care of the critically ill and injured. As a leader in this "triage" concept, the EMS program attracted students from across the nation. The media took notice as well, raising public awareness about Davenport's expansion into a field other than business.

The college created a new enterprise of a different type when in 1983 it purchased the 265-acre Candlestone Inn recreational complex in Belding, Michigan. The property included a 27-room hotel, restaurant, lounge, conference rooms, a championship golf course, and tennis courts. Its primary purpose, however, was to provide a "working laboratory" for students pursuing a degree in restaurant and lodging management. (When established in 1973, the hospitality program itself was the only one of its kind in West Michigan and was eventually emulated by other colleges.) Candlestone helped train hundreds of students before it was sold in 1988.

Hospitality Suite. Students in the restaurant and lodging management program interned at Candlestone Inn near Belding, Michigan. Davenport was the only business college in the country to manage its own resort in combination with an academic degree.

Robust expansion continued as Davenport developed three "Career Centers," two in northern Indiana, and later one in Grand Rapids. These sites offered condensed training formats—one year or less—in word processing, accounting, and legal and medical secretarial skills. Because the concept of a location dedicated exclusively to shorter certificate programs was unproven, college leaders chose to test the model outside of Michigan, but contiguous to major metropolitan areas. Career Centers in South Bend and Merrillville, Indiana, quickly proved popular for employers looking for a certain skill set and also with students looking to earn a specialized credential and enter the workforce quickly. Based on that success, Davenport opened a third Career Center on Eastern Avenue in Grand Rapids. The certificate schools contributed to Davenport's phenomenal growth throughout the 1980s and 1990s.

Meanwhile, enrollment on the main campus created such demand for seats that the need for facilities expansion could not be ignored. In 1983, ground was broken on a 35,000 square-foot addition to the Robert W. Sneden Academic Center. The project featured an expanded library and student center, extra classrooms, and special laboratories for accounting and computer programming instruction.

A President's Legacy. Board of trustees chair Wilbur Lettinga and former President Robert Sneden unveil the new sign in front of the academic center, which was named for Sneden in 1980.

First Responders. Led by cardiologist Dr. C. Mark Vasu, the Center for the Study of Emergency Medical Services provided training for pre-hospital medical care of the critically ill and injured. Because it was one of the first of its kind, the EMS program was able to attract students from across the nation and spawned many competing programs based on its original model. Eventually, as nursing and other higher-level medical programs evolved, the program was discontinued.

Fast Forward. *In 2015, a donation from an original supporter of the EMS program helped establish a scholarship in the College of Health Professions was established for students pursuing a health-related degree.*

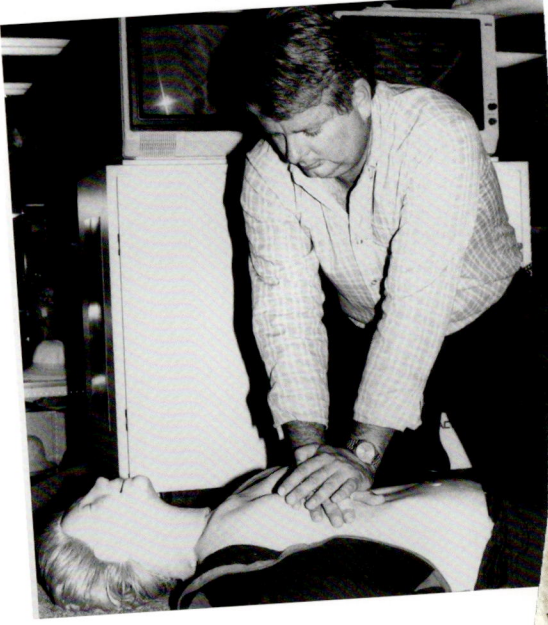

Services to continue at Davenport

GRAND RAPIDS Davenport College is in the final stages of negotiations regarding transfer of Grand Valley State College's Center for Emergency Medical Services (E.M.T.), according to Davenport President Donald W. Maine.

Pending approval by the Davenport College Board of Trustees, the E.M.T. program will be introduced as part of a new Division of Allied Health Sciences.

Having provided valuable service and training to West Michigan communities under the direction of Grand Valley State Colleges, the E.M.T. program will continue in its present form at Davenport College. Students will have the opportunity to earn an Associate Degree in Emergency Medical Systems Management, which includes the paramedic designation.

The transfer of the building lease and staff is scheduled to occur on January 1, 1981, with students being able to continue their winter term classes without interruption.

The new Division of Allied Health Sciences will function as an integral part of the Davenport College Continuing Education Division, directed by Dean Scott Derr.

Grand Rapids Charity Golf Classic

June 23, 1984
Elks Country Club

The community value of the Emergency Medical Services program was further validated when it was chosen from 29 applicants to become the beneficiary of the 1984 Grand Rapids Jaycees annual Charity Golf Classic. Organizers selected EMS because "it benefits the greatest number of people."

PGA champion Tom Watson (left), ranked number 1 in the world at the time, was the headline pro for the tournament, which drew 15,000 spectators and raised $90,000—breaking all previous records for the event.

Road race at Davenport

A 15 Kilometer Road Race will be sponsored by Davenport College on Saturday, Oct. 3, with proceeds used The Center for the Study Emergency Medical Ser-

run will start at 10 a Townsend Park, with all icipants receiving a con ative mug. Plaques will varded to winners in vari ge divisions, while a nu of prizes will also be p ted in a random draw

Th ry fee is $6.00. For regi on information, cor Terry Stiemann or own at Davenport : 451-3511.

Emergency Medical ervices Program at Davenport College prepares people for pre-hospital management of the critically ill and injured. In addition to instructing E-Unit drivers, fire fighters and private ambulance technicians in life-saving techniques, the Center provides advanced life support learning opportunities for people of all walks of life.

Davenport sponsored a 15K road race to raise additional funds for the EMS program.

Classic to benefit CPR training

By Al Palmeri

Choosing the proper charity for the Charity Golf Classic is no easy task.

This year's process involved 29 candidates, which had to be narrowed to 10, then five, then three finalists.

After about three months, the Classic's 10 major sponsors got together and selected the winner, and the result is a first for both the Grand Rapids area and the United States.

Proceeds, estimated at $75,000 by Charity Golf Classic officials, will go toward a computerized learning center for paramedics and the study of cardiopulmonary resuscitation (CPR) at the Davenport College Center for the Study of Emergency Medical Services.

Operating as planned, the center would feature three computers and would help educate several thousand Grand Rapidians in the finer techniques of emergency training. Officials estimate port hopes to build toward a goal of 20-30 percent of the county's residents trained in CPR.

To illustrate the need, statistics show that in Seattle, where about seven out of every 10 people know CPR, survival rate of pre-hospital cardiac arrest victims is 35-45 percent. In Kent County, only six percent of those victims survive.

"It's imperative that the community be involved in emergency medical services," said Candace Otte, a nurse at the Davenport center.

Proceeds from the Charity Classic will go mainly toward three computers, which cost about $23,000 apiece. Each computer includes adult and infant mannequins.

Additional software which educates paramedics on the latest techniques hikes the price of the center, which is slated for opening in September. The center, at 1695 Service Rd. NE, will be open from 8 a.m. to

155

1982

2,100 ENROLLMENT

TUITION $42 Per Credit Hour

DIPLOMAS and ASSOCIATE DEGREES
Computer Programming, Fashion Merchandising, Hospitality Management, Business Management, Marketing

LOCATION 415 East Fulton

Branch Campuses
Lansing
Kalamazoo
Career Centers
South Bend
Merrillville

Students continued to train on electric typewriters into the 1980s, even as "Word Processing" appeared in the college catalog as a new associate degree. Before long, desktop personal computers would make typewriters obsolete.

DAVENPORT COLLEGE TYPING

Throughout its history, Davenport has valued and cultivated strong ties with the business community. In 1984 the college hosted "Open House 100" to recognize and honor centennial businesses that helped build West Michigan into the state's second largest economic region.

Taking its place among centennial enterprises, Davenport itself has been a strong contributor to the regional economy. In this 1984 data sheet, the college breaks out its estimated $59 million fiscal infusion into categories ranging from jobs, salaries, and operational support generated by Davenport itself, to student spending and the future earning power of its graduates. Beyond dollars, Davenport calculates its greatest value as a producer of "talent capital"—an ongoing renewable resource for West Michigan and beyond.

DAVENPORT COLLEGE: CONTINUING OUR COMMITMENT

415 EAST FULTON, GRAND RAPIDS, MI 49503 PHONE (616) 451-3511

DAVENPORT COLLEGE: A $59 Million Asset To West Michigan

Davenport College Faculty, Staff, Students And Alumni Represent A Total Economic Impact Of $59,729,969 On The West Michigan Community

A study completed in January of 1984 used the following variables: total college revenues, student expenditures, tax dollars expended on public and private colleges, and alumni earnings. These variables were multiplied by 2.25, a multiplier recommended by the Michigan Department of Commerce, representing the average number of times that each dollar is "turned over" before leaving the local economy.

Davenport College Revenues Of $7,312,000 Represent An Economic Impact Of $16,452,000

In 1983 Davenport College (Grand Rapids) expended $7,312,000 in West Michigan. This includes salaries, payment to college vendors, and bank deposits. Apply the 2.25 multiplier and this represents a total economic impact of $16,452,000.

Davenport College Students Spent Over $6 Million In 1983, Representing An Impact Of $15,012,931.

Each Davenport College student spends an average of over $3,100 per year for personal and living expenses. This average increases for those students who are married or living independently off-campus away from home. Total student expenditures equal $6,672,414. Apply the 2.25 multiplier and the economic impact is $15,012,931.

Davenport College Provides Assistance To Its Alumni, Earnings Increase $26,136,250

Recent studies reveal that a college graduate receives an average salary of $5,075 more than a person without a degree. The increased earning power of Davenport College's 5,000 plus alumni equals $26,136,250.

Davenport College Saves The Taxpayers of Michigan $2,128,788

A State subsidy of $1,242 per student would be paid if the 1,714 full-time equivalent students of Davenport College were to attend a public community college. Instead Davenport College relies on tuition revenues and private support. Thus, a savings of $2,128,788 to the taxpayers of Michigan.

Davenport College Represents A $59 Million Impact On The West Michigan Community. Davenport College's True Impact, However, Is With The Students It Trains To Be Tomorrow's Business Leaders

1980s Intramural Sports and Student Life

Undeterred by the benching of intercollegiate sports in 1979, students found ways to stay in the game. Men's and women's intramural teams in football, softball, and other sports continued. Pick-up games and spontaneous contests between residence halls, such as a tug-of-war outside Lillian Myners Hall and 'snow volleyball,' kept team spirit vigorous on campus.

Between talent shows, clubs, and gravity-defying celebrations in Mabel Engle hall, students never lacked entertainment.

159

The Davenport University Foundation. Throughout its history, Davenport had relied almost entirely on tuition revenue to fund operations and development. Annual fundraisers to supplement operating revenue had been organized since 1970, but no formal endowment existed to provide funds for scholarships or capitalize major projects.

In 1982 the Davenport College Foundation was established through an employee fund drive. In less than 60 days it raised $30,000 from faculty, staff, college trustees, alumni, and local businesses. Within five years the fund's corpus had grown to $1.5 million; today its assets surpass the $20 million mark.

Every year, hundreds of students receive tuition assistance through endowed, memorial, or annual scholarships

Vitae: Roger VanderLaan

In a career spanning nearly four decades at Davenport, Roger G. VanderLaan was part of leadership teams that achieved major milestones, from program and degree innovations to campus expansions.

After graduating from Ferris State College (now University), he began his career teaching high school business subjects in the just-established Forest Hills school district. In 1963, VanderLaan arrived at Davenport to teach accounting. He served also as Davenport's first athletic director and coached the Panthers basketball team to several league titles. Soon he moved into the administrative ranks, first as director of admissions and later serving in several vice president positions under four successive college presidents.

Before Davenport had an organized development office, VanderLaan coordinated college fundraising efforts, which eventually led to the 1982 establishment of the Davenport Foundation. He had a lead role in implementing some of Davenport's most original concepts and initiatives, including the Candlestone Inn management program and the Lettinga Entrepreneurial Center. For his long record of service he was selected in 1998 to receive the first Tyrus R. Wessell Award for Distinguished Employee Service, given annually to a Davenport employee who exemplifies the mission and ideals of the university. VanderLaan retired in 2001 after 38 years at Davenport.

(Above) VanderLaan at the "tote board" for Davenport's annual fundraiser, which he established and coordinated throughout the 1970s. As a primary source of supplemental revenue, the capital drives were instrumental to Davenport's financial health, and imperative for accreditation. (Right) VanderLaan and President Maine enjoy Davenport's annual golf fundraiser to benefit student scholarships.

In 1984 a new wing on the north side of the Sneden Academic Center added 35,000 square feet of instructional space and featured the college's first "laboratory" classrooms specifically designed to accommodate the rapidly growing use of desktop computers. The project also included a significantly expanded library (top), named after Margaret Sneden. Its 25,000 volumes, 500 periodicals, and resource materials classified the facility as one of the most comprehensive business libraries in the area.

162

Digitally Driven. Although computer training expanded rapidly following the introduction of the personal computer (PC) in the mid 1980s, Davenport first offered computer-related training beginning in 1962 with a short course called "IBM Key Punch." (Even then the class catalog announced that "automation is revolutionizing business and industry.")

Data processing was introduced as an associate degree in 1971 and as a bachelor's degree in 1983. Diplomas and certificates in "word processing" were consistently in demand.

With its emphasis on administration and management, Davenport's early computer curriculum grew from the rise of office applications. This differed from programs at large research universities, where computer education originated in departments of mathematics and engineering which specialized in technological development. As its curriculum matured, Davenport also began to expand into more technical disciplines to offer degrees in programming, networking, and security.

By the end of the 20th century, these disciplines and degrees would be consolidated under the category of "computer information systems."

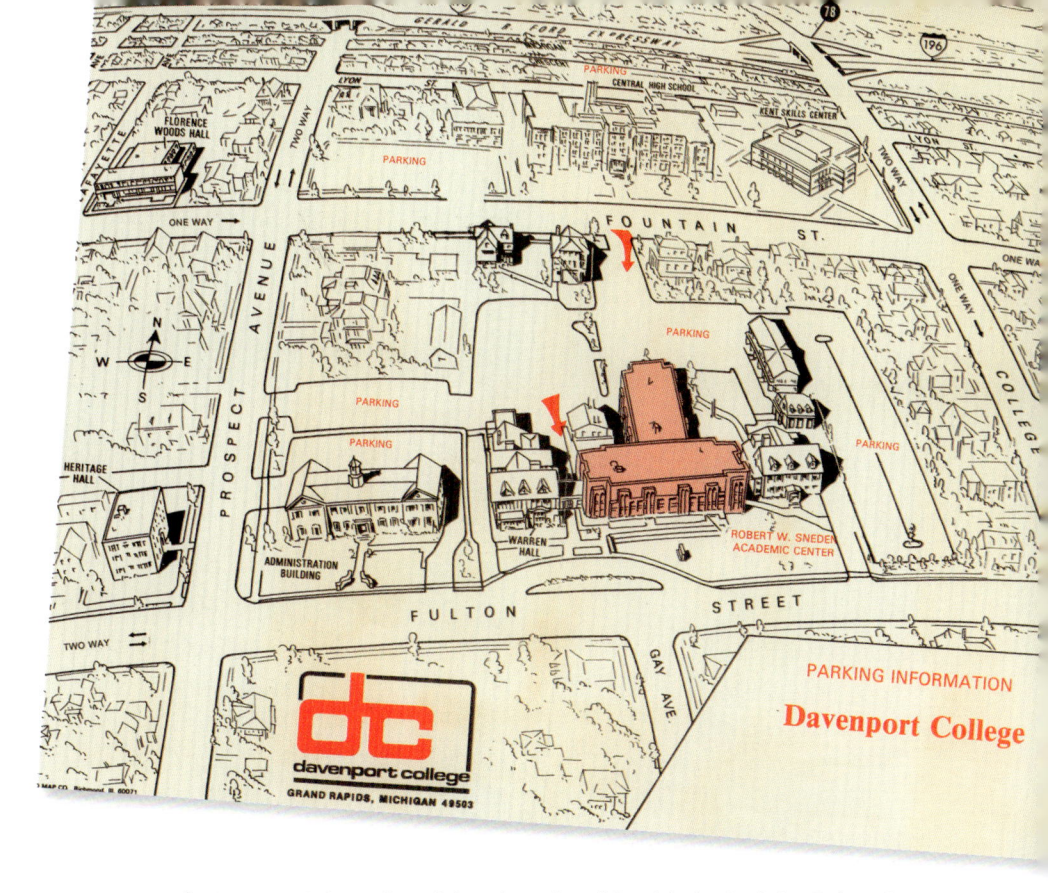

Campus Orientation. A hand-rendered "aerial view" of the Fulton Street campus shows the new wing on the Sneden Academic Center.

Legacies Margaret Davenport Sneden

Margaret Davenport started life at her parents' business school. The family home at 215 Sheldon Boulevard where she spent her early childhood shared an address with the adjacent Davenport Institute classroom building. She herself would go on to devote a lifetime to the school.

Born in 1918 in Grand Rapids, she grew up in the Ottawa Hills neighborhood. After graduating from Ottawa Hills High School, she completed secretarial studies at Davenport-McLachlan Institute, then earned her bachelor's degree from the University of Grand Rapids.

Following graduation she went to work for UGR as assistant to President Paul Voelker. With one other woman she managed the university's main administrative office, including registrations and admissions, tuition, faculty correspondence, and housing. The university office was where she also met husband Robert Sneden in 1942. Two years later they were married and moved to LaCrosse, Wisconsin, where Sneden was stationed as a U.S. Army captain at Camp McCoy.

After Sneden was deployed to Europe, Margaret, expecting the couple's first child, returned to Grand Rapids. When her husband returned in 1946 and accepted a teaching position at Davenport, the pair later joined the family board of control, which directed institutional policy for the growing Davenport organization.

Margaret continued to serve as a director for the next 50 years. She was an original member of the college's first governing board, which awarded her emeritus status upon her retirement in 1999. Concurrently she also served on the boards of Detroit College of Business, Davenport Schools, Inc., and later the M.E. Davenport Foundation.

The demands of a fast-growing organization and the risks of proprietary management—when family assets were used as collateral to finance Davenport's expansion—were always part of Margaret's job as well. She carried her role with pride and gratitude, always considering herself fortunate. Davenport, she said, was "an institution always ahead of its time; training, along with its traditional student body, single women, divorced women, women raising children, the physically challenged, and students in difficult financial straits, all before 'financial aid' as we know it today."

Her commitment to education and her partnership with her husband are evident throughout Davenport University. Gifts directly from Robert and Margaret Sneden established the original

Strong Shoulders. Margaret Davenport (with her father) spent her early years in the family home connected to the classroom building at 215 Sheldon Boulevard.

Margaret Davenport Sneden

scholarship endowment at Great Lakes Junior College, the Sneden Graduate School, and named academic scholarships at the Davenport University Foundation. A prodigious reader and promoter of literacy, Mrs. Sneden's most visible honor is the facility that bears her name, the Margaret Davenport Sneden Library. Its development in 1985 on the Fulton Street campus—made possible with financial support from Dr. and Mrs. Sneden—was pivotal in securing state of Michigan approval for Davenport's baccalaureate program. The library continues under her name at the W.A. Lettinga campus.

Mrs. Sneden's many involvements in civic life included the Blodgett Hospital women's board, service guilds at East Congregational Church and Pilgrim Manor, Ladies Literary Club, Camp Fire Girls, and Alpha Iota business sorority. In 1997 she received a Legacy Award from the Grand Rapids Women's History Council, an honor given to women in various fields who have impacted their community over their lifetimes. That same year, Davenport College awarded her an honorary doctorate degree—recognizing both a birthright and a lifelong commitment.

Margaret Davenport posts a sign for a World War II Victory Garden on the University of Grand Rapids campus.

Reminiscing. Mrs. Sneden and President Gerald Ford share memories of the University of Grand Rapids, where both worked in the 1940s. Ford was visiting Davenport in 2001 for a reunion of the UGR football team.

The Giant Leap: The Baccalaureate Degree

Converting Davenport to a four-year institution was near the top of President Maine's "25 goals" list, and discussion of the prospect began not long after he took office. Surveys of students, faculty, local high school counselors and business leaders all indicated strong support.

College leaders decided to beta test the baccalaureate market by first creating a cooperative arrangement with Detroit College of Business, which had been offering bachelor's degrees for several years. During the trial period beginning in 1980, DCB would host the final two years of a baccalaureate degree on Davenport's Grand Rapids campus. Sixty-five students eagerly enrolled to become part of the college's first group of Grand Rapids baccalaureate candidates.

The Detroit partnership proved so successful that Davenport College made preparations to offer its own Bachelor of Business Administration degree. Approvals were required from the North Central Association for accreditation, as well as the state of Michigan for an expanded charter. College administrators began the monumental task of preparing a self-study report for both authorities.

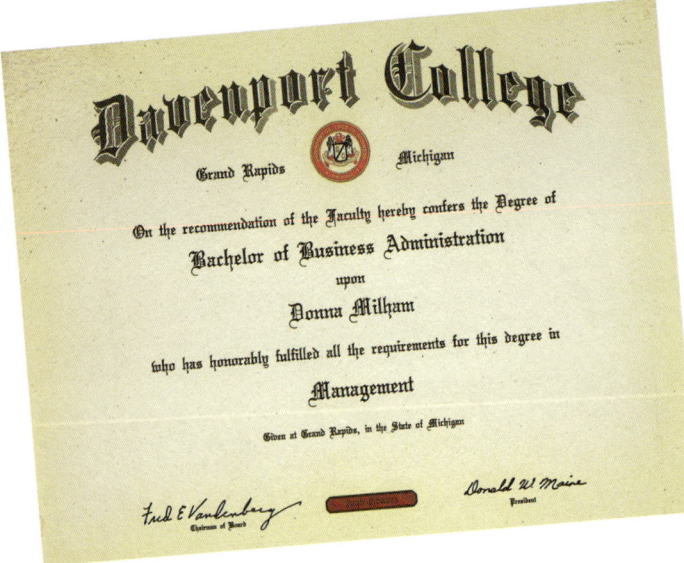

Degrees of Distinction. 1985 was a major year for Davenport College. In that year the school graduated its first class of baccalaureate recipients, completed the expansion of the Sneden Academic Center, and acquired Detroit College of Business in Dearborn. Before this breakout year was over, Davenport would become the largest private college in the state, ready to rank as a major player in business education.

Following concurrent on-site evaluations, NCA recommended approval of the baccalaureate degree without reservation or qualification. The Michigan State Board of Education, however, reported that Davenport's library facilities were not sufficient to support baccalaureate level programs. The board was willing to reconsider if Davenport completed recommended improvements.

A grant from the Sneden family allowed an expanded library to be included in the blueprints for the addition to the Sneden Academic Center. With the final hurdle cleared, Davenport secured state approval and, in 1983, introduced four-year degrees in accounting, general business, management, and marketing. Collectively called the Senior Division, the program was led by Elmer Vruggink, who previously served as deputy superintendent of Grand Rapids Public Schools.

Even with the academic foundations in place, the cultural changes necessary to evolve as a four-year college incurred some reservation and even resistance. Many were reluctant to fundamentally alter an identity that had defined Davenport for more than a century. Full-time faculty members who had spent years specializing in associate degree curricula feared reassignment to entry-level courses only. "They believed, and understandably so," said President Maine, "that if Davenport offered bachelor degrees, they—the faculty who had worked so hard to build the school—were in danger of being left behind."

Arguments supporting the four-year conversion in the end proved persuasive. Becoming a baccalaureate institution would have the most decisive impact on the college's image since accreditation had in the previous decade. It also represented a dream reclaimed from the former University of Grand Rapids: an independent four-year institution combining a well-rounded education with focused bachelor's degrees.

1985
Davenport College acquires Detroit College of Business.

1985
Merrillville Career Center opened.

1986
Saginaw Business Institute renamed Great Lakes Junior College.

1986
W. A. Lettinga Entrepreneurial Center dedicated.

The 1980s witnessed great transformation in the corporate sector, fueled by mergers, takeovers, and downsizing. One effect of this trend was a rise in entrepreneurialism and growth of the small business sector. Davenport College became a strong resource with the creation of the W.A. Lettinga Entrepreneurial Center, located in the renovated Sherman house on the Fulton Street campus. The Center specialized in custom support and training services for small businesses in the West Michigan area, including for-credit classes. Modifications would be made to its programs throughout the years, but always with the same goal in mind: to serve the educational needs of local and regional employers apart from formal campus settings.

Detroit College of Business in Dearborn had a history of association with Davenport dating back to 1954.

Moving into the Motor City

In 1985, Davenport acquired Detroit College of Business—its largest expansion yet. With similar operating philosophies and a long combined history, both schools were poised to benefit from a merger. Moreover, Davenport and Detroit had already partnered successfully in the bachelor's degree matriculation agreement.

The merger enabled the combined Davenport/Detroit system to claim 10 primary locations, multiple continuing education sites, and a combined enrollment of 8,000 students, making it the largest independent college in the state of Michigan. Unlike the previous Lansing and Kalamazoo campus affiliations, however, Detroit College would retain both its name and its separate educational charter—which was one of the oldest issued in Michigan.

An important and unifying accreditation sequence ensued: North Central Association approval for Detroit College in 1986 was followed in 1988 by a 10-year extension of Davenport's baccalaureate program. Immediately after, approval of the Lansing and Kalamazoo campuses as baccalaureate institutions was granted, along with permission for additional locations. This last authorization allowed Davenport to establish two more campuses—Battle Creek and Holland—in 1990 and 1991, respectively.

Meanwhile, at the home campus in Grand Rapids, a cornerstone property was acquired: the Sherman House, at the northwest corner of College Avenue and Fulton Street, completed Davenport's occupancy of the Fulton Street block between Prospect and College. The site became the Wilbur A. Lettinga Entrepreneurial Center, named for the chair of the Davenport College Board of Trustees.

A Decade at Davenport. At a party celebrating ten years in office, President Maine celebrates with his four children, President Emeritus Sneden, and a ride on the "Maine Line Railroad."

Vitae: Frank Paone and James Mendola

Dr. Frank Paone's career spanned more than 25 years from the time he joined Detroit Business Institute as chair of its accounting department, through his retirement in 1987. As the first president of the reorganized and renamed Detroit College of Business, Paone's record included numerous milestones: senior college accreditation, new library and administration buildings at the main Dearborn campus, expansion into several communities in southeast Michigan, and establishing DCB's candidacy for full accreditation. Working with Davenport College, Paone also helped facilitate the bachelor's degree partnership between the two schools, which set the stage for Davenport's own baccalaureate program.

Frank Paone

Dr. James Mendola had served as an academic dean at DCB for 18 years when he was appointed senior vice president, succeeding Dr. Paone. Dr. Mendola spearheaded major facilities improvements at the main campus in Dearborn, the establishment and subsequent expansion of the Warren campus, and the development of a new Flint campus. During his career he was also active and highly visible in the national education community as a consultant for two accrediting associations, and as a professional evaluator for more than 40 higher education institutions throughout the United States. He continued to lead DCB within the Davenport Educational System as president, retiring in 1999 with 30 years of service.

James Mendola

4-B The Grand Rapids Press, Wednesday, November 23, 1977

Davenport Honors 25-Year Recruiter

MRS. WOODS, flanked by Davenport College President Donald Maine, left, and former president Robert Sneden, watches sign unveiling in front of the newly-dedicated residence hall.

Grand Rapids Press Photograph by JIM STARKEY

Rename Hall for Lillian Myners

From left to right: Ty Wessell, Sharon Wohlner, Betty LaCroix, Donna Burns, Miss Myners, President Maine and Clifton Wonders joined with other college friends and employees to honor Lillian Myners when the former Heritage Hall was renamed in her honor.

Naming Opportunities. Conversion of residence halls and expanded parking reflected Davenport's gradual shift from a residential to a commuter campus. Warren Hall and later Mabel Engle Hall were both renovated and converted to faculty and administrative offices. In 1990, Lillian Myners Hall (lower left) was demolished to create space for a new parking structure.

Davenport felt committed to recognizing individuals whose dedication to the school—through both prosperous and uncertain times—epitomized institutional values and gave special significance to the term "naming opportunity." (Top left) Florence Woods Hall at 301 Fountain was named for the director of the school's recruiting office. After the original Lillian Myners residence hall was torn down, the former Heritage Hall was renamed for her. Ms. Myners' career as a Davenport faculty member—from 1936 until 1971—still ranks among the longest, but just as resonant was the statement she made at the dedication ceremony: "I liked being part of and contributing to Mr. Davenport's dream of building for the future."

170

Embracing Change: The Davenport Success System

By design, no amount of change or growth alters Davenport College's commitment to a specific educational fusion of solid academics with intensely focused business training. Davenport leaders have always worked diligently to optimize this model, which requires constant refinement between real-time adaptability and core consistency.

Davenport faculty took a lead role in ensuring the relevance and durability of their institution's unique brand. They created an assessment tool called a Student Success Skills Survey, which asked college trustees, area business leaders, and educators to identify a set of skills they considered most important and most durable for employee success. The highest-ranking qualities were grouped into categories, which then were assimilated into every course across the curricula. The result became known as the Success System.

During the late 1980s, as Davenport climbed to an entirely new level as a statewide accredited independent higher education system—and as its first bachelor's degree graduates began entering the workplace—the Success System was amended and expanded. Eight proficiencies were identified as essential for professional growth and performance: problem solving, communication, teamwork, integrity, interpersonal abilities, decision-making/leadership, self-initiative, and reliability.

On the cusp of a new decade, marked by epochal events (among them the fall of the Berlin Wall and the Tiananmen Square uprisings), these qualities took on special significance. Beyond competencies, they were indicators of the next generation of thinking, working, and living. In the coming century, organizations and systems of all types would favor the lateral over the linear, collaboration over conformity.

Progressive instincts long embedded in Davenport's culture encouraged the fullest expression of the Success System within this paradigm. The faculty embraced the opportunity to prepare students to explore alternative ways of thinking, reimagine their professional environment, and to creatively solve complex problems.

The essentials of the Success System resonate as a distinguishing feature of a Davenport education. Any graduate can articulate the role that the "success skills" play in their chosen degree program.

Trustee Fred E. Vandenberg succeeded Wilbur Lettinga as governing board chair in 1990. A prominent West Michigan healthcare executive, he served as president of Butterworth Ventures and chief operating officer at Butterworth Hospital (later Spectrum Health).

Legacies Wilbur A. Lettinga

As Wilbur Lettinga tells it, the key to his future was the one he put in the ignition of his Chevrolet Bellaire one summer morning in 1953. "I grew up on a farm, not knowing where to go after high school," Lettinga explained. "So I got in my car and drove to Davenport. It was the beginning of my career."

The decision was not quite as spontaneous as it sounded, although it did represent a complete change of direction. 'Bill' (his lifelong nickname) already had been accepted into Milwaukee's Berean Bible College to begin studying for the ministry; but by his own account was "never comfortable with that decision." Fred Kamminga, his boss at Kamminga Auto Wash in Grand Rapids where Bill worked part time, suggested he consider Davenport Institute.

Talented in math, Lettinga enrolled as an accounting major, financing his education by working as a bookkeeper at a nearby Texaco gas station. After graduating in 1955, he apprenticed at the accounting firm of Davenport instructor James Rugg and began studying for his CPA exams. Eager to go into business for himself, Lettinga opened his own office.

Wilbur became a force in the West Michigan community as a leader and creator of multiple businesses. He possessed the entrepreneur's instincts for recognizing opportunities early, including computerized journaling and lasers when they were both emerging technologies. (Laser Alignment, the firm Lettinga founded in 1968, patented a process that helped excavate the route of the Chunnel beneath the English Channel.) From underground sprinkling systems to finance, he pursued virtually every idea that interested him. His original accounting firm, which he later named Lettinga and Associates, and Kentland Corporation, which managed mobile home parks and office buildings, operated successfully for decades.

The son of Dutch immigrant farmers always considered Davenport's modest beginnings analogous to his own. Referring to Davenport Institute's first-floor retail space at 2 East Fulton, Lettinga recalls attending classes on the second floor "above the shoe store." But these memories are infused with loyalty and unwavering support. Prospering with his own successful firms, Lettinga has remained a lifelong major benefactor, helping Davenport grow from the single two-story building he attended to an elegant Heritage Hill campus, and eventually to the 43-acre Caledonia campus that bears his name.

(Left) As board chair, Bill Lettinga always wished for a gavel at meetings. In jest, he was presented with one upon concluding four terms in 1990. (Top) Lettinga welcomes sportscaster Dick Vitale as headline speaker at an Executive 100 event.

Lettinga began giving back to his alma mater by joining the Davenport College governing board as a trustee in 1973. In 1978 he began a 13-year tenure as chair under President Donald Maine and continues to serve on the board to the present day. He also was a founding board member of the Davenport College Foundation in 1982 and the following year was honored with the Distinguished Alumni Award. In 1986, the W.A. Lettinga Entrepreneurial Center on the Fulton Street campus was dedicated to his stature in the business community. As a resource for small businesses and corporate clients alike, the facility represented Lettinga's commitment to business development and excellence in West Michigan.

Other prominent organizations have benefitted from his largesse. Lettinga initiated the Hope Network Foundation in 1987 and named the Coral Lettinga Campus for his granddaughter. He was a founding member of the Butterworth Foundation board and in 1996 donated the funds that made the Lettinga Cancer Center possible. He has also served on many other community boards, including Hospice of Michigan, and holds an honorary doctor of laws degree from his alma mater.

Proud Moment. The Lettinga children present their father with a plaque dedicating the W.A. Lettinga Entrepreneurial Center, established in 1987 on the Heritage Hill campus.

"If independent thinking and seizing opportunity are the hallmarks of an entrepreneurial spirit, Bill Lettinga became the prototype for entrepreneurs everywhere."

—Donald Maine, *Maine Street: A Tribute to 27 West Michigan Entrepreneurs*

The Nineties: The World Goes Online

Davenport in the Digital Age

As influential as the Internet would soon become, in the opening years of the decade it was still little known outside of government and academia. The zeitgeist of "online" had not, as yet, developed.

This would change seemingly in an instant. By mid-decade the World Wide Web had begun to reconfigure almost every measure of the way the world communicated, conducted business, and even shopped. For Davenport, this tremendous shift meant not only integrating the new technology, but leading the charge as educators of new performers in a transformative era.

125 Years in Business. Celebrities and dignitaries helped the college celebrate its 125th year. President Maine is flanked by soon-to-become *Tonight Show* host Jay Leno and Michigan Governor John Engler at a gala held at the Amway Grand Plaza.

All this activity was barely a tremor in 1991 when Davenport College celebrated its 125th anniversary. It was a year filled with celebrations, starting in February, when comedian (and soon-to-become *Tonight Show* host) Jay Leno entertained guests during a gala evening at the Amway Grand Plaza Hotel in Grand Rapids. A second celebration in May hosted hundreds of alumni, friends and members of the college community at the George Welsh Civic Auditorium. As the 1991-92 academic year got underway, a fall gathering at the Grand Rapids campus included students and families from every Davenport location in Michigan.

At the end of 1991, Davenport broke ground on its Holland campus. In the years immediately following, growth strategies began taking a different turn. Instead of adding physical sites, Davenport's expansion focused on developing academic programs and advanced degrees at existing locations. Although at a more moderate pace, classroom access did continue as Davenport pursued markets in the northern part of the state. Through cooperative arrangements with West Shore Community College and Northwestern Michigan College, Davenport began offering classes in Scottville, Traverse City, and Gaylord.

At the same time a major alternative to the conventional classroom was emerging. Already Davenport students had logged on to a campus email network; now they also began taking individual online courses to augment their in-seat studies. These were critical early steps toward what would eventually become Davenport University Online.

Ground is broken in late 1991 for Davenport's Holland campus—as Dean Tom Carey and Vice President Dr. Barbara Mieras shake on it.

Friendly Competition. During the 1990s two area private colleges—Nazareth College in Kalamazoo and Jordan College, which had campuses in Cedar Springs and Flint—ceased operations. President Maine purchased both charters, using the Nazareth document to provide the authorization necessary to add advanced degree programs at Davenport.

Maine sold the Jordan College charter to the University of Phoenix, an online-only for-profit institution, which was seeking entry into Michigan. Some worried about the competition Phoenix presented, but as Maine explained later, his decision represented a management best practice: embracing rather than fearing competition sharpens an organization's performance.

The Virtual Classroom

In the form of institutional networks of connected PCs, internet had been commonly in use throughout the 1980s. In 1995, the Internet exploded into the public arena with the commercialization of the World Wide Web. Enveloping the planet with the ubiquity that its name implied, the web would leave few—if any—segments of society untouched.

In education, the effects of the new technology would prove inestimable. Distance learning through computer connectivity made site accessibility—which had driven so many decisions in previous years—less imperative. Before the decade would end, an entire degree could be earned in one's own home.

Antecedents for a full online degree platform first appeared in 1992 with Davenport's Adult Accelerated Career Education (AACE) program, which offered a condensed degree-completion timeline for working adults. The concentrated course model was adapted into online format and quickly became the delivery of choice for busy professionals. Even after AACE was phased out as a formal program, its legacy found a new incarnation.

In 1998, the distance learning model created for AACE was launched as the Davenport Learning Network. Demand for online classes quickly outpaced both the course options and the accreditation to offer them in greater volume. During the formative years of online education the North Central Association maintained a conservative attitude toward distance learning. After review by the Higher Learning Commission, the Davenport Learning Network was accredited in 1999. In 2000 this would become known as Davenport University Online, with authorization to offer complete degree programs.

In-seat students, meanwhile, were not only being trained in the new technologies, they were also being taught by them, as classrooms became equipped with innovations like WiFi, digital whiteboards, and interactive real-time testing. "Notebook" took on a whole new meaning as most work—from lecture notes to research material to the textbooks themselves—transmogrified from page to screen. Davenport moved rapidly to the forefront of these developments, integrating new technologies into all levels of instructional strategy, from introducing new degrees to meet the career demand, to pedagogical methods in the classroom.

"We are being swept along in this tidal wave of technology. It is reshaping how we approach our various publics, our customer base, business and industry, everything that we do."
—President Donald Maine

The Davenport Educational System

During the second half of the 1990s, major reorganizations took place to regionalize Davenport's various locations. In 1996, Davenport College completed a merger with Great Lakes Junior College (GLJC), the last operating enterprise of the Davenport Schools Incorporated parent company. The new Davenport/Detroit/Great Lakes system now consisted of sixteen campus locations in Michigan and Indiana. Donald Colizzi, dean of Davenport's Lansing campus, was given the additional responsibility of supervising the GLJC system, including the main campus in Midland and its supporting locations in Saginaw, Bay City, Caro, and Bad Axe. Matt Cawood served as vice president and chief operating officer for the five Great Lakes campuses.

Now operating three large colleges—each with its own network of sites—Davenport needed to develop a new managing structure. An umbrella organization called the Davenport Educational System was established, consisting of three separate regions (Western, Central, and Eastern) that delineated the three college groups. Each regional group was managed by a vice president/CEO and governed by its own regional board. Also, each maintained its own separate accreditation.

Because Maine's role became more comprehensive than typically associated with the president designation, he was appointed chancellor of the Davenport Educational System, reflecting his responsibilities as director of the entire organization. Correspondingly, the title of each individual college leader was changed to president. In the Western Region, Dr. Barbara Mieras became president of Davenport College, which included the main campus in Grand Rapids, plus campuses in Lansing, Kalamazoo, Holland, and Battle Creek. Matt Cawood became president of Great Lakes Junior College in the Central Region, with Julia Davis serving as president of Detroit College of Business and its Eastern Region locations.

> A major component of the AACE platform—online classes—later provided the model for the Davenport Learning Network, launched in 1999. More comprehensive in scope, the Learning Network reached students across the globe and became the predecessor for Davenport's Online Division.

1990
Battle Creek branch opens with the acquisition of Argubright College.

1991
The College celebrates its 125th anniversary.

1992
Holland campus opens.

1993
First "internet" network created in Iowa.

1995
World Wide Web commercialized, soon reaching 25 million users.

1996
Davenport acquires Great Lakes Junior College in Saginaw.

1997
Davenport Educational System developed as a holding company comprised of Davenport College, Detroit College of Business, and Great Lakes Junior College.

1998
Donald Maine appointed chancellor of DES; Dr. Barbara Mieras appointed president of Davenport College.

Barbara A. Mieras

While growing up in the Detroit suburb of Redford Township, Barbara Mieras had two interests—science and business—and she knew early on that her future would include at least one of those disciplines. In high school she excelled in business classes and set her sights on becoming a business teacher. In pursuit of that goal she earned both a bachelor's and master's degree in business education from Western Michigan University.

After completing her studies, Barbara joined the faculty of Hartford High School in Hartford, Michigan, where she taught for three years. She next moved to the Van Buren Career Technical Center, gaining experience in the administrative side of education, then joined the Davenport College Kalamazoo campus as director of continuing education in 1984.

Within a few months, Mieras knew she had found the perfect fit for her educational philosophy. "From the moment I met the Davenport administrators, faculty, and staff, I was struck by their deep and genuine interest in students and their success," Mieras recalled. The compatibility was reciprocal, and within a year Mieras was appointed associate dean of the Kalamazoo campus, a promotion that would be the first of many in her long Davenport career.

Recognizing the necessity of an advanced degree for higher education leadership, she returned to school. While working full time and raising three children, she commuted two evenings a week to East Lansing to take classes at Michigan State University, eventually earning her Ph.D. in College and University Administration in 1990.

By this time Mieras had transferred to the Grand Rapids campus to serve as Davenport's vice president for admissions and marketing. During the formation of the Davenport Educational System, she served as chief operating officer.

On October 7, 1998, Dr. Mieras was formally inaugurated as president of Davenport College, becoming the first woman to lead the school in its 132-year history. Dr. Mieras considered her appointment "an incredible honor and the thrill of a lifetime" and immediately dedicated herself to the task of advancing the college to higher levels.

Her many achievements included implementing the plans for the graduate program and the Learning Network (predecessor to Davenport University Online), creating the Learning Academy (a curricula for employee education), expanding the university library, and significantly increasing the assets of the Davenport University Foundation. In her first year as president she launched Davenport's largest capital campaign, Invest in Success, which ultimately raised $15.3 million and ranked her among Davenport's greatest generators of philanthropic support.

(Top) Barbara Mieras began her career in education as a high school business teacher. (Middle) Beginning in 1998, commemorative medallions were issued to Davenport presidents, including a posthumous medal for President Robert Sneden. (Left) With her father, Edward Elsner, at her inauguration. Academic robes, previously belonging to President Robert Sneden and given to Mieras by the M.E. Davenport Foundation, are still worn by her every year at commencement.

Presidential Profile Barbara Mieras

After the three regions of the Davenport Educational System had merged to create a single university, a consolidation of leadership positions also took place. The positions of chancellor and regional presidents were replaced with a single presidency. Mieras assumed a new role as executive vice president for advancement and president of the Davenport University Foundation. In 2007 she was appointed senior vice president for major gifts.

Mieras devotes a generous amount of time to community and professional service on the boards of Davenport University Foundation, Founders Bank and Trust, and Metro Health Hospital. She has served both her alma maters with terms on the advisory boards at Western Michigan University and Michigan State University. Because of her love of the arts she has also immersed herself in the cultural and civic life of Grand Rapids and West Michigan, with a particular devotion to the Grand Rapids Ballet as a board member. Recognition for her accomplishment in both higher education and civic life is abundant. Dr. Mieras was twice nominated for an Athena Award, a prestigious credential that honors dynamic women leaders. She received Davenport University's highest employee tribute, the Tyrus R. Wessell Award for Distinguished Employee Service, for longevity and distinction of service. She counts among her most gratifying recognitions the Michigan State University Crystal Apple Award as an outstanding educator, along with Distinguished Alumni Awards from both Western Michigan University and Michigan State University.

At Davenport University and throughout West Michigan, Dr. Mieras remains dedicated to education through scholarship development, program enhancements, and capital projects.

> "I've always found Davenport people to be especially committed to making a difference in students' lives."

Barbara Mieras

Davenport's First Woman President. For the installation of Dr. Barbara Mieras, the college held its first formal inauguration proceedings, which included the entire Davenport community, government and civic leaders, and representatives from other colleges. A processional was held from the Grand Rapids campus to ceremonies at Central Reformed Church.

Speaking of Success: The "Executive 100" Lecture Series

From the time author-economist Elliot Janeway stepped to the podium as Executive 100's debut speaker, this popular lecture series grew to be one of the college's most successful public relations initiatives and was hugely popular in the community. The program originated in 1973 to give 100 area business executives the opportunity to convene quarterly for lunch and a noted speaker. Popular demand made it impossible to confine attendance to 100, and soon the program was accepting standing-room-only crowds. For 25 years, Executive 100 attracted renowned speakers from all over the country and from all fields, from literature to sports, politics to media, and of course business, economics, and leadership.

Escalating speaker fees, travel, and other costs associated with the program prompted a decision to discontinue the series in 1997.

The "Excellence in Business" Award

In 1998 Davenport launched a new annual signature event, the Excellence in Business (EIB) Gala. Developed to support the Davenport Foundation scholarship fund, EIB's purpose was also to honor—through the Peter C. Cook Excellence in Business Award—a West Michigan leader who exemplifies commitment to excellence, regional economic growth and innovation, and community engagement.

Peter C. Cook Award Recipients

1998   **Peter C. Cook,** Chair, Mazda Great Lakes, Inc. and Cook Holdings, LLC
Speaker: David Gergen

1999   **Frederik G.H. Meijer,** Chair, Meijer, Inc.
Speaker: Dave Thomas

2000   **Richard M. DeVos,** Co-Founder, Amway Corporation
Speaker: Geoge Will

Davenport honors local entrepreneur Cook

▶ *The college tonight will establish the Davenport College Peter C. Cook Excellence in Business Award.*

The Grand Rapids Press

West Michigan entrepreneur and philanthropist Peter C. Cook embodies Davenport College's philosophy like no other, says Davenport President Barbara Mieras.

"He certainly is an example of the college motto: Make a living, make a life, make a contribution," Mieras said.

And that's why Cook is being honored tonight with the establishment of the Davenport College Peter C. Cook Excellence in Business Award.

"Mr. Cook embodies the spirit of the college and is a role model to students and all of us associated with Davenport College," Mieras said.

Each year, the new award will honor "an outstanding business leader who demonstrates a living commitment to those three aspects of the college motto," she said. "Someone who is a good person, who demonstrates quality of character and, thirdly, someone who gives back generously to community and to others."

Cook, 84, chairman and majority owner of Mazda Great Lakes and a Grand Rapids resident, has a long record of community involvement.

Recent activities include a 1996 gift of $2 million to the former Butterworth Hospital for the creation of a health care research center that bears his and his wife, Pat's, name.

Last year, Hope College built a 183-student dorm/conference guest center with the help of $1 million from the Cooks. He helped lead a $13.5 million endowment campaign for Hope's Western Theological Seminary. He invested in The B.O.B. restaurant in downtown Grand Rapids through a trust and last week enlarged his stake in the Grand Rapids Hoops basketball team.

Cook has been affiliated with Davenport since he enrolled there as a student in 1931. He's served as a trustee, received the Distinguished Alumni Award in 1981, an honorary doctor of laws degree in 1987 and saw the Peter C. Cook Administration Building dedicated in his honor in 1985.

The award presentation is part of a fund raiser whose proceeds will fund student scholarships. More than 550 are expected to attend, Mieras said.

"Forty-eight corporations or organizations have purchased tables. We think that's quite a statement, not only for Peter C. Cook, but for their support of Davenport College," she said.

The event will feature keynote speaker David Gergen, editor-at-large of U.S. News & World Report and former advisor to Presidents Nixon, Ford, Reagan and Clinton.

Peter C. Cook, chairman of Mazda Great Lakes, has a long record of community involvement.

Davenport College

Excellence in Business Dinner Gala

May 20, 1998

Honorary Chairs
President Gerald R. Ford and Mrs. Betty Ford
Richard and Helen DeVos
Jay and Betty Van Andel

Co-Chairs
John and Marie Canepa
Dick and Betsy DeVos

(Opposite) From 1973 to 1997, Executive 100 was one of the most popular tickets in Grand Rapids. It gained a national reputation as a lecture forum by featuring the most notable figures of current public life, including author Art Buchwald, political satirist Mark Russell, astronaut James Lovell, Detroit Tigers manager Sparky Anderson, *Detroit Free Press* columnist Mitch Albom, and many others. (Center): Trustees Betty LaCroix and Robert Sadler welcome ABC News reporter Carol Simpson, far right. (Bottom right): Sportscaster Dick Vitale talks shop with local TV sports anchors.

(Top right) Peter Cook, first EIB award recipient, accepts the tribute named for him from Chancellor Donald Maine. From the outset, the EIB event began drawing hundreds of supporters annually, both individual and corporate.

(Above left) Peter Cook, Donald Maine, and Cook Award recipient Richard DeVos in 2000. (Above right) Fred Meijer, the second Cook Award recipient, and Peter Cook in 1999.

Approaching The Millennium

Maine's 20th Year

After two decades of Maine's leadership, statistics from this era vividly illustrate the scope of Davenport's influence. During those 20 years the college grew from one campus with approximately 2,000 students to 16 campuses and more than 75 class attendance locations. Total enrollment exceeded 15,000 degree-seeking students, with thousands of additional professionals from business and industry attending seminars and training. Almost any community in the Lower Peninsula of Michigan was within an hour's drive of one—or more—locations.

It had been more than a dozen years since Davenport's last major academic advance, when it converted from a two-year to a four-year institution. Graduate level training became Maine's next goal.

In 1998 the Margaret and Robert Sneden Graduate School began offering the Master of Business Administration (MBA) degree. Geared for working professionals, areas of concentration focused exclusively on strategic management, marketing, and general management. Dr. Thomas Brown was named vice president and dean of the graduate school after having served as vice president for the Grand Rapids campus. The school graduated its first class of 34 MBAs in 2000.

The college's momentum was undeniable, and it may have appeared that nothing could impede its pace of advancement. Before long, however, Davenport would be compelled to address the possibility of over-expansion. The organization would also be tested by an event far more upsetting: the departure of the leader who had guided Davenport for a generation.

A contemplative moment for Chancellor Donald Maine.

1999

ENROLLMENT
14,836
Undergraduate & Graduate

SCHOOLS
School of Business
School of Health Professions
School of Technology
Margaret and Robert Sneden Graduate School

108 FULL-TIME FACULTY
3020 Total Staff

UNDERGRADUATE TUITION
$196 Per Credit Hour

LOCATION
415 East Fulton

Reimagined…and Realized. By the end of the 1990s both Davenport College and the city itself were immersed in new eras of development. A number of major civic construction projects brought an array of business, residential, entertainment, and educational venues within a few city blocks of each other, achieving at last the urban renaissance Grand Rapids had long pursued.

Davenport had a key connection to all this revitalization through Chancellor Donald Maine's membership in Grand Action, a development consortium that initiated the DeVos Place Performance Hall and Convention Center, Van Andel Arena, Meijer Majestic (Civic) Theatre, Millennium Park, and the Michigan State University College of Human Medicine. Over the course of a dozen years, Grand Action projects represented more than $400 million in community development and established a new era of private–public partnership in civic investment.

1998
Margaret and Robert Sneden Graduate School launched, led by Dr. Thomas Brown.

1999
Davenport Learning Network begins offering online classes and one year later is approved by North Central Association to offer full degrees online.

2000
Plans announced to create a single university from the three Davenport regional divisions.

We Built this City. (Above) The 12,000-seat Van Andel Arena is home ice for the Grand Rapids Griffins hockey team and a performance venue for countless acts and events. Members of Grand Action include (back row): Tim Wondergem, Steve Heacock, Dick DeVos, Jon Nunn, David Frey and Donald Maine. Front Row: Bob Hooker, John Canepa, Casey Wondergem, and Marty Allen.

(Left) Van Andel Arena ceremonial brick laying 1995. (L-R) Bob Hooker, Dick DeVos, David Frey, and John Canepa.

An Unexpected Farewell

In 1999, Chancellor Donald Maine was diagnosed with a progressive neuromuscular disease requiring him to take an early medical retirement. It was a devastating announcement for the entire Davenport community. Maine's longevity and prominence had made him both synonymous with and symbolic of Davenport in the public arena; but for many the ties were deeply personal. Said governing board chair Fred Vandenberg: "Don is a guy you learn to love real quick."

Determined to prepare the institution for its next iteration before stepping down, Maine set in motion two major initiatives: first, he introduced a plan to restructure the Davenport Educational System—with its three separate colleges—into a single accredited university. The implications were both exhilarating and staggering: the transition would require a standardized curriculum, a common academic calendar, and a single administration with one governing body for the entire university. It also would include a shift in culture greater than Davenport had ever experienced.

"University status is a logical outcome of the evolution of Davenport College over the years," stated Chancellor Maine in a communication to college trustees. Increasing collaborations between the colleges, such as graduate and online programs, Maine felt, supported the case for unification.

The North Central Association approved the name change, and on May 8, 2000, the college officially went forward as Davenport University. Two years of preparation for full accreditation lay ahead, thus setting the agenda for Maine's successor.

Maine's second major announcement was equally influential: the future establishment of a new campus. While only in the conceptual stage, a potential location with abundant space to grow was already being evaluated on the outskirts of Grand Rapids. "It will be a high-tech millennium campus," Maine said. "We need to continue to meet the needs of our students, and the only way to do that is to stay on top of technology."

> "I can't imagine a more successful university CEO than Don Maine. He's taken a good institution and made it an outstanding institution."
> —Arend Lubbers, former president of Grand Valley State University

Parting Embrace. Chancellor Donald Maine and President Barbara Mieras.

Davenport to lose its guiding force

Donald Maine is stepping down as the school's chancellor because of health reasons.

By LZ Granderson
The Grand Rapids Press

Donald Maine, who took Davenport College from a small Grand Rapids business school to a thriving institution with 20 locations, said today he will step down because of health reasons.

Maine, who two years ago took the title of chancellor of the Davenport Educational System Inc. after serving 21 years as president, said he will continue working until a successor is found.

I'm writing a book about the greatest entrepreneurs of West Michigan," said Maine, 57. "Their stories are incredible."

In 1999 Maine was diagnosed with mitochondrial myopathy — a form of muscular dystrophy with no known cure.

"It's going to be a huge loss," said Fred Vandenberg, chairman of the school's board of trustees. "It's a clear and personal loss for all of us ... Don is the kind of person you learn to love real quick."

When Maine took the job as president in 1977, Davenport operated at one location on East Fulton Street, preparing about 1,800 students for secretarial and accounting careers. The school operated with an annual budget of $1.8 million.

Over the next 23 years, Maine

Authoring a new life: Donald Maine, who took over at Davenport in is writing a book about West Michigan entrepreneurs.

PRESS PHOTO/LORI NIEDENFU

25 Check Marks

Reluctantly, Davenport prepared its farewells for the leader who had brought the institution such a great distance. Chairman Vandenberg, presenting a board resolution honoring Chancellor Maine, spoke for everyone: "The story of Davenport College and Davenport University from 1977 to 2000 is truly the story of Don Maine's vision, leadership, and integrity."

Maine's friend Arend "Don" Lubbers, president of Grand Valley State University, concurred. "I can't imagine a more successful university CEO than Don Maine. He's taken a good institution and made it an outstanding institution."

Maine had both practiced and modeled the consummate balance of leadership: proving himself a formidable visionary, innovator, and executive while staying in sync with Davenport's culture. With both professionalism and respect, he had negotiated the delicate transition from family to independent leadership, in the process completing the job begun by President Sneden—distinguishing Davenport from its "proprietary" counterparts and installing it unequivocally in the category of a higher education institution. With exciting plans already unfolding, Davenport was about to embark on a new era with a heritage uniquely its own: a specialized school that offered a full university experience.

Looking back, Maine himself recalled the list he'd kept throughout his Davenport career. Each time a goal was realized, he placed a red check mark next to it.

When he left Davenport, there were 25 check marks on the list.

Davenport College becomes a university

▶ Officials expect enrollment to explode at the system's three business schools with the status announcement.

By Cami Reister
The Grand Rapids Press

Students who thought they were getting a college education at Davenport these past four years now can say they have received a university education.

The business school, one of three colleges making up Davenport Educational System Inc., announced today that all three schools will operate as Davenport University.

Davenport College, Detroit College of Business and Great Lakes College now known as Davenport University-Western Region, Davenport University-Eastern Region and Davenport University-Central Region.

Fred Vandenberg, chairman of the board of trustees overseeing the schools, said the path to becoming a university started when Davenport was established as a secretarial school.

It now includes more than 20 campuses in Michigan and Indiana, offering more than 55 associate and baccalaureate majors, plus master's degrees in business administration in several specialties.

"One of the things we really tried to focus on is doing a better job for the students because that is what it's about," Vandenberg said. "A change from Davenport University would be better for our students than a change from Davenport secretarial to all of the things in between."

Davenport's switch to a university was approved by the state and the North Central Association of Colleges and Schools, officials said.

Michigan is one of few states requiring a college to have at least two graduate programs that are nonprofessional degrees before it can call itself a university.

---

2 schools now offer degrees in e-business

▶ Davenport and the University of Phoenix help students get caught up in the Web world of commerce.

By LZ Granderson
The Grand Rapids Press

Two area colleges are introducing programs to better prepare students for a business world that is becoming dominated by the Internet.

Davenport University and the University of Phoenix recently have added e-commerce degrees to their business programs.

DAVENPORT
UNIVERSITY
reINVENT U.

Leveling Up. In May of 2000, the North Central Association officially approved Davenport's request to reconcile its three separate colleges into a single university. The name became official, and the school that had begun the 20th century as Grand Rapids Business College would go forward in the 21st as Davenport University.

185

Presidential Profile Donald W. Maine

For a man who devoted his entire professional life to education, Donald Maine ironically was not a good student himself. Born in Detroit and raised in Grand Rapids, Maine graduated from Comstock Park High School in 1960 with a scholastic record that was less than exemplary. Still, he chose to pursue a college education, earning an associate degree from Grand Rapids Junior College (now Community College) before transferring to Michigan State University. Still not a serious academic, he neglected his studies so consistently that as graduation loomed, he found himself hopelessly behind.

The self-described 'class cutup' decided to get serious. He jammed 24 credit hours into his final semester in order to finish on schedule, then enrolled in graduate school to earn his master's degree in education. From that point on, his commitment was complete.

Maine started his career as a middle school teacher, first in the Grand Rapids Public Schools, then in the Kenowa Hills system. For his early accomplishment he was honored by the Grand Rapids Jaycees as Outstanding Young Educator of the Year.

After several years in the classroom, Maine wished to move into the post-secondary environment. His fascination with entrepreneurial thinking found a natural outlet at Davenport College. Its record of innovation was the perfect foundation for Maine's vision of growing Davenport into an accessible, multi-degree-granting university. Inspired by Davenport's motto—"Make a living. Make a life. Make a contribution"—Maine spent the next 27 years doing just that.

Maine first came to Davenport College in 1971 as director of special programs, which included the College Achievement and Transition (CAT) program, Operation Outreach, and others. In 1975 he accepted an appointment as dean of occupational education at Grand Rapids Junior College. He returned to Davenport in 1977 to become its president, succeeding the retiring Robert W. Sneden. Maine's selection marked the first time in nearly seven decades that Davenport would be led by a nonfamily member.

As his own leadership imprint emerged, the growth of the college reflected his tremendous energies and vision. The baccalaureate program, the graduate school, and ultimately the attainment of university status mark his most notable achievements. From a single campus in Grand Rapids offering associate degree programs to 2,100 students, Davenport College expanded into a multi-campus university offering undergraduate and graduate degrees in business, technology, and health professions

Donald W. Maine

"When you're leading an organization, you watch successful people, and I tried to surround myself with successful folks. I learned all that I know from those people."

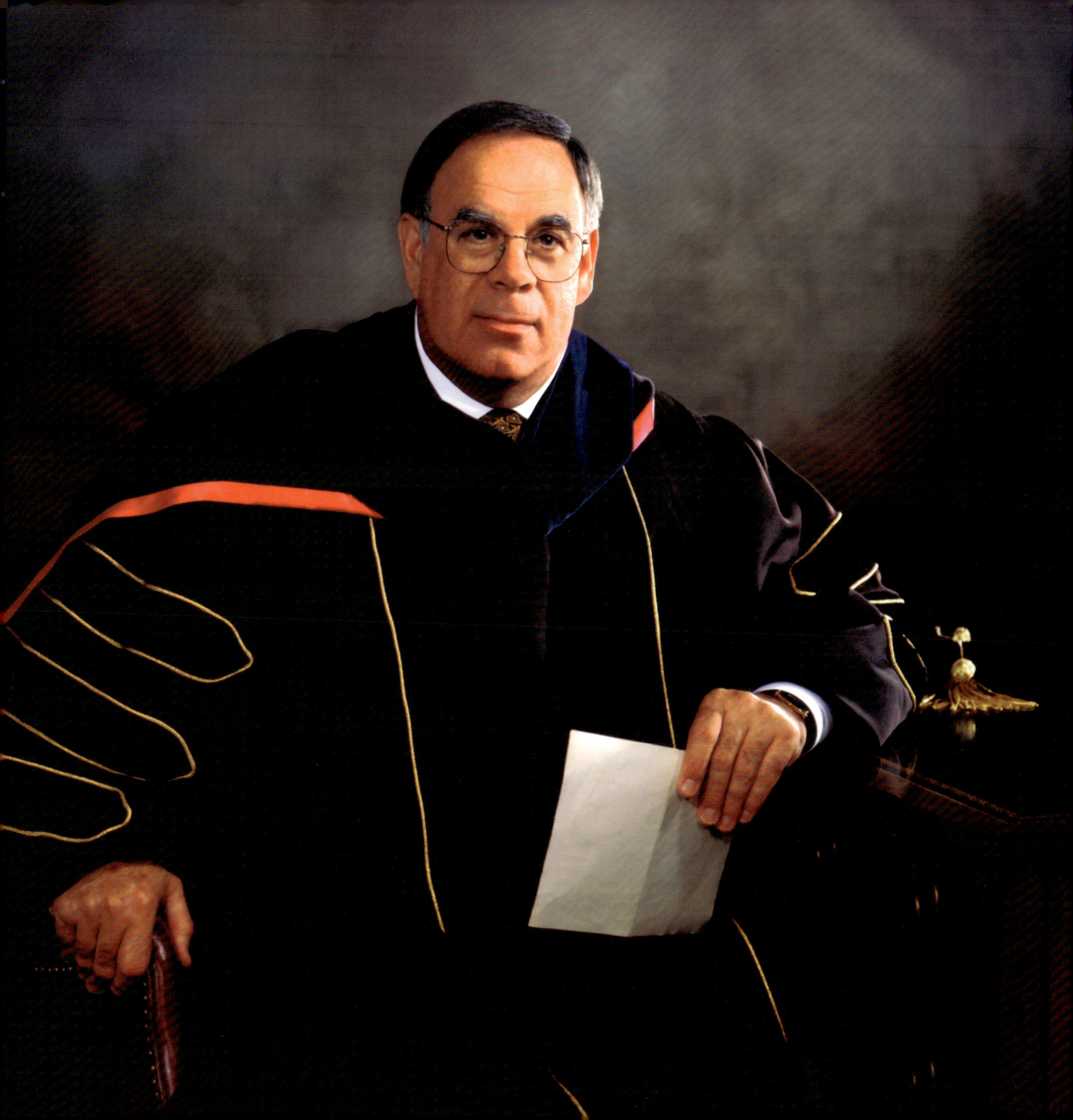

to nearly 16,000 students. Throughout this exponential development, Maine was a "hands-on" leader and friend who provided support and mentorship to faculty, administrators, and students alike.

Most important to the school's institutional profile was Maine's focus on the expansion of academic programs leading to bachelor and eventually MBA degrees. Maine himself cites the college's conversion to a four-year institution as the legacy piece of his career, elevating Davenport to an important level of perception in the educational and business communities.

Organizational realignments in the late 1990s brought Maine a new title: chancellor of the Davenport Educational System, which consisted of more than 30 branch campuses and satellite locations throughout Michigan and northern Indiana.

One of Maine's most auspicious accomplishments—and one of the most influential for the institution's future—would be among his last as Davenport's leader: initiating the process of transforming Davenport from college to university. While his every intention was to lead Davenport into the 21st century with this status, the discovery that he had developed a degenerative neuromuscular disease forced Maine to retire when he was just 57.

"Don's absence will be a clear and personal loss for all of us," governing board chair Fred Vandenberg said when the news was made public. But he added, "Because of Don's leadership and vision, Davenport is solidly positioned to continue its track record of success." As Maine closed more than a quarter century of achievement with the school he loved, the Donald W. Maine School of Business was named in his honor.

Despite his prognosis, rigorous treatment enabled Maine to return to the active community involvement that characterized his entire professional life. His range of service encompasses corporate, economic, cultural, and civic life in Grand Rapids and West Michigan. Organizations like Opera Grand Rapids, Celebration on the Grand, the Public Museum of Grand Rapids, Grand Rapids Area Chamber of Commerce, and Grand Rapids Economic Club owe much to his commitment. Through his work with the economic development group Grand Action, he has helped instigate some of the city's most visible facilities—among them DeVos Place Convention Center and Van Andel Arena, both of which have had tremendous and sustained impact on the vitality of downtown Grand Rapids.

Maine's guidance is also linked to the region's rapidly emerging health and medical community. In addition

As academic leader, hands-on participant in college activities, or surrounded by his family, Donald Maine is equally comfortable in many roles. Also an author, he wrote a collection of biographical profiles of leading West Michigan CEOs in his 2002 book *Maine Street*.

Presidential Profile Donald Maine

to serving the Van Andel Institute—a medical research institution with a global reputation—the Fred Meijer Heart Center Patient Advisory Board, and Metropolitan Hospital, Maine cochaired the Michigan State University College of Human Medicine fund-raising campaign, which raised $10 million to build its medical school, the Secchia Center, in Grand Rapids.

Confirmation of Maine's stature in academia is abundant. In 1985 he graduated from the Institute of Educational Management at Harvard University, an experience he credits as one of the most valuable in preparing him for success as a leader in higher education. He also completed a year of doctoral studies at the University of Michigan. His professional affiliations include member and past chairman of the board of the Association of Independent Colleges and Universities of Michigan (AICUM); he has served as a consultant/evaluator for both the North Central Association of Colleges and Schools and the Association of Independent Colleges and Schools and was a former member and past chair of the Michigan Higher Education Assistance Authority. Recognition of his work and leadership earned him many honors, including an honorary Doctor of Laws from Davenport University, Distinguished Alumni Award from Michigan State University, the Peter C. Cook Excellence in Business Award, a place in the Junior Achievement of the Michigan Great Lakes Hall of Fame, and the Grand Rapids Economic Club George Slykhouse Lifetime Achievement Award.

Like his predecessors Robert Sneden and M.E. Davenport, Maine loves the outdoors—hunting, canoeing, and skiing have been among his passions.

Maine even found time to become an author. His 2002 book, *Maine Street*, profiles 27 West Michigan entrepreneurs and business leaders. Proceeds from the book were generously donated by Maine to the Davenport University Foundation.

Maine challenged his successors by leaving them this question: "How should Davenport now function and behave as a university? We've met the threshold; now—what do we need to do to become a great university worthy of its name?"

"Our new university will not change what we do best; it will allow us to make our best even better in an increasingly competitive education market."

—President Randolph Flechsig

THE NEW MILLENNIUM
2000-2009

One Student Body, One Purpose

AT THE TIME RANDOLPH FLECHSIG BECAME chancellor in the fall of 2000, Davenport had not experienced a leadership change in nearly 25 years. Raised in Ohio and educated at Xavier University and St. Louis University, Flechsig began his career in healthcare administration in Saginaw. In the early 1990s he was approached by Great Lakes Junior College to advise on the development of a nursing program and soon after was asked to chair the college board of trustees. When GLJC merged with Davenport College in 1996, Flechsig remained on the combined board of the Davenport Educational System. His position as president and CEO of Saginaw Cooperative Hospitals would prove valuable to the university's planned expansion into health professions. His contributions to Davenport's growth and transition during the 1990s made him a prime candidate to succeed Chancellor Donald Maine.

Merging the three regional operations of the former Davenport Educational System was already underway, and the name change introduced in May of 2000 presented both a goal and an imperative: to begin developing a singular culture. The term "university" itself connoted an entirely different set of expectations in the minds of students, alumni, accrediting bodies, and the public at large.

"The unification of Davenport University means we must view ourselves differently," said Chancellor Flechsig. "We are one university with one student body and one purpose."

> "The unification of Davenport University means we must view ourselves differently. We are no longer a loose federation of far-flung campuses, but one university with one student body and one purpose."
> —Randolph Flechsig

"A Davenport degree is proof to the work world that our graduates know how to be successful in their chosen career. When potential employers see a Davenport graduate, they see an energetic, prepared worker who should be at the top of their list."

First Steps

The North Central Association of Colleges and Schools (NCA) had set a two-year timetable to complete the university conversion. To form a leadership structure more consistent with a university paradigm, Chancellor Flechsig created the first President's Cabinet, charged with administering the new institution. To develop transition strategies, Flechsig and the cabinet conducted numerous site visits to the North Central Association and to several other universities.

Through this process the immensity of the conversion began to reveal itself: Davenport would have to reconfigure its entire administrative infrastructure, including curricula, calendars, and its credit-hour systems. Also required were cohesive financial and quality control systems, and a single-brand image for the entire campus network. A unilateral academic calendar and curriculum would mean that—for the first time in the institution's history—every campus would offer the same programs and classes, would follow a set of unified academic policies, teach on the same schedule, and share one common catalog.

The logistical implications alone were staggering. Each of the three regional colleges had different courses, credit-hour structures, and term lengths. The semester basis used by the Central Region presented the most logical model to adopt, given that it was by far the most widely used throughout the state. Half of Davenport's students were transferring in semester credits from other institutions.

Executive leadership and governance were also realigned. Unified governance under a single board of trustees no longer required separate governing boards or presidents. The title of chancellor would be discontinued, and Flechsig would continue as both CEO and president of Davenport University. Previous regional presidents would assume new responsibilities. Matthew Cawood of the Central Region was appointed executive vice president for operations and enrollment; Western Region President Dr. Barbara Mieras became executive vice president for advancement and president of the University Foundation.

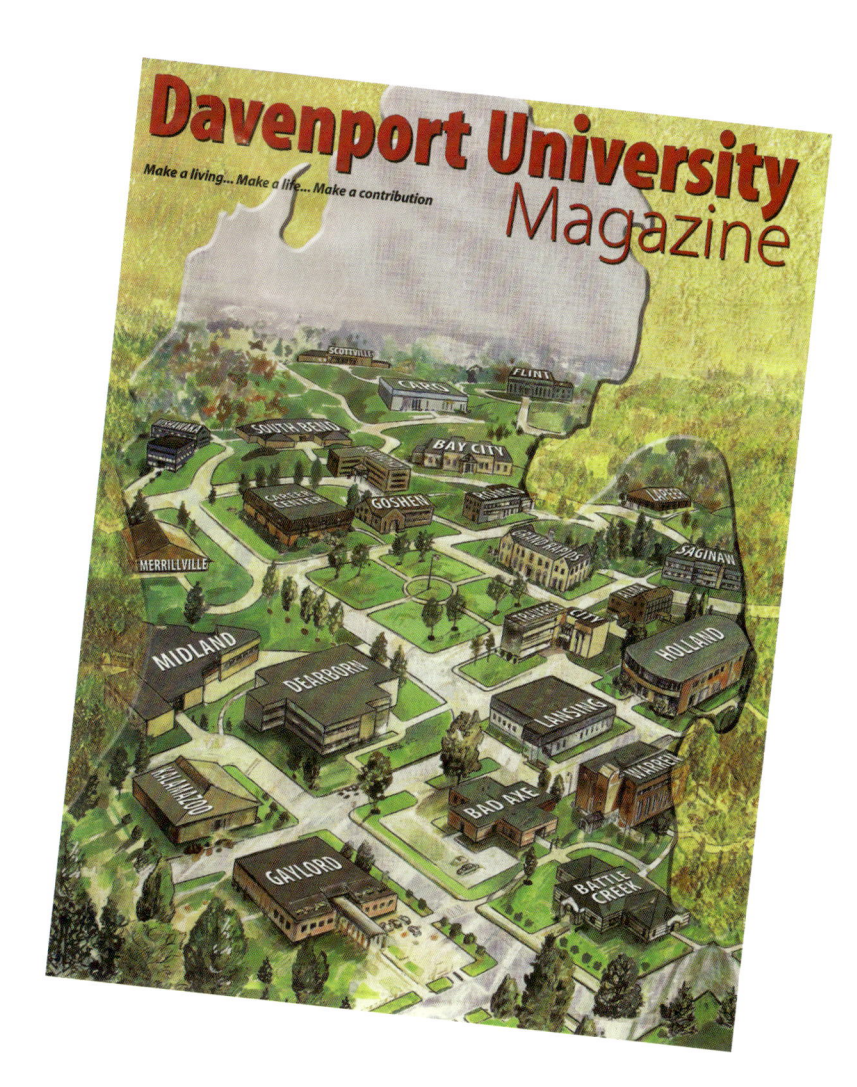

As the new century began, more than 30 Davenport campuses and classroom sites covered Michigan and northern Indiana. The complexity of unifying all the individual locations would require three years of intense effort and preparation.

Shortening the Stack. Each campus functioned with its own course selections, calendar, and catalog. Among the "softer" benefits of unification would be considerable economies in paper and printing costs.

James Meyer, president and CEO of Spartan Stores, Inc., served as Davenport University board chair from 2000 to 2008. Meyer attended Davenport College in the 1960s.

The Drawing Board

With the major structural and administrative pillars identified, much larger philosophical considerations awaited. Davenport needed to determine, for itself and its many constituents, what it meant to be a university: what should it look like and represent? How would admissions and the student body be affected? What kind of faculty was needed, what new services should it extend, what new degrees should it offer? In sum, how did Davenport need to change? These fundamental elements of purpose and direction were the most significant Davenport had encountered in decades.

In an effort to answer these questions, President Flechsig and his senior staff prepared a planning document called *Framework for Success: Propelling the University Toward Its Vision*. In describing how Davenport would build on its previous success while retaining unique features as a specialized institution, the *Framework for Success* set out its priorities: an innovative curriculum, a highly qualified faculty, a commitment to customer service, an aggressive student recruitment and retention strategy, a marketing plan, a vigorous fundraising effort, strategies for financial controls and investments, and a plan to develop new facilities and utilize new technologies.

With its vision articulated, the administration felt ready to request an NCA Higher Learning Commission comprehensive visit for the spring of 2004 to accredit Davenport as a single university. For the next two years all of the institution's energy was mobilized toward this goal.

Davenport University's
FRAMEWORK FOR SUCCESS
Propelling The University Toward Its Vision

November 2001

Prepared by
Randolph K. Flechsig
President

"Curriculum unification was a fascinating exercise. We all began forming strong bonds with colleagues at other campuses, which made it easier for us to begin thinking of becoming a single university as opposed to a collection of individual campuses. We started to think as one—and that was a very empowering moment."

—David Fleming, member of the president's cabinet and university provost.

The More Things Change. President Flechsig's 2001 *Framework for Success* guided Davenport into its third century with the same convictions from its first: "Learning is our highest purpose and first priority. We will deliver innovative academic programs that offer students a truly practical business education. We will be responsive to a changing business environment and will prepare students for the world of work."

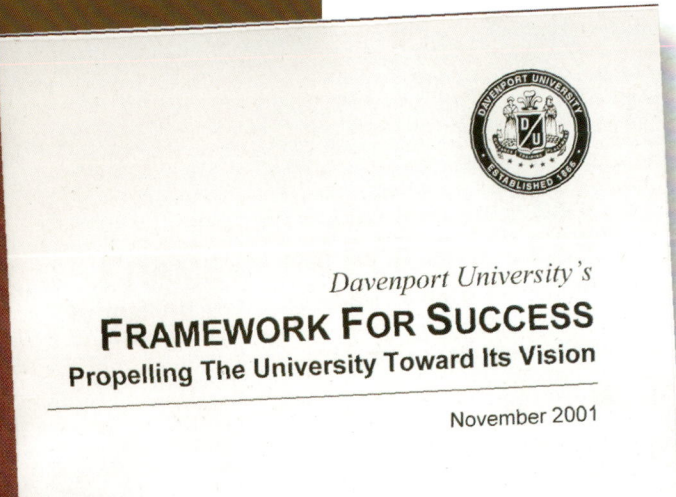

National Recognition. Davenport University's MBA program was listed among the "Best of the Online Grad Programs" in 2001 by *U.S. News and World Report*. Davenport was one of only 38 schools nationwide listed in the business programs category.

The Lanting Welcome Center, named for alumnus James Lanting and wife Clarine, became the main entrance for the Fulton Street campus. Mr. Lanting also served on Davenport's governing and foundation boards. (L-R): Group Vice President Colleen Wolfe, President Randy Flechsig, donors Clarine Lanting and James Lanting, Chair Emeritus Wilbur Lettinga, and Dr. Barbara Mieras, executive vice president for advancement and president of Davenport University Foundation.

Work in Progress: Composing the University

The volume of this task—imposing in its own right—was matched by the nature of reshaping an operating culture that had defined Davenport for decades. Individual Davenport campuses, operating in diverse communities all across Michigan, had a tradition of autonomy widely regarded as effective in addressing the needs of their individual student bodies. "It proved difficult," noted Vice President David Veneklase, "to move from an entrepreneurial culture to one that would rely on standardized policies and practices."

One source of anxiety involved the shift to a common semester system and academic calendar. Many were concerned that the confusion would overwhelm students, or perhaps discourage them from registering. Others pointed out that the term-to-semester depreciation involved in credit-hour conversion might create financial hardships for students, as they faced the possibility of additional classes to make up for the "exchange rate." Advisors had to create revised academic plans for approximately 13,000 students, followed up by individual consultations with each and every one. Understandably, students needed extra assurance that the change wouldn't disrupt their educational timetable or their budget.

Perhaps most daunting of all was the effort required to create the new curriculum. More than 100 faculty members spent thousands of hours on this monumental process, which involved an exhaustive audit and comparison of more than a thousand classes system-wide. Program by program, degree by degree, they identified logical areas of consolidation, eliminated duplication, and organized cohesive new classes on a semester model. When they finished, they had reduced 1,030 classes to just over 350 and streamlined 225 separate programs into 60.

In the meantime, facility renovations in Grand Rapids began updating the main campus to accommodate the reconfigured programs. Classrooms were retrofitted with new technology, the Cook Administration Building underwent a complete remodel, and a new atrium connector, called the Lanting Welcome Center, created a large main foyer and reception area between the Sneden Academic Center and Warren Hall.

But Davenport was just beginning to grow into its new identity; many other important transformations were gathering momentum.

BUSINESS
THE GRAND RAPIDS PRESS

Business school named for Don Maine

Honoring a Legacy. The new university master plan organized the college's three primary concentrations—business, allied health occupations, and computer applications—into formal 'schools.' The business division would become the Donald W. Maine School of Business in honor of Davenport's chancellor emeritus.

Forever Altered. The 2001 academic year was barely underway when the September 11 terrorist attacks on New York City's World Trade Center staggered America and the world. With fears and emotions running high everywhere, a letter from President Flechsig reminded the campus community of Davenport's abiding principles of multicultural respect.

DAVENPORT UNIVERSITY

September 19, 2001

Dear Davenport Family:

The events of the past week have deeply affected our nation as well as nations around the world. Shock and disbelief are changing to sadness and grief for the tremendous loss of lives and the hardships placed on businesses and their employees across the land. In our quest for answers many Americans are rediscovering fundamental beliefs that are sustaining them and helping them recover from our collective tragedy. My wish is that all of Davenport University can find comfort in this time of suffering.

In higher education we have a fundamental belief in the ultimate quest for a free society. We are on the front line, guarding the rights that keep America so great...freedom of speech, freethinking, and free enterprise. We are educating our students in a free and open learning environment and supporting those students in their quest to rise above the hatred that comes from closed, uneducated minds. As the largest independent business university in Michigan and northern Indiana, we have a responsibility to continue on our mission to prepare new generations of students for the support of free enterprise, the very institution that was attacked by these terrorists. As associates of Davenport University, you are serving your country in a very fundamental way, and I am proud to be among you in this mission.

As classes begin, I'd like to ask you to think of the fundamental values for Davenport University as reflected in our guiding principles. "Diversity enhances a strong and healthy organizational culture. Davenport University values the contributions of diverse populations, ideologies and educational perspectives." I remind you of this as a source of strength for you as you come across the inevitable anger. I am hopeful that you will not encounter harassment on our campuses, but I recognize that history shows we must be on alert to stop this behavior if it occurs. We have a zero tolerance policy for any type of discrimination or harassment, and I expect you all to support me in enforcing this policy university-wide.

I would also like to confirm that we will follow the directive of President Bush to return to business as usual and will plan to function normally in our support of students.

As a final note, I'd like to extend my personal sympathies to those who have lost friends or loved ones as a direct result of recent events and to those who find themselves actively grieving. I'd also like to thank all the campuses that have set up fund drives, blood drives or other activities to respond to this crisis on a local level. I strongly encourage these local efforts. We will be exploring ways in which Davenport University can continue to assist those in need in future months and will keep you informed of any opportunities for further contributions.

God Bless America!

Thank you all.

Randolph K. Flechsig
President

2000
Randolph K. Flechsig appointed university chancellor. (The title of "chancellor" is replaced with "president" in 2001).

Davenport Online—originally called The Learning Network—is accredited by North Central Association to offer online degrees.

September 2001
Terrorists crash two commercial airliners into New York City's World Trade Center, collapsing the twin towers and killing thousands. A third hijacked jet hits the Pentagon and a fourth is crashed into a Pennsylvania field.

2002
Davenport's athletic program is reinstated with men's hockey and women's basketball teams.

September 2003
Unified curriculum and semester system implemented for all Davenport campuses.

Davenport joins National Association of Intercollegiate Athletics (NAIA) and begins competing in the Wolverine-Hoosier Athletic Conference.

October 2004
Davenport accredited as a single university by North Central Association.

September 2005
W. A. Lettinga Campus opens in Caledonia Township.

Roaring Back: Return of the Panthers

Mothballed for nearly a quarter century, Davenport's athletic program was restored in the early 2000s. It was a major leap forward in Davenport's return to a fully integrated college environment designed to attract more traditional-age students. Two teams were inaugurated for the 2002-03 school year: men's hockey (with just 14 players) and women's basketball (with a squad of 8). The university's first athletic director, Paul Lowden, joked that he and the coach of the Lady Panthers worked out of "broom closets" during those first seasons.

Numerous teams followed in both varsity and nonvarsity sports, and by 2005 Davenport would become a full member of the Wolverine-Hoosier Athletic Conference (WHAC), consisting of local and regional institutions like Aquinas College, Indiana Tech, and the University of Michigan–Dearborn. By the time it reached its 10th year, hundreds of Panther athletes were playing on 26 teams in conference and nonvarsity sports. The athletic program itself became a "major player" in attracting traditional-age students and building a more complete university environment.

"The athletic mission has to tie with the mission of the university. At Davenport it is not a right to be an athlete; it's a privilege."
—Athletic Director Paul Lowden

After starting with three teams and an office in what he described as a "broom closet," Paul Lowden launched a fully integrated and staffed sports program that would grow to include hundreds of student athletes and more than 30 teams.

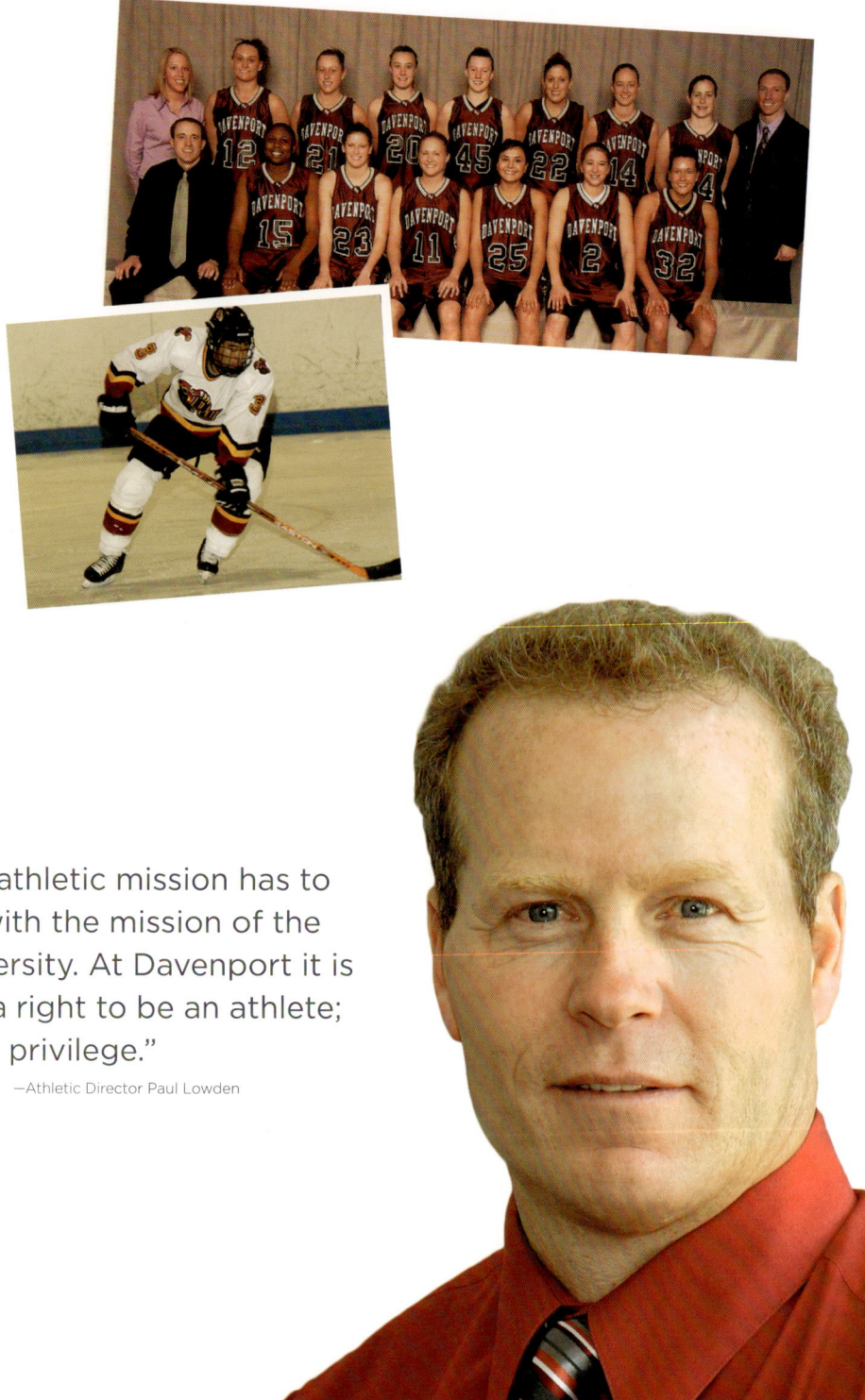

One DU

On September 3, 2003, for the first time in its history, all students throughout the system started classes on the same day, using the same credit-hour system and the same curriculum. There was little, if any, disruption attributable to the changes.

Exhilaration combined with a sense of profound accomplishment for the inestimable hours spent on converting dream to reality. As the academic year progressed, apprehension dissipated as the benefits of consolidation were revealed. Predicted cost savings began to materialize: faculty and students adjusted smoothly to the new class rhythms and routines.

The following spring, the completion of the pilot academic year synchronized with the scheduled accreditation visit by the Higher Learning Commission. The university community was well-acclimated to its new identity and confident in its presentation to the review committee. That fall, the announcement was official: Davenport was accredited by the North Central Association as a single university. The final report stated that "the university serves as a model for the successful merger of three institutions" and that "the unified institution was stronger than any one of the three."

Davenport University could now move forward in galvanizing its culture around the individual schools it had established: the Donald W. Maine School of Business, the School of Health Professions, the School of Technology, and the School of Arts & Sciences, also known as the University School. All its efforts went behind branding the university with these specialties—cornerstones of what was becoming regarded as the new "knowledge economy."

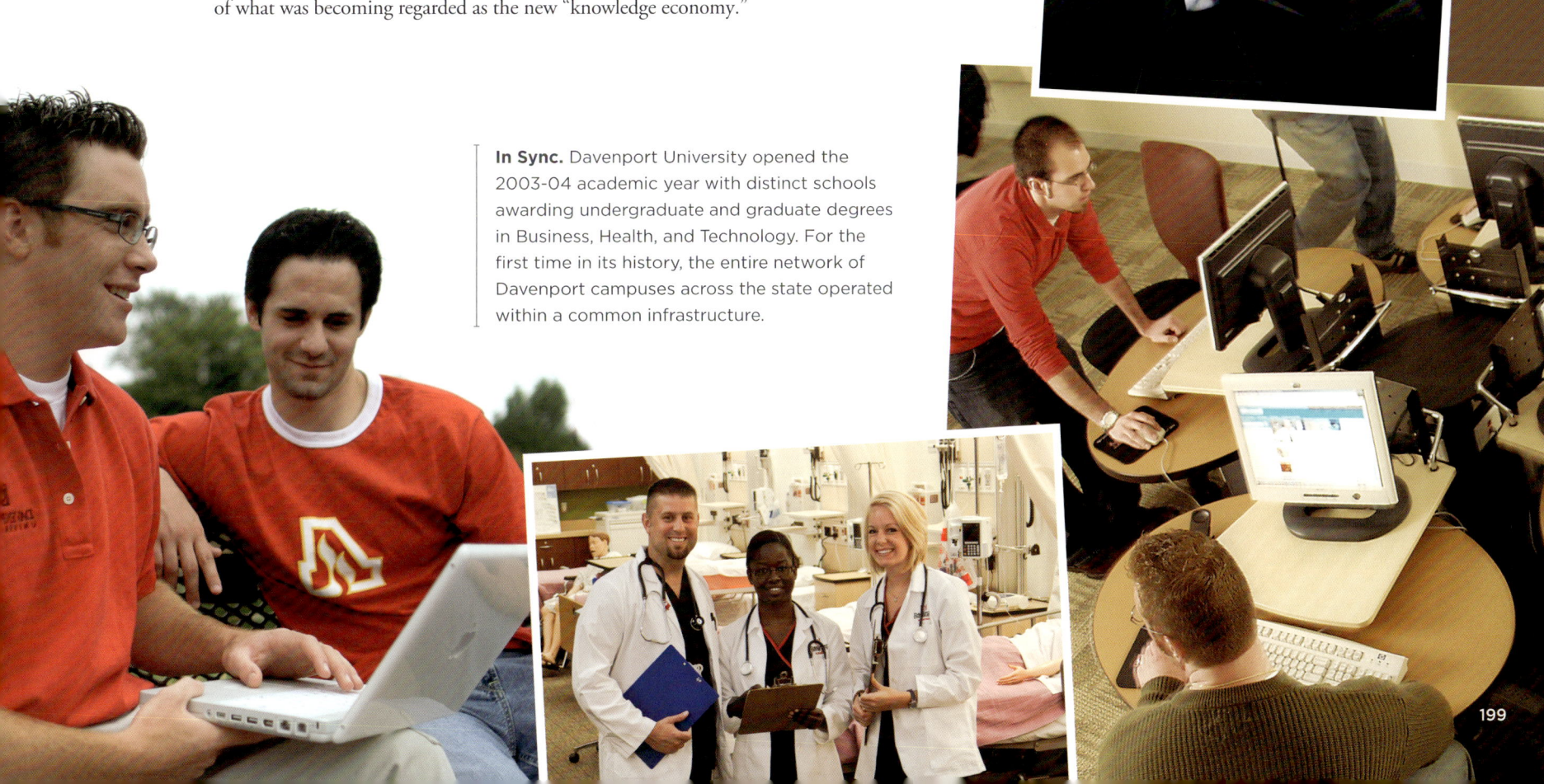

In Sync. Davenport University opened the 2003-04 academic year with distinct schools awarding undergraduate and graduate degrees in Business, Health, and Technology. For the first time in its history, the entire network of Davenport campuses across the state operated within a common infrastructure.

'Brick and Click:' The Online Option

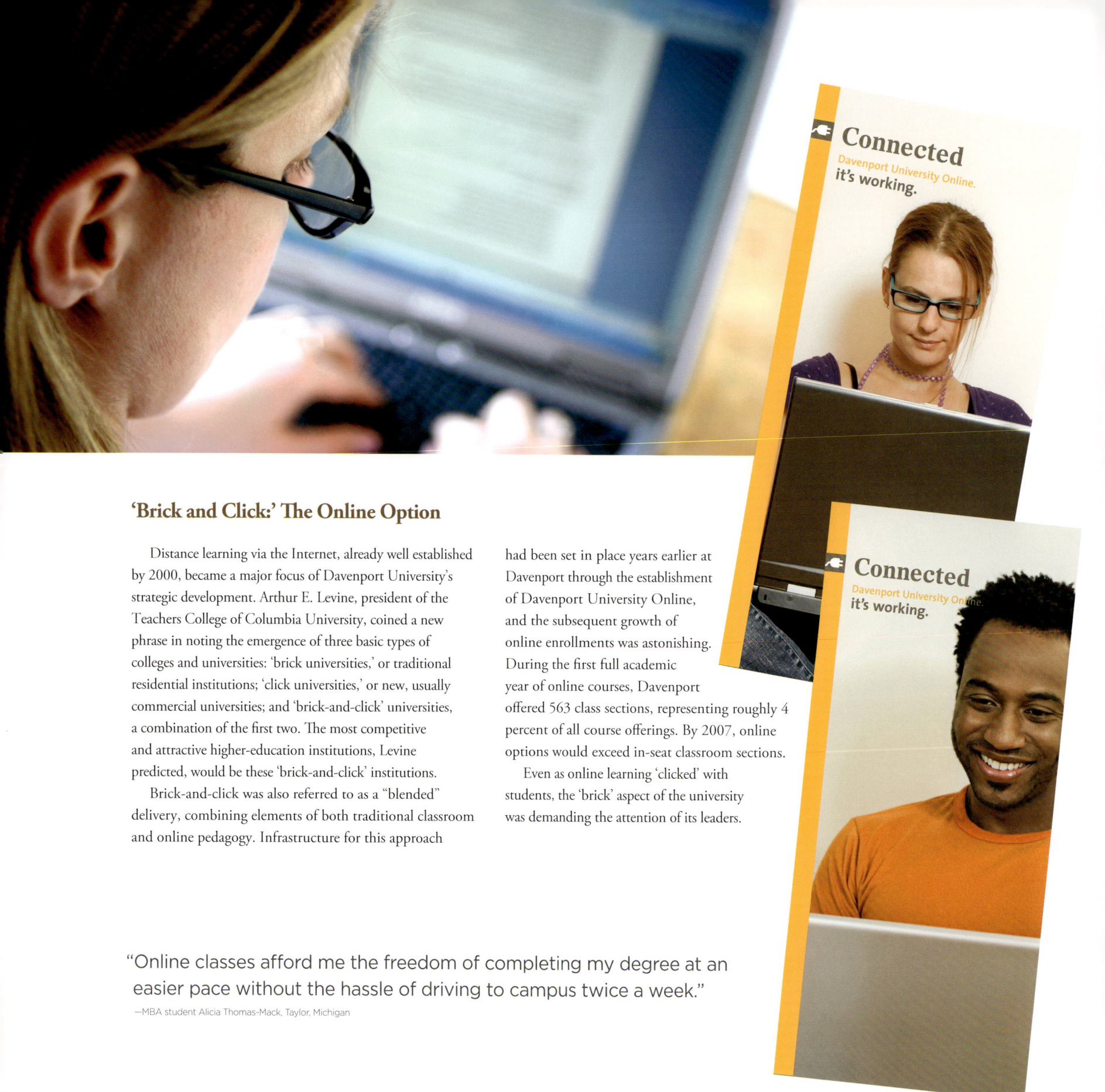

Distance learning via the Internet, already well established by 2000, became a major focus of Davenport University's strategic development. Arthur E. Levine, president of the Teachers College of Columbia University, coined a new phrase in noting the emergence of three basic types of colleges and universities: 'brick universities,' or traditional residential institutions; 'click universities,' or new, usually commercial universities; and 'brick-and-click' universities, a combination of the first two. The most competitive and attractive higher-education institutions, Levine predicted, would be these 'brick-and-click' institutions.

Brick-and-click was also referred to as a "blended" delivery, combining elements of both traditional classroom and online pedagogy. Infrastructure for this approach had been set in place years earlier at Davenport through the establishment of Davenport University Online, and the subsequent growth of online enrollments was astonishing. During the first full academic year of online courses, Davenport offered 563 class sections, representing roughly 4 percent of all course offerings. By 2007, online options would exceed in-seat classroom sections.

Even as online learning 'clicked' with students, the 'brick' aspect of the university was demanding the attention of its leaders.

"Online classes afford me the freedom of completing my degree at an easier pace without the hassle of driving to campus twice a week."
—MBA student Alicia Thomas-Mack, Taylor, Michigan

Davenport University's proud relationship with President Gerald R. Ford encompassed 65 years, beginning with his position as an instructor and assistant football coach at the University of Grand Rapids in the 1940s. (Above) "Coach" Ford shares a special moment with former UGR football players at a 2001 reunion. On Ford's right and left, respectively, are Dallas Braden and quarterback Jack Barrows. (Left) A gathering of presidents: Dr. Barbara Mieras, Randolph K. Flechsig, Gerald R. Ford, Donald W. Maine.

Before his passing in 2006, President Ford personally granted Davenport University the extraordinary opportunity to name a prestigious scholarship in his memory.

Vitae: Dr. Therese (Terri) Tomaszek

Professor of humanities and social sciences, Dr. Therese (Terri) Tomaszek has personified teaching excellence at Davenport for more than 40 years.

Her distinguished career encompasses three concentrations: academic assessment, international education, and service learning. Among her most influential contributions to Davenport's instructional culture was the Success System (now called the Excellence System): a composite of cross-professional attributes and competencies integrated throughout all Davenport programs and courses. For decades, this has been the pedagogical and philosophical model of a Davenport education.

Tomaszek also instigated and developed a thriving international culture on campus. As Davenport's first Fulbright Scholar, she created the Study Abroad China Program, which subsequently grew to include other countries. Dr. Tomaszek's signature Global Perspectives class expanded into a suite of courses focused on world cultures.

As the faculty liaison for experiential learning, Dr. Tomaszek throughout her career has been the champion of meaningful applied learning outside the classroom, including community involvement and volunteerism.

Equally respected by her students and her colleagues, Dr. Tomaszek has been honored with awards both within and outside the university.

Shovel Ready. Participating in the 2004 W.A. Lettinga Campus groundbreaking ceremony are (from left): Group Vice President Colleen Wolfe, Mike Van Gessel of Rockford Construction, university governing board Chair James Meyer, Michigan State Senator Glenn Steil (R-Grand Rapids), Barbara Steil, Sharon Lettinga, Wilbur A. Lettinga, President Randy Flechsig, Executive Vice President for Advancement Dr. Barbara Mieras.

The New Campus

As Davenport approached its 2004 accreditation review, it was clear that the university's future could not be fully realized on its Heritage Hill campus alone.

As early as January 2003 university officials were considering a new campus on the outskirts of Grand Rapids adjacent to the new M-6 freeway, a south connector linking two of the city's major interstates. The initial phase of campus development called for a main classroom building and residence hall designed to serve 2,400 students.

Excitement for the project was tempered by considerations of greater scale and scope. The new campus was being proposed while the university was operating more sites than at any time in its history, and the university governing board was uncomfortable making a commitment to a major new campus in Grand Rapids without broader attention to the viability of all locations.

After studying various scenarios over 18 months, the board concluded that adding capacity to the downtown campus would be complicated and excessively expensive. Even a fully implemented Fulton Street expansion still would limit enrollment to a maximum of 2,100 students. A revised macro-plan emerged: further improvements at the existing campus would be curtailed, the Eastern Avenue Career Center closed and its shorter career programs transferred to Fulton Street. Purchase of a 42-acre site located on Kraft Avenue in Caledonia Township was approved. The new campus would serve as the university's flagship location while administrative headquarters would remain in Heritage Hill.

A June 2004 groundbreaking launched the $22 million project. The site, to be named the W.A. Lettinga campus, had space for up to 4,000 students—nearly double the capacity of the Heritage Hill location.

The creation of a "suburban" campus prompted some concern and disagreement. While acknowledging the realities of a landlocked location and constrictions on growth, many expressed regret for the cultural upheaval of leaving the city core. Davenport and its predecessor schools had belonged to downtown Grand Rapids for nearly 140 years; departure represented a severance that felt much deeper than geographical relocation.

'Framework' for a New Campus. Steel girders outline the three-story Richard M. DeVos and Jay Van Andel Academic Center, anticipating the completed vision (below). The flagship building was the first in Grand Rapids named for both cofounders of Amway Corporation.

"I appreciate Davenport's commitment to communities by allowing us to serve on 'university time'. The volunteer time-off policy has a great impact on the lives of those we serve."

—Terri Cardon-Weiss, member of the Saginaw Campus Community Engagement Team

Like these undergraduates rebuilding houses in the aftermath of Hurricane Katrina, Davenport students and staff have always been encouraged to "Make a Contribution" to their communities…even if that means traveling nearly a thousand miles to provide help where needed.

Vitae: Dr. Thomas Brown

Dr. Thomas H. Brown earned the distinction of having served Davenport through five college presidential administrations. Beginning with Robert Sneden, Brown joined Davenport College in 1966 as a faculty member, where he also chaired the Business Administration Division. Under President Donald Maine he held several top positions in academic affairs and research and strategic planning. In 1998 while Dr. Barbara Mieras was president, Brown was named the first dean of the Margaret and Robert Sneden Graduate School and concurrently served as director of transition during Davenport's conversion to a university. Brown became a charter member of the first President's Cabinet appointed by President Randy Flechsig, who also chose Brown to lead the Donald Maine School of Business as its first dean. For President Richard Pappas, Brown served as provost before retiring in 2011. He was recognized with Davenport's highest employee honor, the Tyrus R. Wessell Award for Distinguished Employee Service.

Dr. Brown holds a doctorate in college and university administration from Michigan State University. His career contains numerous professional appointments, including service on more than 30 accreditation evaluation teams through the Higher Learning Commission of the North Central Association of Colleges and Schools.

Davenport's New Home

The W.A. Lettinga campus opened in the fall of 2005, accompanied by a formal dedication ceremony, a legislator's tour and a community open house. The flagship of the campus was the three-story Richard M. DeVos and Jay Van Andel Academic Center, the first structure to be named for both cofounders of Amway Corporation. The 127,000-square-foot facility combined classrooms, faculty offices, private conference rooms, student and fitness centers, a cafeteria, the campus bookstore, and an expansive library/information commons. It was a millennial building in every sense—classrooms and labs featured changemaking learning technology, and the entire facility complied to Leadership in Energy and Environmental Design (LEED) certification.

For the first time in many years, Davenport also reintroduced on-campus living to its students. The campus's first residence hall, named for Davenport alumnus Peter C. Cook and wife Pat, was designed to house 80 students.

Mark Griffin, a long-time member of the Grand Rapids full-time faculty, called the new campus a result of "bold thinking [that] changed how people perceive Davenport."

2003 — 12,700 ENROLLMENT

133 Full-Time Faculty

TUITION $339 Per Credit Hour

45 Degrees (graduate and undergraduate)
College of Business 25
College of Technology 16
College of Health Professions 4

The university's second residence hall, completed in 2006, was later dedicated to Fred and Lena Meijer, when the couple made a generous land gift to Davenport for future expansion. (Center inset) Doug Meijer, celebrates the dedication with Wilbur Lettinga and Interim President Michael Volk.

The Campus Expands

Within a year preparations began for a second residence hall to shorten the wait list that had already developed for Cook Hall. Another prominent West Michigan name appeared on campus with the dedication of the Fred and Lena Meijer Residence Hall, honoring the founder of Meijer Incorporated and his wife.

Davenport's new location adjacent to a main metropolitan highway afforded a major advantage in visibility. Davenport leaders began to visualize a signature facility that would prominently showcase the university and contribute to its on-campus environment: a student center offering a full range of programs and activities. The centerpiece of the new structure would be a state-of-the-art fieldhouse for the expanding athletic program. Soon, plans for an 85,000-square-foot facility on the western edge of the new campus were on the table.

Davenport: Educating Across Three Centuries | The New Millennium

Legacies Peter C. Cook

Ambition and Drive. Peter Cook was introduced to imported automobiles early in his career and went on to become one of the region's largest distributors of foreign cars.

Among West Michigan's leading philanthropists and community benefactors, few can parallel the legacy created by Davenport-McLachlan alumnus Peter Cook. Passionately devoted to his work, family, and community, Cook personified the institutional philosophy of "Make a Living, Make a Life, Make a Contribution."

While he moved easily in corporate circles, he considered himself first and foremost a citizen of the community where he lived. He was born in southwest Grand Rapids and graduated from South High School in 1932 (one class behind fellow graduate Gerald Ford). Dreams of a college education were difficult to fulfill in the Great Depression, particularly with an unemployed father and four younger brothers at home. In order to help support the household, Cook put his college hopes on hold to take a job on the assembly line at the Leonard/Kelvinator Refrigerator Corporation. The starting wage was 17 cents an hour.

Not willing to abandon his educational ambitions, he came to Davenport-McLachlan Institute. While most work was scarce at the time, administrative help was still in demand—particularly for men—so Mr. Davenport advised Cook to enroll in the secretarial course. Cook took classes at night while working days at Kelvinator and gradually worked his way up in the company. Gaining experience in accounting and finance through various positions, he eventually accepted a partnership at Import Motors, Ltd. By 1954 he was president of the company, which supplied Volkswagen, Audi, and Porsche automobiles to 60 dealerships around Michigan. In 1977, Cook and his partners formed Mazda Great Lakes and went regional with their business. Even though he sold the distributorship in 2000 he was not the "retiring type," and formed Cook Holdings, a wealth management firm, which he chaired until his death in 2010.

While running a thriving automobile business, service never took a back seat. Cook worked on the boards of dozens of organizations during his career: Rotary Club, United Way, Spectrum Hospital, the Grand Rapids Chamber of Commerce, and many others. Working with friend and Davenport President Donald Maine on the Grand Action Committee, he helped usher in the 1990s development surge that produced major cultural and event venues such as DeVos Place Convention Center and Van Andel Arena. His many passions and interests included Dixieland jazz (he played trumpet), Western American history and art, and his family.

But few things gave him as much satisfaction as giving back, which he engaged in prolifically. Philanthropy came naturally to Cook, who once told an interviewer, "I enjoy giving it away." Success cultivated within him a sense of gratitude and generosity that touched every sphere: arts, medicine, community and civic enrichment, and particularly higher education, where his gifts helped finance projects, programs, and buildings at every college in the West Michigan region.

But Davenport—his alma mater—always held a special place in his life.

Devoted to Davenport. Cook's ties to Davenport lasted far beyond his student days. He was a member of the board of trustees, Distinguished Alumnus of 1981, and namesake and first recipient of the Peter C. Cook Excellence in Business Award established in 1998. Also named for him were the Cook Administration Building on the Fulton Street campus, the Peter and Pat Cook Residence Hall on the W.A. Lettinga Campus, and the Peter Cook Center for Graduate Studies in downtown Grand Rapids.

Peter Cook

Davenport University Career Fairs 2006

- American Express Financial
- Cintas Corporation
- Target
- FedEx
- Charter Communications
- Lowe's Home Improvements
- Blue Cross Blue Shield
- Fifth Third Bank
- State Farm Insurance
- SBC Global
- Internal Revenue Service
- Trinity Health

In the past, we've attracted the biggest names. Who will you attract?
Davenport Career Fairs connect our brightest students with the area's best employers. These events are invaluable networking experiences that can result in job placement. Take advantage of these great opportunities, FREE to all Davenport students.

Davenport University
it's working.

"My focus is always [on] the students and helping them prepare for what lies ahead in the world of business. This has been the strength of Davenport and what has sustained its success for the past decades."

—Ron Draayer, faculty advisor for Davenport's Business Professionals of America chapter and faculty member since 1977.

Business Professionals of America (BPA) and DECA (formerly Delta Epsilon Chi) are both national cocurricular organizations focused on leadership and entrepreneurship. Academic competitions are held each year at the regional, state, and national levels. Both groups have had prosperous histories at DU for decades. Since chartering in 1981, the Davenport chapter of BPA has entered more than 1,000 contestants in BPA competitions. Davenport teams consistently outperform rivals from some of the most prestigious business programs in the country, and Davenport holds the national BPA record for the highest number of first-place finishes.

"The decision to build a residential campus was a game changer for the university. Students have a better opportunity to learn in an environment where they have close relationships with faculty, staff, and other students. A residential campus provides those important connections and enables students to truly enjoy a university experience, and as alumni they will have a place to come back to and identify with for the rest of their lives."

—DU Trustee Kenneth Bovee, (chair, 2008–2010)

Students get acquainted with their new campus, from corridors and classrooms to the comforts of home in the apartment-style Peter C. and Pat Cook Residence Hall.

Davenport: Educating Across Three Centuries | The New Millennium

Fulton Street Farewell. Unparalleled in beauty of both nature and architecture, the Heritage Hill campus stood for decades as a distinguished gateway into the downtown area. In maintaining the character of this historic corridor, Davenport left a legacy to the city of Grand Rapids as well as the educational community, as the site became a branch campus of Grand Rapids Community College.

In 2007 Davenport announced its departure from downtown Grand Rapids and put its historic Heritage Hill campus up for sale. Among interested parties was Grand Rapids Community College, whose main campus was just a few blocks away.

End of an Era: Fulton Street Farewell

The investment in the Lettinga campus had presented university leadership with a sobering reality: it was no longer financially viable to retain the historic Heritage Hill location. Maintaining the pace of capital projects and new degree programs, along with the expense of maintaining two full campuses in the Grand Rapids area, was proving unsustainable. In 2005, Davenport leaders made the decision to close the Fulton Street campus altogether.

Releasing this distinguished location became a study in mixed emotions. This city block had been Davenport's first independent campus—and just as the new location symbolized a major development milestone, 415 Fulton Street had represented a comparable transformation from "institute" to "college." Perhaps most conflicting was the distancing from the city itself; Davenport, in tracing its ancestry back to 1866, had always been at the heart of the city.

Gradually, presence was reduced at the campus as programs and staff were transferred to Lettinga Campus and various auxiliary locations. Grand Rapids Community College purchased the Heritage Hill campus in its entirety in 2009, and by 2010, the transfer of ownership was complete. A Fulton Street Memory Garden is located on the W.A. Lettinga Campus.

The university's School of Technology became the first in the country to offer degrees in network security and information and computer security, a fact noteworthy of coverage on CNN. In an interview with the news network, Dean Reid Gough called security the "one area of expertise that holds the 'key to the castle' for all organizations."

Deep in Study. Whether among the stacks or at the screens, students at the Margaret Davenport Sneden Library are serious about their work.

2006
Fred and Lena Meijer Residence Hall opens on W.A. Lettinga campus.

May 2007
Closing of Heritage Hill campus in downtown Grand Rapids announced.

September 2008
Lehman Brothers files for bankruptcy, triggering a stock market crash and subsequent decline that reduces the Dow Jones Industrial Average by nearly half. U.S. enters the 'Great Recession.'

October 2008
Student Center opens on W.A. Lettinga Campus.

President Flechsig resigns from Davenport University; Executive Vice President for Finance Michael Volk named Interim President.

November 2008
Barack Obama elected as America's first African-American president.

May 2009
Heritage Hill campus on East Fulton Street sold to Grand Rapids Community College.

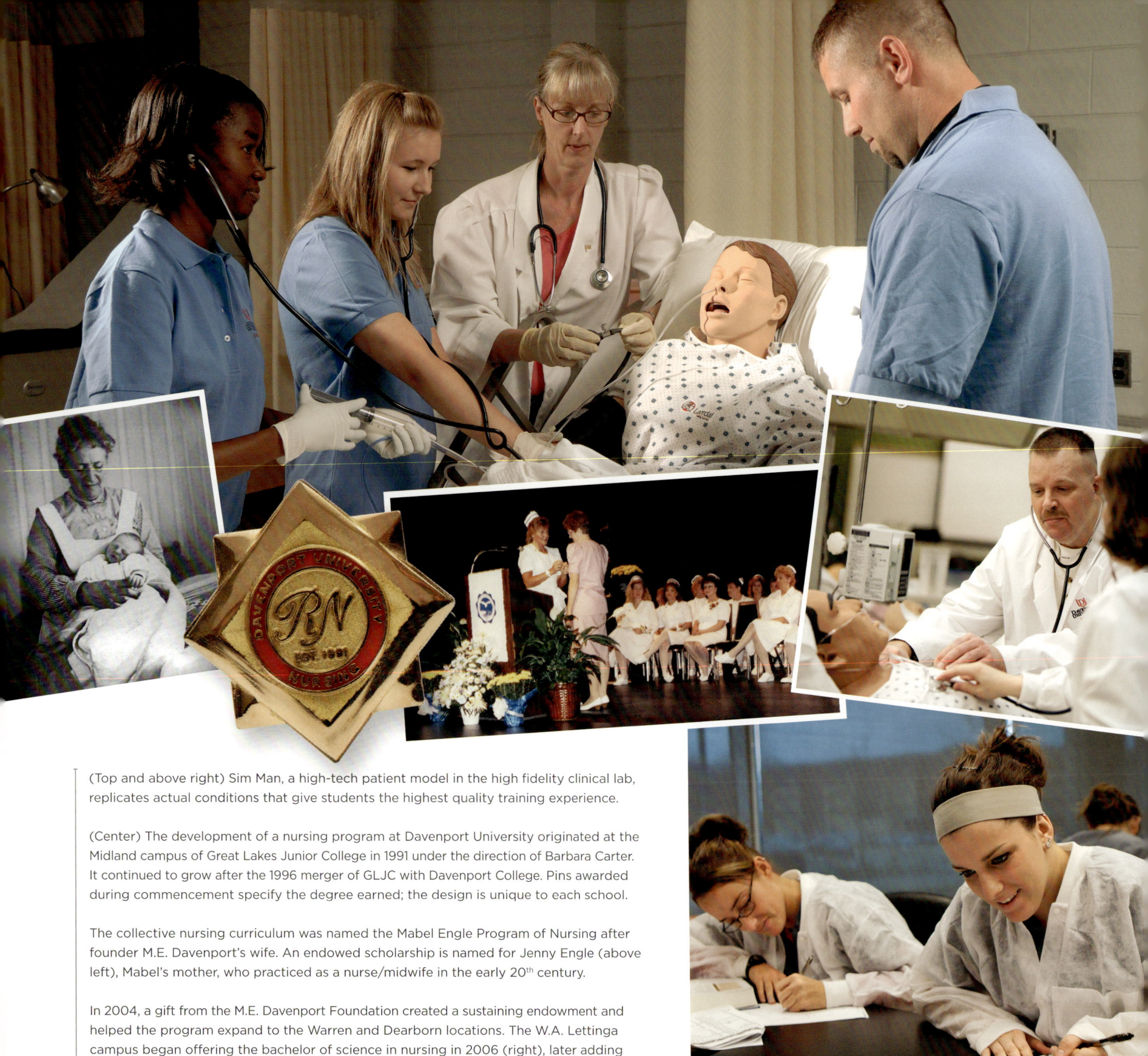

(Top and above right) Sim Man, a high-tech patient model in the high fidelity clinical lab, replicates actual conditions that give students the highest quality training experience.

(Center) The development of a nursing program at Davenport University originated at the Midland campus of Great Lakes Junior College in 1991 under the direction of Barbara Carter. It continued to grow after the 1996 merger of GLJC with Davenport College. Pins awarded during commencement specify the degree earned; the design is unique to each school.

The collective nursing curriculum was named the Mabel Engle Program of Nursing after founder M.E. Davenport's wife. An endowed scholarship is named for Jenny Engle (above left), Mabel's mother, who practiced as a nurse/midwife in the early 20th century.

In 2004, a gift from the M.E. Davenport Foundation created a sustaining endowment and helped the program expand to the Warren and Dearborn locations. The W.A. Lettinga campus began offering the bachelor of science in nursing in 2006 (right), later adding a master's degree. It is one of Davenport's most demanded programs, with a highly competitive admission process.

212

The Dean Team. First university deans (L-R): Dr. Denise Oleske, School of Health Professions; Dr. Kojo Quartey, Donald W. Maine School of Business; Reid Gough, School of Technology. Far right: Dr. Thomas Brown, provost.

School deans guide quality, progress

213

Commencement 2008: A University First

In the spring of 2008, Davenport held its first-ever commencement ceremony as a single university.

Academically, the university's prestige was growing with groundbreaking new programs and degrees. Bachelor's and master's degrees anticipated new career trends in fields like sports management, accounting fraud investigation, and information assurance. The acclaimed nursing program, which had originated in Midland, was extended to Grand Rapids.

The most visible evidence of the university's growth was the new Student Center, completed in time for the start of the 2008-09 academic year. Along with first-rate fitness and training facilities, spaces for club meetings, activities, and intramurals, the centerpiece of the facility was a 1,500-seat fieldhouse, which gave the Davenport Panthers—for the first time ever—a home court.

Home Court Advantage. On October 31, 2008, Davenport dedicated its new Student Center. The 87,000-square-foot facility included a 1,500-seat fieldhouse for men's and women's basketball, an indoor track, fitness center, climbing tower, and a café/commons area. Adjacent outdoor athletic fields for soccer and lacrosse completed the complex. For the first time in their history, the Panthers had a place to call their own.

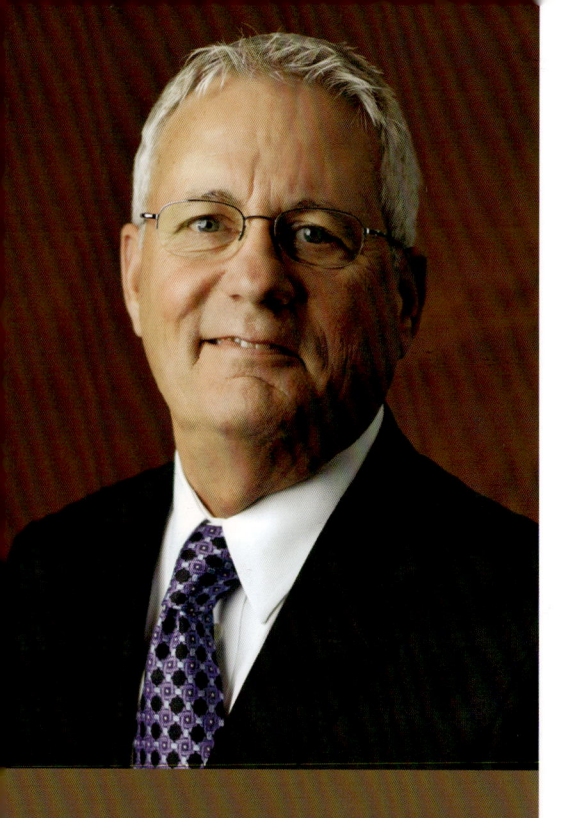

Kenneth C. Bovee served on Davenport's Board of Trustees for 10 years, including 4 as chair. He led the presidential search committee that selected Richard J. Pappas, and he worked closely with Dr. Pappas on Vision 2015. Mr. Bovee was CEO and president of Keystone Management Group.

Interim and Introspection

In the fall of 2008, President Flechsig tendered his resignation for personal reasons. The ensuing months provided an opportunity for reflection and evaluation, as university leaders worked to continue progress while reinforcing important aspects of Davenport's culture.

The board of trustees unanimously approved the appointment of Davenport University's Executive Vice President of Finance Michael Volk as interim president while a candidate search for a new president was initiated. Volk was able to provide continuity and a stabilizing influence while Davenport prepared for its next leader.

Michael Volk served as interim president from 2008 until 2009. He continued as executive vice president for finance following the selection of Davenport's next president.

"It will be the next great evolutionary challenge of the university to measure and find ways to continuously improve quality." —Randolph Flechsig

Presidential Profile Randolph K. Flechsig

While growing up in suburban Cleveland, Randy Flechsig never envisioned becoming a university president. Like most boys, he spent his time rough-housing with neighborhood friends and frequently wound up in the emergency rooms of local hospitals being sutured or x-rayed. From those experiences he developed an early interest in medicine. He dreamed of becoming a doctor, but throughout school struggled academically.

In college at the University of Cincinnati, an academic advisor introduced him to non-medical hospital careers. He transferred to Xavier University in Cincinnati, changed his major to business, and diligently applied himself to his studies, graduating second in his class.

Randy decided to continue for an advanced degree and enrolled in a rigorous master of science program in healthcare administration at St. Louis University. A one-year residency in suburban Detroit brought him to Michigan. After launching his management career at hospitals in Marshall and Hudson, he moved to Saginaw to become president and CEO of the Hospital Council of East Central Michigan, overseeing 21 hospitals in a 14-county area.

There he helped create the Health Care Alliance Pool, a unique local healthcare provider-based insurance plan for small businesses.

Flechsig had no plans whatsoever to change direction. But his expertise was sought by Great Lakes Junior College in Saginaw in establishing their new nursing program. Shortly after, Randy was invited to join the college's first public governing board and was soon named chairman.

By virtue of the 1996 GLJC merger with the Davenport Educational System, Randy next became a member of the DES governing board and was suddenly part of a much larger organization and network of schools. It was through this experience that he began to contemplate a role in higher education. In the fall of 2000 he was appointed to succeed retiring chancellor Donald Maine.

Randy Flechsig's personal narrative is similar to that of many students—and leaders—who choose Davenport. He was the first in his family to attend college; his home environment didn't emphasize higher education or a professional career; and like his predecessor Don Maine, he struggled academically until the realities of marginal performance ignited in him a passion for success through education.

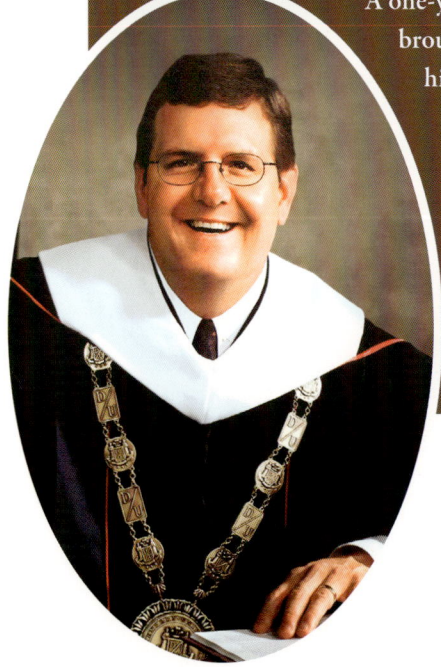

Randolph K. Flechsig

With his intense focus on improvement, it was no coincidence that Randy was attracted to Davenport at a time when it was planning its greatest restructuring in 1999. Davenport's board of trustees recognized the match between Flechsig's skills and the institution's future and selected him to implement the university model in the new century. While president, Flechsig served also on the executive committee of the Association of Independent Colleges and Universities of Michigan (AICUM), as a member of the Council of Presidents for the National Association of Intercollegiate Athletics, and was a founding board member of Legacy Trust Bank. His community commitments included the Grand Rapids Economic Club, Grand Rapids Griffins Youth Foundation, Hope Network Foundation, and the Michigan Chamber of Commerce.

Flechsig challenged future leaders to continue the university's upward trajectory. "One of the big challenges of the next generation of leaders at Davenport will be to develop more and better measures of quality and performance. It will be the next great evolutionary challenge of the university to measure and find ways to continuously improve quality."

> "We tell our graduates that a Davenport degree is proof to the work world that they know how to be successful in their chosen career. We work very hard to make sure that when potential employers see a Davenport graduate, they see an energetic, prepared worker who should be at the top of their list."
> —Randolph Flechsig, 2006

LEFT: Joining President Flechsig at the dedication of the campus commons named for him are governing board chair James Meyer (at right) and past chair Wilbur Lettinga.

During President Flechsig's administration, Davenport was accredited as a university, established a new residential campus, and reinstated its athletic department.

Crossroads:
Educating in the New Economy

By the 21st century, America's reign as the world's 'Captain of Industry' was over. Companies that typified American dominance—like Bethlehem Steel and Polaroid—had disappeared. Production outsourcing to other countries, begun in the latter 20th century, was recalibrating the world economy.

More than most other states, Michigan symbolized the industrial muscle age and suffered disproportionately. During the 2000s nearly one million payroll jobs disappeared as the state fell from 18th to 36th in per capita income. Unemployment in 2009 averaged 13.4 percent.

In Grand Rapids, the loss or contraction of signature industrial facilities reflected the national decline. Gone from the economic landscape were Reynolds Metals, the General Motors Stamping Plant, and Steelcase's nearly mile-long complex of factories on Eastern Avenue. Gone also were the well-paying jobs that guaranteed a secure future while not requiring education beyond a high school diploma.

Faded Era. Once a symbol of manufacturing vigor, the Reynolds Aluminum water tower on Grand Rapids' southwest side signified the decline of the manufacturing age by its distressed façade.

New technologies—fiber-optics, digitized data, software—were forming an entirely reimagined economic base. In corporate leadership, names like Jobs, Zuckerberg, Gates, and Bezos became the Rockefellers, Carnegies, Morgans, and Vanderbilts of the new "genius age." As a result, the millennial may rate as one of the greatest transformative eras in history, with the Digital Age taking its place alongside other epochs. Author Thomas Friedman, in his bestselling book *The World is Flat*, suggested that the extraordinary confluence of major 20th and 21st century trends figuratively changed the 'shape' of the world itself.

Poised at this convergence, with its university identity established, Davenport University prepared for its own next era of development. At Davenport University—for 143 years an institution whose specific educational purpose was to prepare individuals not only to perform but to excel in changing environments—a new president was about to take over.

"Davenport will be renowned nationally and internationally as a quality institution that will help even more students realize their career dreams and generate positive change for their employers and communities."

—President Richard J. Pappas, Ed. D.

VISION FOR
CONTINUED EXCELLENCE
2009 - PRESENT

Dynamic Vision, Enduring Values

IN ITS OPENING DECADE, THE 21ST CENTURY HAD already far outdistanced the 20th. With breathtaking speed the world had become digital, instant and mobile, spawning an entirely new way of living, working, and communicating. "Viral" now referred to the contagion of information while "apps" performed thousands of functions at one's fingertips. Institutions and individuals raced to embrace and apply this surging flood of new developments.

Davenport University was riding a fast track of its own as Dr. Richard J. Pappas assumed the presidency in August of 2009. As one of the largest private, nonprofit universities in Michigan, Davenport offered dozens of associate, bachelor, and graduate degrees in business, technology, and health professions. More than two dozen men's and women's sports teams competed in the National Association of Intercollegiate Athletics (NAIA) and in club leagues. Like the world itself, Davenport had become a much different place since the beginning of the new millennium.

Social media made its debut, with Facebook posts and Twitter feeds announcing not merely the daily activities of ordinary citizens, but contributing to world events such as the "Arab Spring" wave of uprisings in countries like Egypt, Libya, and Syria.

> "Even though our vision continues to change, our values have never wavered throughout every era of the institution's leadership."

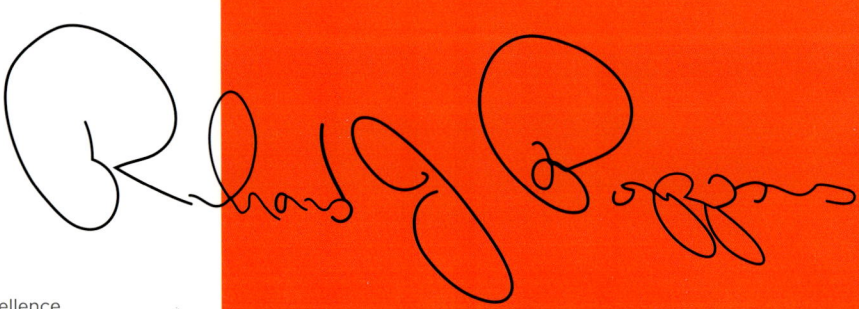

Richard J. Pappas

Davenport: Educating Across Three Centuries | Vision for Continued Excellence

Davenport's core mission had not changed, however, as it continued to prepare students through career-focused programs delivering solid academic content and real-world skills taught by accomplished faculty to small classes. President Pappas at once recognized the university's deep commitment to developing the whole person for career and life success. "Employers desire more than just subject matter expertise," Pappas said. "They want employees who demonstrate creative and critical thinking, ethical reasoning and action, and civic and social responsibility." Clearly Davenport's newest president valued the traditions embodied in Make a Living … Make a Life … Make a Contribution.

While Rick Pappas was attracted to Davenport's record of innovation and its dynamic history, Davenport also was attracted to Dr. Pappas because of his history. He had served higher education for 35 years, including 20 as a college or university president. He came to Davenport from National-Louis University in Chicago, an institution resembling Davenport in educational mission. His experience and credentials—and perhaps most persuasively, his philosophy—aligned with the Davenport culture. "The combination of entrepreneurship plus educational and business sense has defined each of my presidencies," Pappas said.

Richard Pappas is inducted as Davenport University's seventh president, congratulated by governing board chair Kenneth Bovee. Congressman Vernon Ehlers, Michigan Third District representative, addresses the ceremony.

June 2009
General Motors files for Chapter 11, becoming the largest American corporation to declare bankruptcy.

August 2009
Richard A. Pappas appointed president of Davenport University.

May 2010
Remaining Davenport administrative operations depart Heritage Hill campus.

September 2010
Robert W. Sneden Center opens on W.A. Lettinga Campus.

May 2011
The FBI's most-wanted, Osama Bin Laden is killed by a Special Forces operation in Abbottabad, Pakistan.

September 2011
Peter C. Cook Center opens in downtown Grand Rapids, offering MBA degrees.

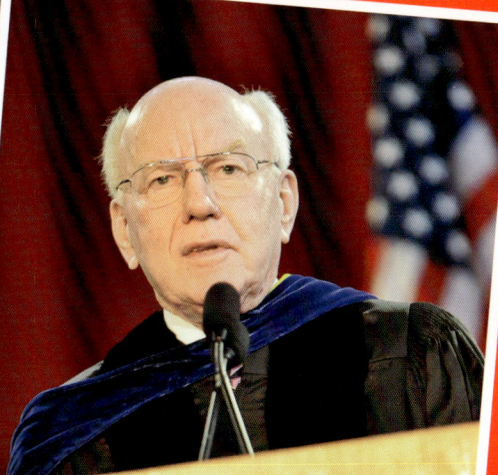

Vision 2015

Each of Davenport's presidents had launched their administrations with well-conceived leadership plans imprinted with their own professional vision for the school. Working closely with faculty, administration, and the board of trustees, Dr. Pappas completed a signature planning outline called Vision 2015. Organized around the pursuit of excellence through continuous quality improvement, the document integrated strategic initiatives at every level. It promoted a thoroughly engaged academic community enriched by superiority in teaching and learning, meaningful cocurricular and experiential activities, deep engagement with employers, and other elements of a broad education that would optimize the value and meaning of every Davenport degree.

The plan committed to "understand better than anyone else" the educational needs of every business, health, and technology leader in the communities Davenport served. Vision 2015 reflected important influences from two acclaimed figures in organizational dynamics and management. The first was W. Edwards Deming, whose groundbreaking applications in productivity and quality had tremendous impact both in Japan and the United States. Also prevalent in Vision 2015 are signature principles of Malcolm Baldrige, former U.S. Secretary of Commerce during the Reagan Administration. The Baldrige model emphasizes performance excellence at every level of institutional culture to maximize productivity, competitiveness, and value to all stakeholders of the organization. The process is dynamic, relying on continuously refined performance goals and ongoing measurement of outcomes.

As his administration gathered momentum, President Pappas energetically promoted those beliefs he held most closely, particularly the inclusion and integration of all university functions into policy, strategy, and operations. He also represented Davenport as "a relevant asset and unique resource for employers"—a driver of, as well as contributor to, emerging economic sectors and activity.

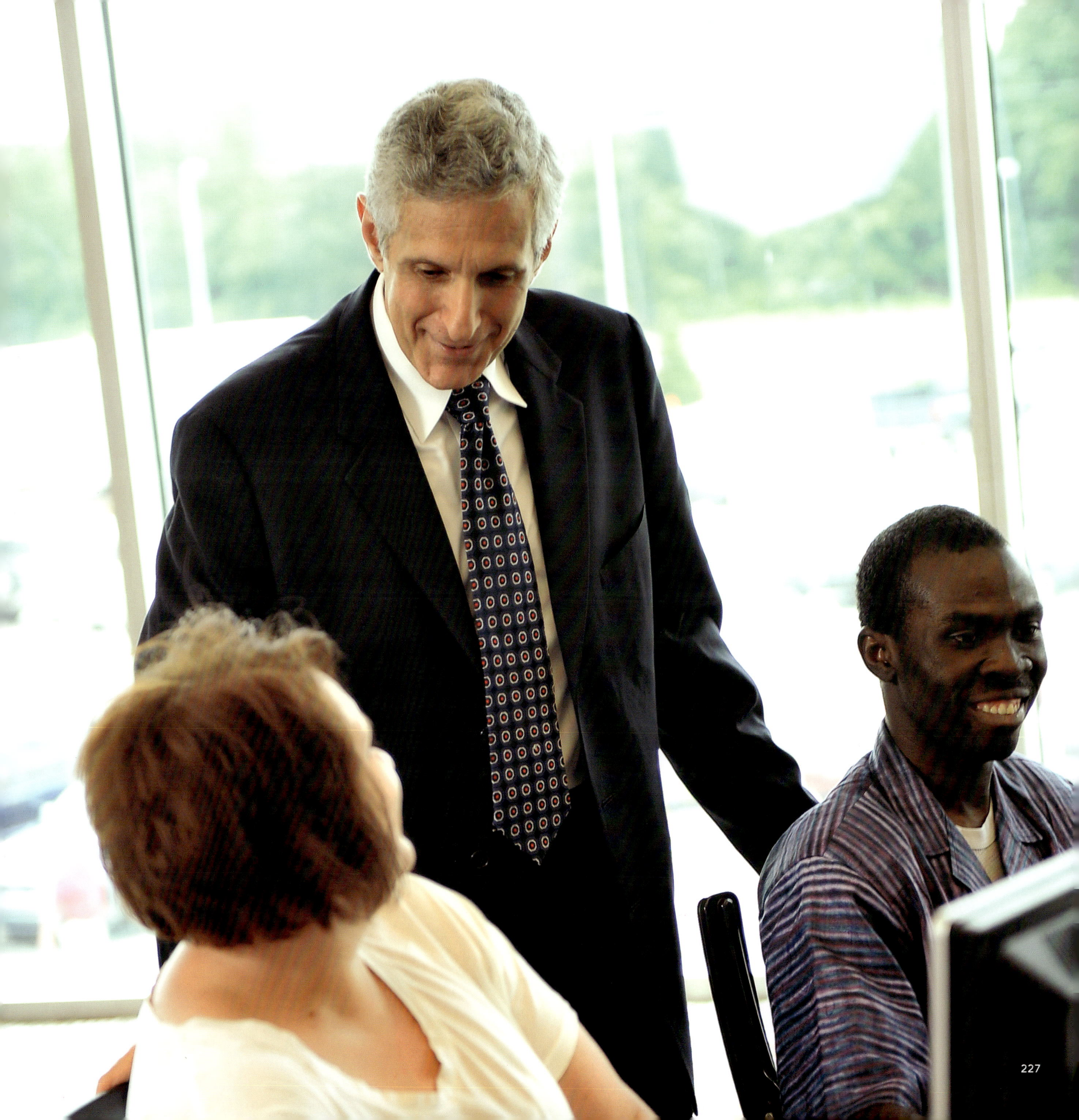

Building New Competencies

A first step toward realization of Vision 2015 was building new competencies within the university to obtain and act upon market intelligence and to drive process improvement. An understanding of the marketplace would help DU better decide what degree programs to develop and where to offer them. Process improvements, meanwhile, would help improve the university's effectiveness in developing and offering its programs and services. Early process improvement work, for instance, reduced the time required to approve new academic programs at Davenport from a few years—standard in higher education—to just 60 days.

Another early victory of data analysis and process improvement resulted from research into why some DU students were unable to achieve success in their studies. Analysis of student performance data revealed that weakness in math or English was a leading cause for new students to discontinue their studies with Davenport. In response, the university introduced entry-level and bridge programs for these subject areas, added instructors into classes and beefed up tutoring programs, helping to dramatically improve performance of new students. Developmental math pass rates increased from 59 percent to 73 percent within two years and introductory English improved from 55 percent to 84 percent during that same time frame, contributing to strong growth in Davenport's retention rate. At the same time, Davenport further strengthened and refined its admissions requirements to ensure admitted students would have a realistic opportunity to earn a degree.

Additional academic advisors were hired and other concerns that students had expressed were addressed, helping to improve upon student success and satisfaction. As a result, DU's graduation rate increased an incredible 110 percent in five years—unheard of in higher education—and student satisfaction rose to an all-time high score of 6.0 on a 7-point scale. Graduate satisfaction also was at an all-time high, and surveys of employers indicated a high level of satisfaction with the preparedness of DU graduates. When Vision 2015 was launched, Davenport University lagged behind all of Michigan's public universities. At the end of five years, it has surpassed the rates of five of those same universities, with its sights set on another five.

"Davenport understands the market better than any other institution and uses that understanding to change the lives of our students by preparing them to achieve their dreams."

—Excerpt from *Vision 2015*

Prominent throughout Vision 2015 are principles that serve as the basis for the prestigious Malcolm Baldrige Award, which annually honors U.S. organizational excellence in the business, health, education, and nonprofit professions.

Vitae: James DeBoer

While a young lawyer just starting practice in the early 1950s, James DeBoer was approached at home one evening by a neighbor who needed legal counsel for an upcoming business matter. That informal inquiry from Robert Sneden began a decades-long relationship between attorney Jim DeBoer and Davenport.

The "business matter" at hand was the 1952 conversion of Davenport Institute from a proprietary to a nonprofit corporation—one of the most important transformations in the school's history. DeBoer continued to serve as the school's chief legal counsel as partner at Varnum, Riddering, Schmidt, & Howlett (now Varnum LLP), and in 1970 became a charter member of Davenport's first public governing board. His term of service continued longer than any other trustee—over 40 years.

Jim and wife, Joy, also became lifelong supporters, gifting to virtually all of Davenport's major growth initiatives. An executive conference room in the Robert W. Sneden Center on the Lettinga Campus bears their name and honors their long friendship with Davenport and the Sneden family.

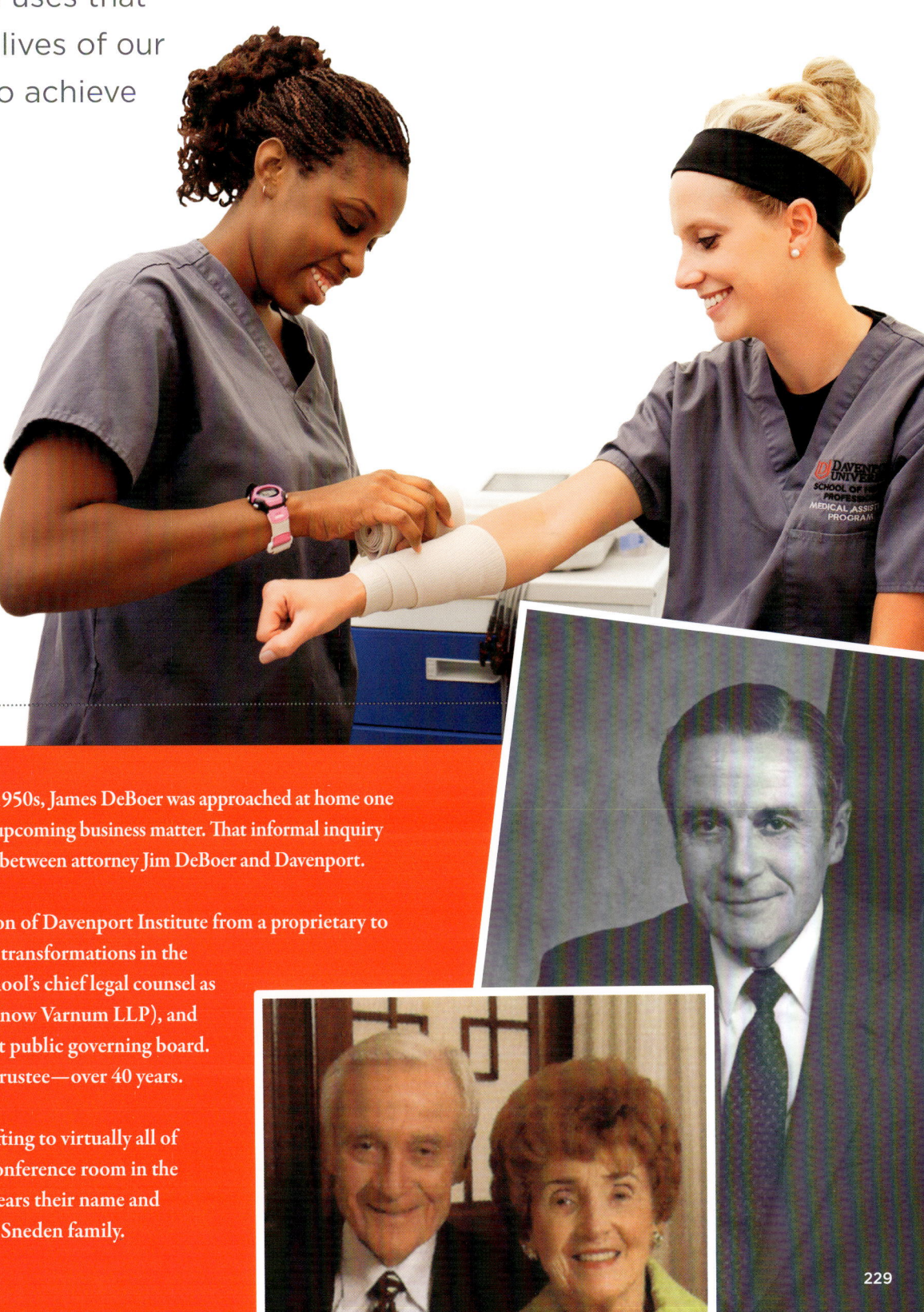

In Pursuit of Academic Excellence

Under the leadership of its new Provost and Executive Vice President for Academics, Dr. Linda Rinker, the academic wing underwent a reorganization, including the formation of a new College of Arts and Sciences. In response to market intelligence, Davenport launched 17 new degree programs between 2010 and 2015, including master's degrees in occupational therapy, nursing, management, health informatics and information management, technology management and more. Davenport also launched a new Executive MBA and the innovative Competency-based MBA that would allow business leaders to progress through an MBA program at their own speed and earn credit based on expertise they already possessed. Also, work was well underway to develop Davenport's first doctorate, in physical therapy.

Among the most ambitious developments of 2013 was the creation of the College of Urban Education. Addressing systemic challenges and differences in urban learning environments, the master's degree in urban education was developed to transform the way teachers prepared for service in urban classrooms. Operating in partnership with Grand Rapids Public Schools (GRPS), the first cohort began classes in 2015, embedded at GRPS' Innovation Central High School. After one year, ICHS student performance showed extraordinary gains in key metrics. Perhaps equally gratifying was the confirmation that Davenport's long-valued tradition of equipping students with grade-commensurate skills could now occur directly at the secondary level, where it could be most beneficial. Additional planned programs include a bachelor's degree in urban education and programs to develop administrative leaders for urban school districts.

In 2014, Davenport began to deliver on the Vision 2015 promise to guarantee employment for its graduates, beginning with all accounting students. The program requires students to meet certain requirements, such as a GPA of 3.0 and at least one internship, to qualify for up to three additional semesters of education if unable to find employment in their chosen field within six months of graduation. The program was launched with the intention of increasing the university's accountability to equip students for jobs in their chosen fields. More than 80 percent of accounting students applied to be a part of the program during the 2014–15 academic year.

Launch of the College of Urban Education and the Employment Guarantee earned Davenport the Higher Education Newsmaker of the Year honor from the *Grand Rapids Business Journal* in 2015. A year earlier, the Grand Rapids Area Chamber of Commerce bestowed its coveted EPIC Award for Excellence in Business on Davenport University in recognition of its ongoing transformation through Vision 2015.

Green Living. At LEED-certified, environmentally friendly South Hall, four floors of apartment-style living provided room for 300 students. Packed with eco-features it also offered some notable firsts: private bedrooms for every resident, and the first all-campus meal service in its dining hall.

Expanding Facilities

New facilities also would improve students' experience and help them to "Get Where the World is Going," as Davenport's brand campaigns declared. In 2009, Davenport's third and largest residence hall, South Hall, opened to students. In 2010, the Robert W. Sneden Center was completed, adding sophisticated classrooms, conference rooms, faculty and administrative offices, an executive conference room for the governing board, and a 220-seat auditorium—the first dedicated space of its type on a Davenport campus. With the opening of this facility, the final migration of staff and faculty to the W.A. Lettinga Campus was completed. Grand Rapids Community College took over the Fulton Street campus.

232 Davenport: Educating Across Three Centuries | Vision for Continued Excellence

Reflective of the integrative and participatory goals of Vision 2015, the Robert W. Sneden Center was designed to accommodate every aspect of university operations: teaching and learning, governance and administration, and events for campus and community. The facility also provided Davenport's first-ever dedicated auditorium space with the 220-seat Wilbur and Sharon Lettinga Auditorium.

In the fall of 2011, Davenport returned to downtown Grand Rapids with the opening of its Peter C. Cook Center, created as a graduate center for the MBA and master of management programs. It also houses the Institute for Professional Excellence (IPEx), the professional development arm of the university that helps employers statewide provide training for their emerging leadership.

Additions and improvements also took place at Davenport campuses across the state. State-of-the-art health labs were added to the campuses in Midland and Warren, and in Lansing a new, high-visibility campus was established in the heart of the city, just two blocks from Michigan's Capitol.

2011

12,400 ENROLLMENT

152 Full-Time Faculty

41 Degrees (Graduate and Undergraduate)
College of Business
21
College of Technology
7
College of Health Professions
13

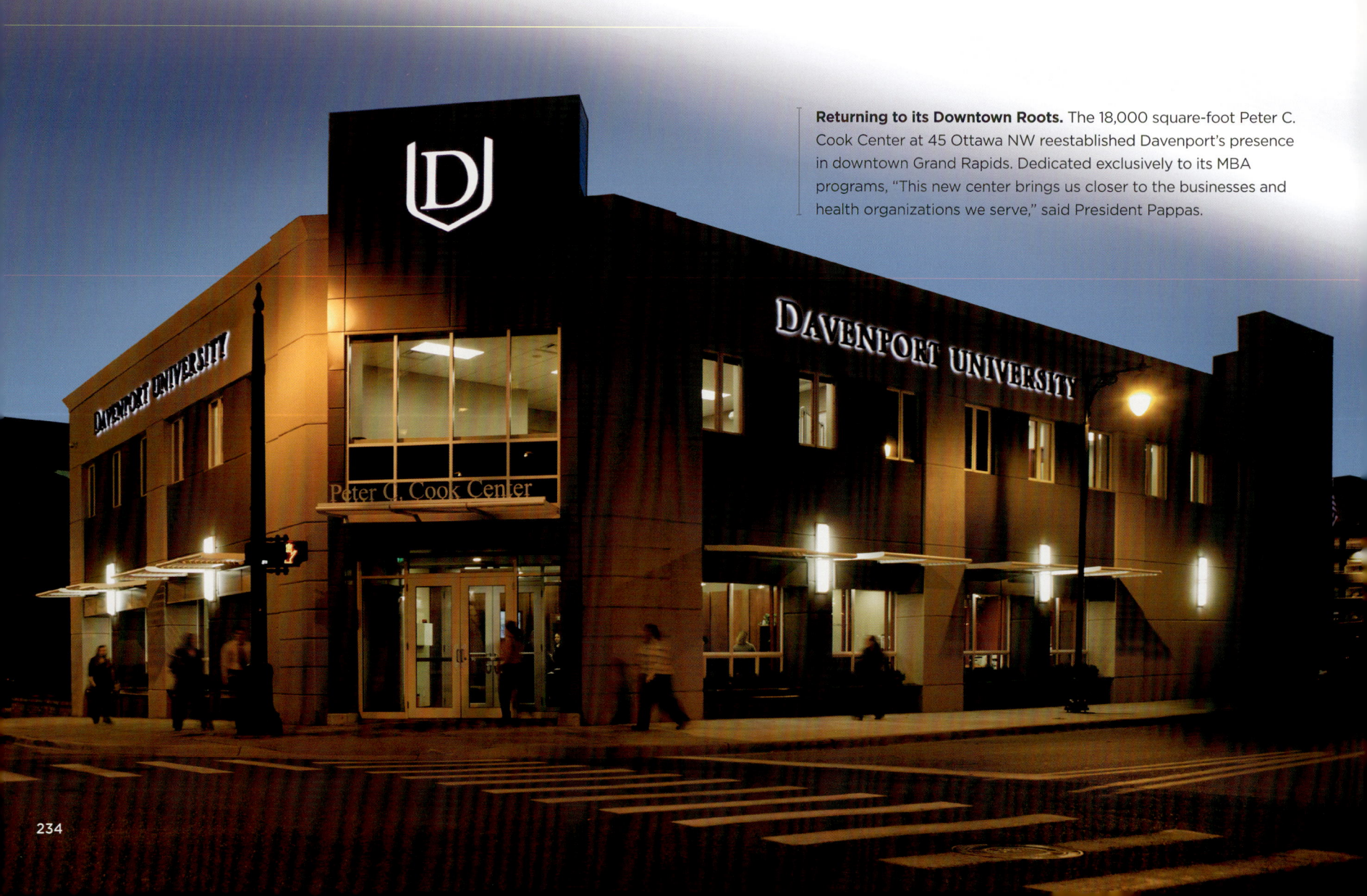

TUITION **$481** Per Credit Hour

Returning to its Downtown Roots. The 18,000 square-foot Peter C. Cook Center at 45 Ottawa NW reestablished Davenport's presence in downtown Grand Rapids. Dedicated exclusively to its MBA programs, "This new center brings us closer to the businesses and health organizations we serve," said President Pappas.

Davenport on the Skyline. More than 60 years after it was acquired as Davenport's first additional school, the Lansing location received a major upgrade in 2013. Moving from the East Kalamazoo Street address it had occupied since the 1970s, the university refurbished a nine-story building on West Grand Avenue, just blocks from the state capitol building. It was crowned by a 5,000-pound illuminated glass beacon.

Under the board leadership of Tracy D. Graham, Davenport University executed its Vision 2015 strategic plan. Graham also oversaw the creation of a new campus in Lansing and the development and expansion of the Farmers Insurance Athletic Complex.

The founder and managing principal of Graham Allen Partners, a private holding company focused on the incubation of early stage, high-growth technology businesses, Graham also cofounded and served as president of GramTel, Inc., the largest privately held provider of managed data services in the Midwest.

March 2013
Farmers Insurance Athletic Complex dedicated.

July 2013
Detroit becomes the largest American city to declare bankruptcy.

August 2013
New Lansing campus opens.

November 2013
The establishment of a football program announced, with competition to begin in 2016.

2014
College of Urban Education established.

Davenport introduces one of the first employment guarantees in the nation, for its accounting program.

Athletics continued to play a tremendous role in university growth and profile. With an average GPA of 3.2, student athletes contributed to growing DU's retention and graduation rates. The Panthers celebrated their 10th anniversary of collegiate league play in 2012 with three national championships and numerous other conference and regional titles. Dedicated in March of 2013, the Farmers Insurance Athletic Complex was established less than a mile from the W.A. Lettinga Campus, featuring baseball and softball fields, tennis courts, and clubhouse facilities. That same year, DU announced plans to develop a football program at the W.A. Lettinga Campus, strengthening its strategy to increase traditional student enrollment. This led to further expansion at the Farmers Insurance Athletic Complex, completed in 2015, with a new turf field and facilities to support the growing track and field program.

As its five-year plan came to a close in 2015, the university looked like a very different organization than the one that had begun the decade. New operating standards, new programs, and new facilities were all in place as DU prepared for the challenges it would face in its push toward 2020.

Playing Hard. Student athletes work and play hard on more than 30 men's and women's teams. School spirit continues to grow with national title wins like men's soccer in 2014 (left), a strong women's basketball program (right), and new playing fields (below). No matter what their sport, all Panthers look forward to graduation day (lower left).

Basking in Victory. Athletic teams at Davenport have won numerous Wolverine–Hoosier Athletic Conference (WHAC) titles plus national titles in the NAIA and other league affiliations. (Left) Men's hockey won four consecutive national titles (2008–2011), (middle) men's baseball took top honors in the WHAC in 2015 to participate in the Avista-NAIA World Series, and (right) the men's rugby team celebrated back-to-back national championships in 2012. Davenport took the WHAC all-sports trophy banner for five consecutive years between 2011 and 2015.

Vitae: Louis V. Buzzitta

The qualities that led Lou Buzzitta to Davenport in 1959 epitomize the story of so many Davenport students—ambition, self-direction, and the desire for a meaningful professional future.

In 1959 Buzzitta was already working in a factory and raising a family when he enrolled at Davenport. After graduating he founded Hughes Management, a healthcare facility development and management company. Eventually two of his sons joined the business and continued to operate the company after he retired.

With business as one passion and baseball another, the family became lead supporters of the development of the Farmers Insurance Athletic Complex, which is the home field for Davenport's spring sports program, including men's baseball and women's softball. Louis and his wife established the Louis V. and Catherine Buzzitta endowment scholarships to assist working students seeking to advance their career goals.

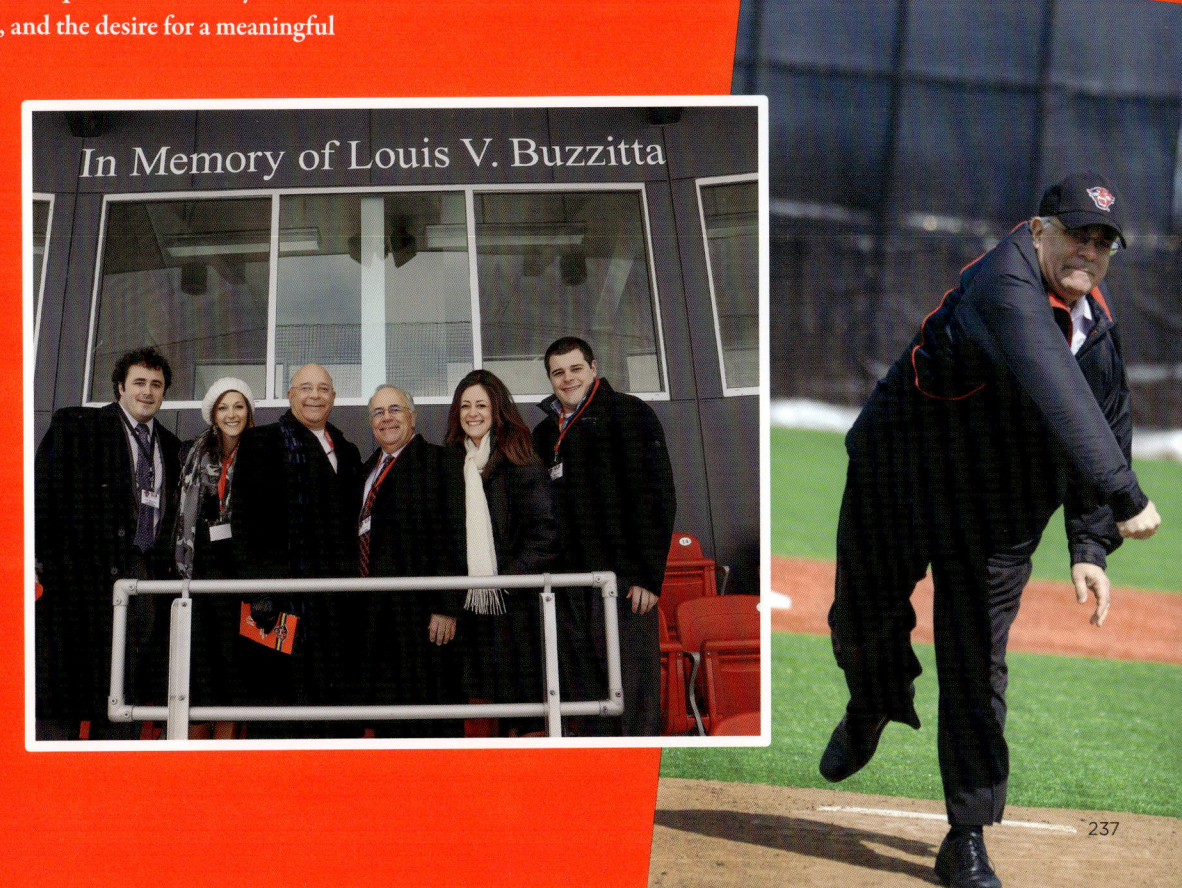

Diversity

LOCAL BEAT
THE GRAND RAPIDS PRESS

Trailblazer for minorities dies at age 95

▶ Hazel Grant, former president of the local chapter of the NAACP, was the first black graduate of Davenport Business College.

Hazel Grant pursued and landed a job at Grand Rapids' City Hall in 1932 after listening to former Mayor George Welch say at a meeting that there were few blacks qualified to work as secretaries and office personnel.

The former president of the local chapter of the NAACP died Monday. She was 95.

Mrs. Grant was a trailblazer who became the first black graduate of Davenport College — now Davenport Business College.

She worked at City Hall as a registrar for 31 years, retiring in 1963.

Mrs. Grant pursued and landed a city job in 1932 after listening to the late Mayor George Welch say at a meeting that there were few blacks qualified to work as secretaries and office personnel.

She organized a Christmas party for city workers in the 1950s and realized half way through the party that a vocal group that was entertaining was giving their rendition of a racist song. Mrs. Grant ushered the group off the stage.

She later learned the first site chosen for the party became "unavailable" as soon as it was learned a black woman was organizing the event.

Mrs. Grant served as president of the Grand Rapids NAACP from 1965-66. In 1966, the NAACP joined the Congress of Racial Equality to hold one of the largest marches in Grand Rapids' history, to protest an Alabama church bombing in which four young black children were killed.

Grant told The Press in 1993 that she remembered the marchers — black and white — striding down the street hand in hand.

"It was a beautiful thing," she told those assembled for the NAACP dinner in 1993. "Everyone was so outraged at the death of those children, and we were all together in our feelings."

She also described the state of race relations: "We're consumed with this (racism) in the high schools and colleges now. But if the civil rights movement had continued to go forward — it hasn't for the last 12 years — we wouldn't have had this."

Mrs. Grant also served as the secretary of Church Woman United for two years and was a member of the founding organization of the Women's Guild of Grand Rapids Urban League.

She was honored in 1993 by the NAACP — an organization she joined in 1922 — at the Freedom Fund Dinner.

She was awarded The Bishop's Cross for her years of dedicated service to the Episcopal Church.

Mrs. Grant was born in Cassopolis and was the only black in her graduating class.

All of Mrs. Grant's immediate family have preceded her in death, including her husband, Ralph C. Grant.

Services will be at St. Philip's Episcopal Church at 10 a.m. Thursday.

Memorials may be made to the St. Philip's Office Renovation Fund.

Davenport University has long been an institution that has valued and celebrated diversity, providing an opportunity for students to obtain an education that leads to growing careers, regardless of race, gender, sexual orientation, religion, disabilities, veteran status, and more. Nearly a quarter of all DU degrees granted between 2006 and 2015 were to members of minority populations. Acknowledging diversity as a core value and an important aspect of its vision, Davenport established the Office of Diversity, Equity, and Inclusion in 2010. In 2011, DU became one of the first private universities in Michigan to extend same-sex partner health benefits to employees. Davenport seeks to cultivate a community where similarities and differences are leveraged for full inclusion of a diverse workforce and student body. It values and benefits from the full participation and contributions of all members of our university community.

For years, Martin Luther King Day has been celebrated annually with on-campus marches (left). Former Davenport basketball player Thomas Drew shows Grand Rapids Public High School student Rashaud Orange how to tie a tie at an outreach event with the Urban Education program (above).

Digging In. At the ceremonial groundbreaking for the new Donald W. Maine College of Business facility opening in late 2016, Dr. Rick Pappas, Board Vice-Chair Ken Yerrick, Board Chair Frank Merlotti, Chancellor Emeritus Don Maine, Board Trustee Michelle Van Dyke, Board Trustee Carol Van Andel, Rockford Construction CEO Mike Van Gessel, and Dean Pamela Imperato line up with their shovels.

A New Vision for 2020

In the spring of 2015, Dr. Pappas publicly announced the "Investing in the Vision" Campaign, which included key elements that would be part of Vision 2020. Entering the public phase, the campaign had already raised over $20 million of its $25 million goal to build a new facility for the Donald W. Maine College of Business, to further develop the College of Urban Education and to continue building the endowed scholarship fund.

Vision 2020, announced in July 2015, called for accelerated continuous quality improvement across Davenport's operations to generate student outcomes that would compare favorably with those of the upper third of Michigan's public universities. Developed through the collaboration of Davenport's employees and leaders with input from students, donors, alumni, and the Board of Trustees, the new Vision would help to establish a bold direction for the university's progress in academic offerings, student and graduate services, employee engagement, diversity, fundraising, operational efficiencies, and more. "This Vision helps Davenport move forward toward becoming a model for what higher education could look like," said Dr. Pappas.

In addition to expanding upon the W.A. Lettinga Campus with the new Donald W. Maine College of Business facility, Davenport was exploring the opportunity for a new campus in metropolitan Detroit, seeking to be part of the economic renaissance and job growth in southeast Michigan. "We have a long history of serving the Detroit region. With a resurgence of business, technology, and health industries in southeast Michigan, plus a continuing demand for well-prepared educators who will make a difference in urban school districts, we believe our career-focused education model can be an important part of that region's renewal," said Dr. Pappas in announcing Vision 2020.

Davenport also announced new strategic partnerships with community colleges that would expand its access to community college students wishing to continue toward their bachelor's and graduate degrees. The new partnerships would include DU classrooms within community colleges, creating operational efficiencies for the partner institutions and new opportunities and enhanced services for students. By the end of 2015, DU opened within the University Centers of Mott Community College, Kalamazoo Valley Community College, and Wayne County Community College, with several other agreements nearing completion. Davenport also announced it would enhance its online Global Campus, providing access to DU's life-changing education regardless of borders.

In November of 2015, Chancellor Emeritus Don Maine helped Dr. Pappas, board members, and university leaders break ground for the new Donald W. Maine College of Business building at the W.A. Lettinga Campus. The facility will become the new home of DU's business school and a new entrepreneurship center with a "business accelerator" to help small businesses get to the next level of growth.

In December, additional visitors to the W.A. Lettinga Campus signaled further progress toward Vision 2020 goals. The Baldrige Award had been held up as an aspirational goal, since that recognition would provide strong third-party verification for Davenport's approach to building quality. A required first step, however, was DU's 2015 application for the Michigan Performance Excellence Award, which generated a rare (for first-time applicants) site visit by MPE examiners in December. A month later the University learned it had earned Honor Roll recognition, only the second time a college or university had been so honored in more than 20 years. Later that same week, Davenport was accepted as a member of the Great Lakes Intercollegiate Athletics Conference (GLIAC), pending NCAA Division II approval, the realization of another long-standing goal for DU's athletic program. Davenport's progress toward Vision 2020 realization was well underway.

Through most of Davenport's history, its leaders have devoted time and effort to envision the future of their institution. Just as Conrad Swensberg likely could not have imagined what his small business school would eventually become, it is hard to fathom what Davenport University's future still holds. If the future remains consistent with the institution's history, however, it is fairly certain that Davenport University will continue to be true to its core mission of preparing students to succeed in their chosen careers, making a living, a life, and a contribution. While leaders and strategic plans may change, it is not difficult to envision that a growing, vibrant Davenport University will continue to be an important part of the Michigan landscape for the next 150 years.

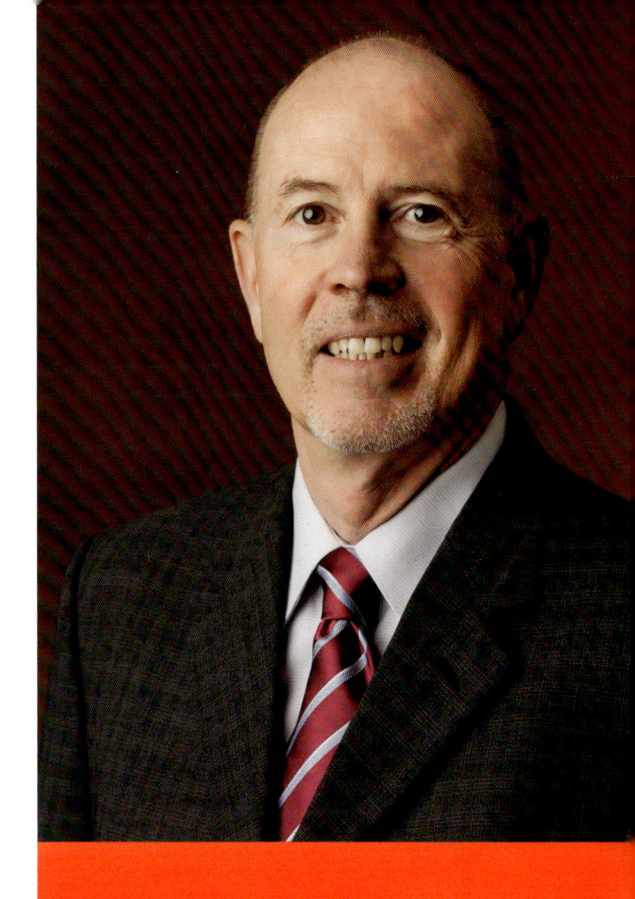

Frank Merlotti, Jr. joined the Davenport University Board of Trustees in 2006 and, in 2015, became its chairman, helping to usher in the university's Vision 2020 strategic plan. Merlotti serves as the lead director of the board of directors for Trex Company and previously was president of Coalesse, president of Steelcase North America, president and CEO of G&T Industries, and president of Metro Furniture

"'Innovation' is a buzzword, but it's really true for Davenport in terms of what we're doing across the board."
—Frank Merlotti, Jr.

Excellence in Business

Established in 1998, the prestigious Peter C. Cook Excellence in Business Award exemplifies the highest principles of business practice and integrity, entrepreneurial vision, and civic leadership. Across a spectrum of professions and enterprises, recipients have epitomized these values.

Growing every year, Davenport University's signature EIB Gala has raised more than $2.4 million for scholarships. Notable headline speakers share the spirit of the evening.

Peter C. Cook Award Recipients

2001 **Wilbur A. Lettinga,** Chair/CEO, Kentland Corporation and W.A. Lettinga Investments
Speaker: Tim Russert

2002 **David G. Frey,** Chair, Frey Foundation
Speaker: Lou Dobbs

2003 **John Spoelhof,** Chair, Bayside Capital
Speaker: Al Roker

2004 **Robert L. Hooker,** President, Cook Holdings, LLC
Speaker: Terry Bradshaw

(Clockwise from left) A thumbs-up to DU from *Today Show* cohost Al Roker. 2004 Cook Award recipient Bob Hooker accepts the tribute from Peter Cook and previous year recipient John Spoelhof. Ted Koppel of ABC News reflects on his *Nightline* career covering world headlines. In a special exchange from award namesake to EIB founder, Peter Cook honors Davenport University Chancellor Emeritus Donald Maine. Best-selling author Mitch Albom with Cook honoree Ralph Hauenstein, a revered figure in the West Michigan business and civic community. Michigan State Men's Basketball Coach Tom Izzo shares thoughts on teamwork. EIB speaker Rudy Giuliani, former mayor of New York City, enjoys 2005's event.

Year	Recipient	Speaker
2005	**Betsy DeVos, Chair,** Windquest Group/Dick & Betsy DeVos Foundation	*Speaker: Rudy Giuliani*
2006	**Donald W. Maine,** Chancellor Emeritus, Davenport University	*Speaker: Regis Philbin*
2007	**John C. Canepa,** Consulting Principal, Crowe Chizek	*Speaker: Dick Vitale*
2008	**Fred P. Keller, Chair/CEO,** Cascade Engineering	*Speaker: Lou Holtz*
2009	**Peter F. Secchia,** Chair Emeritus, Universal Forest Products, Inc., and former U.S. Ambassador to Italy	*Speaker: Ted Koppel*
2010	**Steve Van Andel, Chair/Co-CEO and Doug DeVos, President/Co-CEO,** Amway Corporation	*Speaker: Sugar Ray Leonard*
2011	**James P. Hackett,** President/CEO, Steelcase, Inc.	*Speaker: Helen Hunt*
2012	**David Van Andel,** CEO, Van Andel Institute, **and Carol Van Andel, Executive Director,** David and Carol Van Andel Foundation	*Speaker: Tom Izzo*
2013	**Michael J. Jandernoa,** Former Chair and CEO, Perrigo Co.	*Speaker: Laura Bush*
2014	**Blake W. Krueger,** CEO/President, Wolverine World Wide, Inc.	*Speaker: Capt. Richard Phillips*
2015	**Ralph W. Hauenstein,** Colonel, U.S. Army (Retired)/Founder, Hauenstein Center for Presidential Studies and Hauenstein Parkinson's Research Center	*Speaker: Mitch Albom*
2016	**Birgit Klohs,** President/CEO, The Right Place, Inc.	*Speaker: Anderson Cooper*

Wallace J. Bronner Award Recipients

Year	Recipient	Speaker
2002	**Wallace J. "Wally" Bronner,** Founder/Board Chair, BRONNER'S CHRISTmas WONDERLAND	*Speaker: Sam Donaldson*
2003	**John R. Burt,** Founder, Dura-Last Roofing, Inc.	*Speaker: Mary Matalin and James Carville*
2004	**Dr. E. Malcom Field,** Founder, Field Neurosciences	*Speaker: Steve Bridges*
2005	**Richard J. Garber,** President, Garber Management Group	*Speaker: Lou Holtz*
2006	**Spencer T. Maidlow, President/CEO,** Covenant Healthcare, Inc.	*Speaker: Dick Vitale*

(Clockwise from left) For their inestimable contributions to the West Michigan community, David and Carol Van Andel, shown with President Rick Pappas, were the first recipients honored as a couple. Prominent in West Michigan business and philanthropy, John Canepa proudly displays the cut-crystal sphere. Exemplary leader Blake Krueger accepts the Cook award. Michael Jandernoa and wife, Sue, pose with First Lady Laura Bush. Dr. Barbara Mieras with Wally Bronner, namesake of the Saginaw EIB award. Donald and Kathy Maine with headline speaker Sugar Ray Leonard, world champion boxer. Famed basketball announcer and former coach Dick Vitale, previously an Executive 100 guest speaker, pays a second visit to Davenport. Peter Secchia is recognized for accomplishment both at home in West Michigan and abroad as U.S. ambassador to Italy.

Presidential Profile Richard J. Pappas

Born in Midland and raised in various cities across Michigan, Richard (Rick) Pappas was brought up in a home where expectations were high. Dr. Charles and Sydell Pappas encouraged their three sons to excel in all that they did. Their youngest, Rick, achieved his first college presidency by age 37.

Aside from aspirations to be part of the business world, Rick had no specific career direction in mind while earning a marketing degree at Eastern Michigan University. College marketing internships at the Chevrolet and AC Spark Plug divisions of General Motors were instructive; but like many learning experiences, they also helped filter choices that were not for him. Uncertain about his future, Rick turned to his father for advice.

Charles, serving as president of Mott Community College in Flint, encouraged his son to enroll at the University of Michigan's School of Education. While pursuing his master's degree in higher education and business management, Rick discovered an affinity for academic leadership. He was encouraged by his academic mentor, Professor Joe Cosand, to aim for the top—a college presidency.

After graduation, Rick joined the faculty of Jackson Community College as an associate professor of marketing. After five years of full-time teaching, he pursued an opportunity in business, but soon felt the academic world tugging him back. He earned a doctorate in higher, adult and continuing education at U of M, then returned to Jackson Community College as dean of community and business services/marketing. In this position he could combine his passions for business and education.

Two initiatives he helped create demonstrated his dual interests: an entrepreneurial center that included an industrial incubator, and a quality initiative that involved Dr. W. Edwards Deming, considered the father of the quality movement. These accomplishments helped define the organizational and educational principles—including strategic planning and collaborative leadership—that would prove effective in four successive college presidential positions.

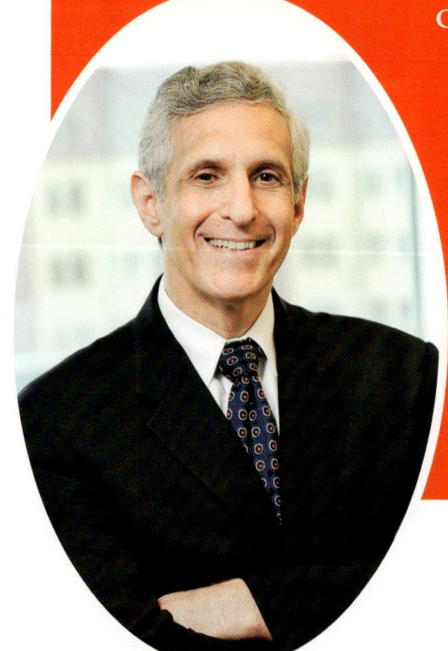

Richard J. Pappas

"Davenport is a community asset and valuable resource that is both worthy of support and a smart investment for the success and sustainability of our economy and communities."

—President Richard J. Pappas

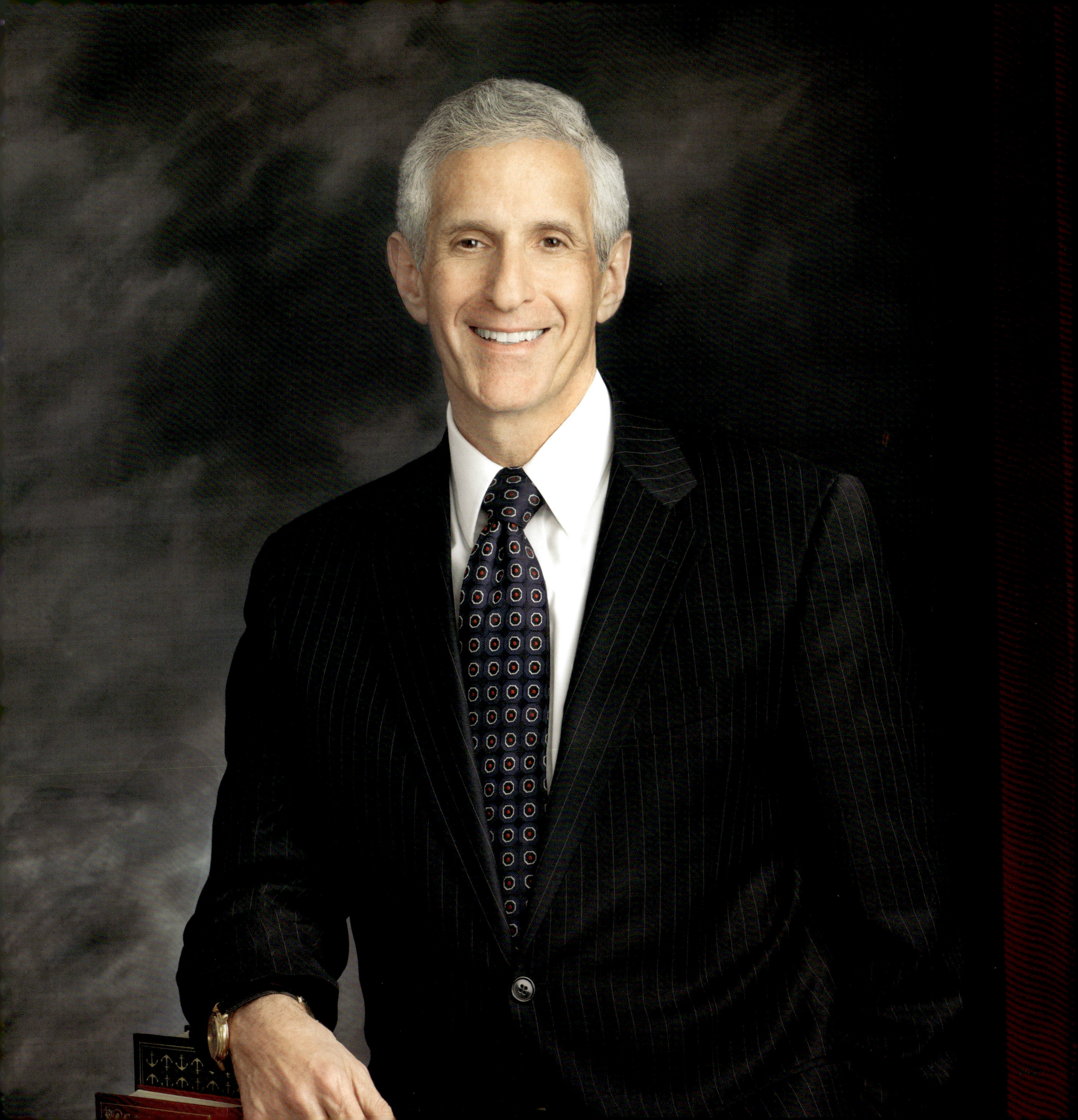

Presidential Profile Richard J. Pappas

The first, in 1989, was at Harford Community College in Bel Air, Maryland. While there he received the Pacesetter Award from the National Council of Marketing and Public Relations. When the opportunity to return to his home state presented itself in 1994, Rick took over as president of Lake Michigan College in Benton Harbor. During his 11-year tenure there, LMC experienced unprecedented growth, reaching the highest enrollment in its history and adding three campuses. In recognition of his leadership and contributions, the college's student services building is named for him.

Dr. Pappas' achievements generated notice beyond southwest Michigan. In 1999, he was awarded the CEO of the Central Region award from the Association of Community College Trustees and, in 2005, the University of Michigan School of Education awarded him the prestigious Norman C. Harris alumni award for outstanding accomplishments in higher education. That same year, he assumed the presidency of his first four-year institution, National Louis University in Chicago. Similar in many ways to Davenport University, NLU is a private, not-for-profit institution with multiple campuses and three major colleges: education, business, and arts and sciences. During his tenure at NLU, Dr. Pappas led an inclusive strategic planning process that helped reverse enrollment declines, improve student retention, restructure the College of Business, and launch an urban initiative to develop principals for Chicago Public Schools.

Following a national search effort, Dr. Pappas was selected as Davenport's new president in 2009. Within a year, the new president's model of inclusive strategic planning and measurable quality outcomes led to the collaborative development of Vision 2015, a long-range strategic plan that would guide the quality transformation of Davenport University. In the first two years, fundraising increased by 20 percent, a Diversity Council and a student government were created, Career Services was largely rebuilt, and new leadership positions were created to guide quality initiatives and conduct market research.

Dr. Pappas quickly became immersed in both civic and economic development in West Michigan, serving as chairman of the Grand Rapids Area Chamber of Commerce and The Heart of West Michigan United Way, and as a board member for The Right Place, Inc., the Economic Club of Grand Rapids, and Fifth Third Bank.

"A president must be both an academic leader and a strong manager. Other qualities include an entrepreneurial style, strong fiscal skills, being a proven communicator with no surprises, and a desire to make a difference for students."
—President Richard J. Pappas

He participated in the West Michigan Strategic Alliance's "Talent 2025" initiative to attract and retain young talent in the region, and was a member of the CEO Advisory Council for the Lakeshore Ethnic Diversity Alliance. Dr. Pappas' higher education profile continued to increase on a regional and national level as well, including executive board service with Michigan Independent Colleges and Universities (MICU) and the American Council on Education, where he chaired the membership committee.

At the five-year milestone of Dr. Pappas' presidency, the horizons first imagined in Vision 2015 were being reached. Retention levels were at the highest levels in the university's modern history and the institution's graduation rate had more than doubled. More than a dozen new degree-granting programs had been launched, a new Lansing campus developed, and construction begun of the new Donald W. Maine College of Business building on the W.A. Lettinga campus. In addition, the new College of Urban Education had launched its first cohort of master's degree candidates.

Proven success and major momentum supplied the energy for Vision 2020, which would guide the University further toward its goal of being a premier institution of higher education and a model other colleges will seek to emulate.

While emphasizing excellence at the institutional level, Dr. Pappas' strongest leadership convictions are directed toward the individual. "I look at the adults and the traditional-aged students who come to Davenport, and see that they all have dreams," says Pappas. "I want to help them achieve those dreams. What we do here can change the trajectory of people's careers and lives."

Opposite page: Dr. Rick Pappas and Steve Boshoven, president of the Foremost Division of Farmers Insurance, at the dedication of the Farmer's Insurance Athletic Complex on March 20, 2013.

Top (from left to right): Louie Boji, founder, Boji Group, LLC; Don DeLuc, president, Thomas M. Cooley Law School; Dr. Richard Pappas, president, Davenport University; Virg Bernero, mayor, City of Lansing; Dr. Brent Knight, president, Lansing Community College; Ron Boji, president, Boji Group in front of Davenport's soon-to-be Lansing Campus.

Right (from left to right): Pounce, Shannon Daley, Dr. Rick Pappas, Dean of Health Dr. Karen Daley, and Alexander Cogbill claim front-row seats for DU's Homecoming games.

DISTINGUISHING DAVENPORT

"What the world's now asking for, Davenport's been doing for 100 years."

—Tracy Graham, governing board chair 2010–2015

Davenport's advance from a sole proprietorship where students earned skill certificates, to a full university offering doctoral degrees, is a trajectory any organization would envy—and in the higher education sector exceedingly rare.

Throughout its evolution, Davenport has intentionally maintained its unique position and identity. This section illustrates enduring commitments that continue to guide the university's ongoing dedication to educational excellence.

AN INDEPENDENT JOURNEY:
DAVENPORT'S IDENTITY IN HIGHER EDUCATION
ANTICIPATORY, ADAPTIVE, AND ALWAYS AUTONOMOUS.

DAVENPORT'S STATEWIDE EDUCATIONAL PRESENCE
LONG BEFORE OTHER COLLEGES, DAVENPORT BEGAN TAKING ITS SUCCESSFUL APPROACH ACROSS MICHIGAN.

THE DAVENPORT CLASSROOM
"PRACTICAL EDUCATION:" A LEARNING MODEL WITH PROVEN VALUE

VETERANS: SERVICE AND SCHOLARSHIP
A PROUD HERITAGE OF EDUCATING AMERICA'S MILITARY STUDENTS.

DISTINGUISHING DAVENPORT

An Independent Journey: Davenport's Identity in Higher Education

DISTINGUISHING DAVENPORT

While the terms "private" and "independent" are often used interchangeably in education, there are relevant distinctions, particularly involving sources of funding as well as sources of influence. Textbook publisher McGraw-Hill describes an independent school as a "nonpublic school unaffiliated with any church or other agency." In the case of Davenport University, there was also no original wealthy benefactor, founding endowment or bequest, or entity of any type to furnish perpetual support.

For many years, differences of a more fundamental nature separated 'traditional' colleges from career or trade schools, giving students a clearly divergent choice: pursue a four-year education, typically in humanities or the sciences, or train in a specific occupation at a career college.

These distinctions began to dissolve in the wake of the Higher Education Act and other programs of the 1960s and '70s. Traditional colleges and universities created separate "schools" or "colleges" in the professions, including business. Expanding knowledge and complexity demanded greater depth and sophistication in the traditional business disciplines. Curricula expanded and degrees multiplied to reflect this trend.

Career-directed schools, meanwhile, experienced transformations of their own. As the pace of change accelerated, the shelf life of skill programs shortened. Certificate and diploma programs were expanded into—or sometimes replaced by—associate and baccalaureate degrees, which required more general education courses. Similarities between traditional and career colleges have continued to develop into the 21st century.

Because its "practical education" traditions have always emphasized the fusion of training with academic quality, Davenport has placed itself at the advancing edge of many of these trends. Major organizational decisions, such as nonprofit conversion and accreditation, have helped Davenport capitalize on developments that drove many similar schools into extinction.

More recently, with tuition costs and student loan debt far outpacing other fiscal trendlines, debate has focused on the proven value of a college degree. Economic and labor trends show a renewed interest and appreciation for efficient training options that lead directly into skilled trades and careers with viable salaries and advancement potential—and by extension the rejuvenation of a prosperous middle class. Increasingly, higher education institutions are expected to demonstrate return on investment. Again, Davenport has long recognized this obligation to its students.

The vast majority of schools listed in this 1950s membership roster from the United Business Schools Association no longer existed by the time the 20th century ended.

According to the U.S. Department of Education, approximately 3,500 post-secondary institutions in the country have closed since 1986. Most were proprietary career and trade schools—including a large number of business and commercial schools—offering less-than-degree programs. Four-year colleges have also closed, including Michigan's Jordan and Nazareth Colleges.

Davenport's organizational affiliations have changed over time. This reflects its own institutional advancement as well as trends in post-secondary education.

The 1950s and '60s: The United Business Schools Association.

A professional organization representing career-oriented schools, UBSA was the most influential and respected organization of its kind. At peak membership it represented well over 100 member schools nationwide, most of them business training institutions like Davenport.

Economic and educational changes profoundly impacted UBSA's membership. In the 20 years following the Higher Education Act of 1965, nearly three-quarters of its affiliates would go out of business. Many schools that did not fail outright were merged into other entities or acquired by nationwide for-profit educational corporations—such as DeVry and ITT Technical Institute—which began to deliver most of the shorter skill-specific courses once taught exclusively by local schools like Davenport. Nationwide, only 10 original UBSA members—including Davenport—went on to become regionally accredited on their own.

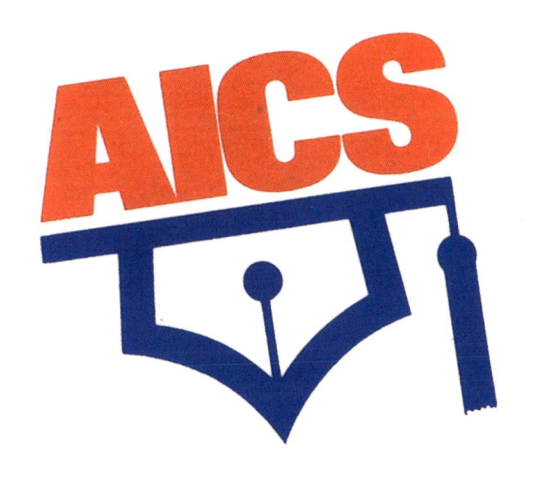

The 1970s & '80s:

UBSA became the Association of Independent Colleges and Schools (AICS) to reflect a wider range of skilled trade and occupational training. Although it maintained connections to AICS for many years, rapid institutional development took Davenport in different directions.

The 2000s.

Following accreditation as a university in 2003, Davenport joined the National Association of Independent Colleges and Universities (NAICU) and took its place among a much larger classification of institutions—all of them four-year and beyond—as diverse as Amherst College, Kettering University, and the Rhode Island School of Design. This solidified Davenport University's alignment with the degree-driven higher-learning environment rather than the paraprofessional school.

DISTINGUISHING DAVENPORT

Davenport's Statewide Educational Presence

From the Postwar Era to the New Millennium

The journey from Davenport Institute to Davenport University spans several decades and three distinct eras, each characterized by various acquisition, reorganization, and consolidation strategies leading ultimately to unification under a single university structure. Each phase responded to the demands of the times, but the focus never wavered from optimum educational delivery and effectiveness.

- Current/historical campus
- Current campus
- Historical campus
- Former satellite campus

Davenport Schools, Incorporated: 1951–1977

When Davenport Institute first embarked on an ambitious expansion program beginning in 1951, the idea of a multi-site college was unusual. By acquiring schools across the lower half of Michigan, Davenport anticipated by many years a pattern other colleges, public and private alike, would emulate.

As the era of the proprietary school began to recede, opportunities to rescue failing for-profit institutions developed. Beginning with Lansing Business University, Davenport went on to acquire several new properties until it was operating campuses in most major lower-Michigan cities. Schools in Lansing, Kalamazoo, Bay City, and Saginaw were ultimately consolidated under a separate nonprofit corporation known as Davenport Schools, Incorporated—an educational franchise of independently managed locations. A fifth campus, in Detroit, was operated as a separate for-profit entity. Over time, similarities developed among the campuses, including common programs and operating procedures.

During the 1970s, the affiliates in Lansing, Kalamazoo, and Bay City were purchased by their respective directors to continue on their own as independent proprietary institutions. The Detroit and Saginaw schools had also grown substantially and developed branch sites of their own in nearby communities.

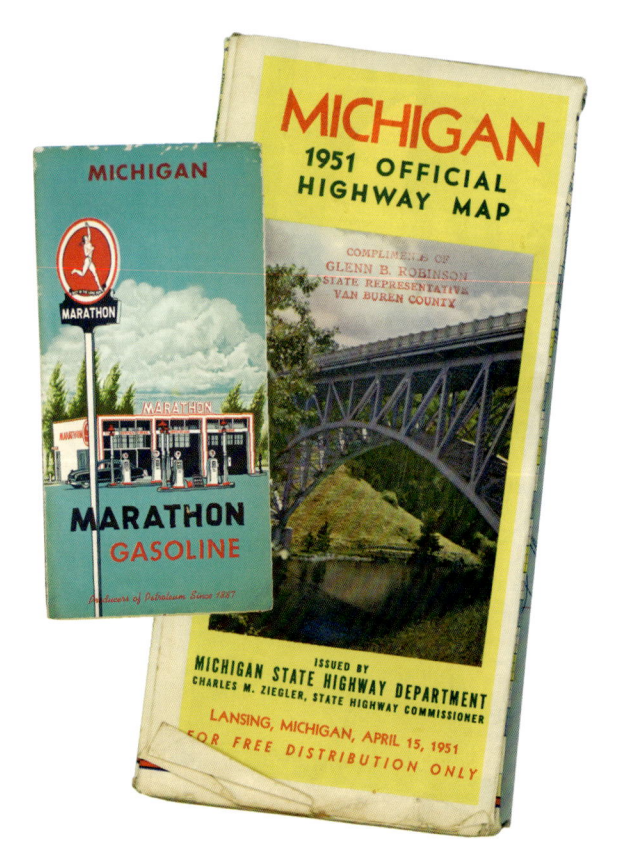

DISTINGUISHING DAVENPORT

253

Creating the Davenport Educational System: 1979–1997

During this remarkable phase of expansion, Davenport College became the largest private independent college in the state. Its coverage extended from the Straits of Mackinac south into Indiana and from the Lake Michigan shoreline to the Thumb area.

Beginning in the late 1970s, the changing jobscape sent many adults back to college to complete unfinished degrees or acquire additional training. For working adults with schedules to keep, convenience and proximity were top priorities.

Davenport responded in two primary ways: by establishing (or in some cases re-acquiring) degree-granting campuses in major markets; and by entering new venues to offer in-demand classes and shorter skill-based formats.

Between 1979 and 1997, the college established a presence in almost every major Lower Peninsula city: Lansing, Kalamazoo, Detroit, Saginaw, Holland, and Battle Creek. Career Centers established at several sites in Indiana specialized in shorter diploma and certificate programs.

In northern Michigan, Davenport classes were offered at community colleges serving Ludington, Gaylord, and Traverse City. Expansion in the state's Thumb area occurred through the 1996 acquisition of Great Lakes Junior College, which served Saginaw, Midland, Bay City, and surrounding communities.

By the end of the 1990s Davenport operated more than 30 sites training a combined enrollment of almost 15,000 students.

APEX. Crossing from the 20th into the 21st century, Davenport University had the largest geographic coverage in its history. Grouped into regions, campuses and classroom locations included:

Davenport College (Western Region±)

Battle Creek	Kalamazoo
Gaylord	Lansing
Grand Rapids*	Scottville
Holland	Traverse City

Career Centers

Goshen	Mishawaka
Hammond	South Bend
Merrillville	

Great Lakes Junior College (Central Region±)

Alma	Lapeer
Bad Axe	Midland*
Bay City	Romeo
Caro	Saginaw

Detroit College of Business (Eastern Region±)

Dearborn*	Warren
Flint	

* Denotes flagship campus

± "Region" designations and individual college names were discontinued as part of the university conversion

The University: Redefining Growth in the 21st Century

The new millennium reversed the trends of previous decades. Global competition and emerging markets demanded optimum organizational performance everywhere, including higher education.

During the opening decade of the 21st century, the number of existing sites offering full degrees was reduced by half, with plans in place for even further consolidation and relocation. Gone were familiar names such as Merrillville, South Bend, Caro, Bad Axe, Bay City, Alma, and Dearborn.

Competition for students accounted for much of the reconfiguration. The model that Davenport had initiated so successfully decades earlier was now widely emulated by other colleges. By 2009, five major institutions—Western Michigan University, Central Michigan University, Ferris State University, Grand Valley State University, and Northwood University—had expanded well beyond their main campuses. These schools alone accounted for 60 locations that had not existed a mere decade earlier, and many other colleges had expanded as well. Additionally, higher level credentials in the workplace required expanded facilities and faculty—a commitment of resources that could not be sustained at small sites.

From Commuters to Computers. More than any other single factor, the emergence of the "virtual classroom" affected directions and decisions in higher education. The all-online model introduced in the 1990s by the University of Phoenix and other large for-profit schools proved so successful that many public and most private institutions began to build their own online programs.

Because Davenport was among the earliest to capture this momentum, its own students switched to the online option in droves. In 1999 only 4 percent of students took any courses online; by 2003, well more than half—58 percent—were taking a least one course online.

The Campuses: A City-by-City History

Year Founded: 1867
Original Name: Lansing Business University
Acquired by Davenport: 1951

LANSING BUSINESS UNIVERSITY. One of the oldest enterprises in the state capitol, LBU was founded in 1867 by Henry P. Bartlett. The school experienced numerous ownership changes before merging with Lansing Commercial Institute prior to World War I. In 1951 the school was privately purchased by Davenport Vice President Robert Sneden, redeveloped under the Davenport model, and then sold to Davenport Schools, Inc. Davenport Institute executive Martin Wynalda (also M.E. Davenport's son-in-law) was appointed managing director.

Wynalda purchased the school from DSI in 1974 and operated LBU as a proprietary institution until retiring in 1979. Davenport College reacquired the organization as a branch campus, which became part of the Davenport University conversion 25 years later.

Top: Lansing Business Institute during the 1960s was located in the Michigan Miller's Insurance Building in downtown Lansing. Its next home on East Kalamazoo Street (middle) was developed by Martin Wynalda. In 2013 the university purchased and renovated a former nine-story bank building in the heart of the state capitol.

Martin Wynalda served as assistant treasurer and director of veterans affairs for Davenport Institute before being appointed manager of Lansing Business University. He was vital to the development of this first Davenport Schools, Inc. satellite location as it grew to prominence in the capitol area.

Marian Davenport Wynalda, like her older sister Margaret, worked for Davenport-McLachlan Institute and University of Grand Rapids. After her husband's selection to run LBU, the couple relocated to the Grand Ledge area, where they raised their family of four. Marian continued to serve on the Davenport Institute family board for many years and also served 10 years on the Grand Ledge school board. The Marian Wynalda Teaching and Learning Institute at Davenport University recognizes her lifelong commitment to education.

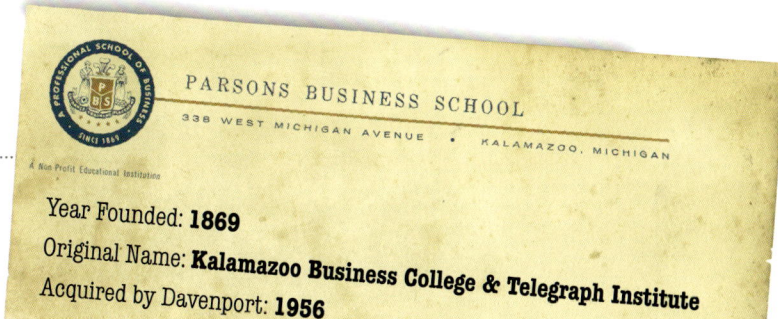

Year Founded: 1869
Original Name: Kalamazoo Business College & Telegraph Institute
Acquired by Davenport: 1956

PARSONS BUSINESS SCHOOL. William F. Parsons established Kalamazoo Business College & Telegraph Institute in 1869. Eventually renamed Parsons Business School, it remained a family enterprise until 1935. Edgar C. Stewart bought and operated Parsons successfully for a dozen years, but the school foundered after his death in 1947. In 1956 Parsons became the second property acquired by Davenport Schools, Inc.

In 1966 Davenport Institute alumnus C. Dexter Rohm, Jr. became managing director. From 1977 until 1981 he owned and operated Parsons privately then sold the school back to Davenport College. He remained dean of the college's Kalamazoo branch until his death from cancer in 1994. Kalamazoo continued as a main campus of Davenport University for more than two decades. In 2015, a partnership with Kalamazoo Valley Community College resulted in a move of the campus to KVCC's new University Center.

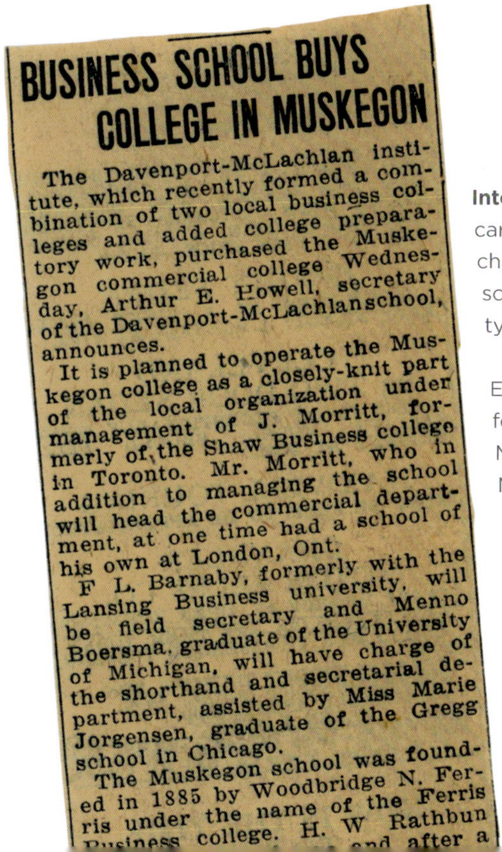

Originally located in a downtown office building, the Kalamazoo campus had its own building on West Main Street for 45 years.

Intertwined History. The early history of proprietary career schools often involved multiple management changes and mergers that blended the backgrounds of schools still in operation today. Muskegon College was typical of this pattern.

Established in 1888 by Woodbridge Ferris (who also founded Ferris Institute, now Ferris State University), Muskegon College was briefly owned by Davenport-McLachlan Institute in the 1920s. A few years later, Arthur Howell, a DMI administrator, bought the property and ran it as Howell's School of Business. He later sold the operation to the Jewell family, who successfully ran the school for decades under its original name, Muskegon College. In 1965 the Jewells purchased Flint-based Baker Business University to create today's Baker College.

DISTINGUISHING DAVENPORT

DISTINGUISHING DAVENPORT

NORTHEASTERN SCHOOL OF COMMERCE. Although the exact date of its founding is obscure, 1880 is accepted as the year Thumb-area entrepreneur Cyrus Devlin started Devlin's Business College. In the 1890s he merged it with another proprietary school to form the Bay City Business College, then disappeared from the education scene.

After World War II, Bay City Business College became Northeastern School of Commerce (pictured at right). Louis Bork, an NSC graduate, joined the faculty in 1948 and five years later became interim director. The school was acquired by Davenport Schools, Inc., in 1954. With Bork as managing director, NSC operated as a DSI subsidiary until 1977 when it was purchased by the Bork family. NSC closed in 1995.

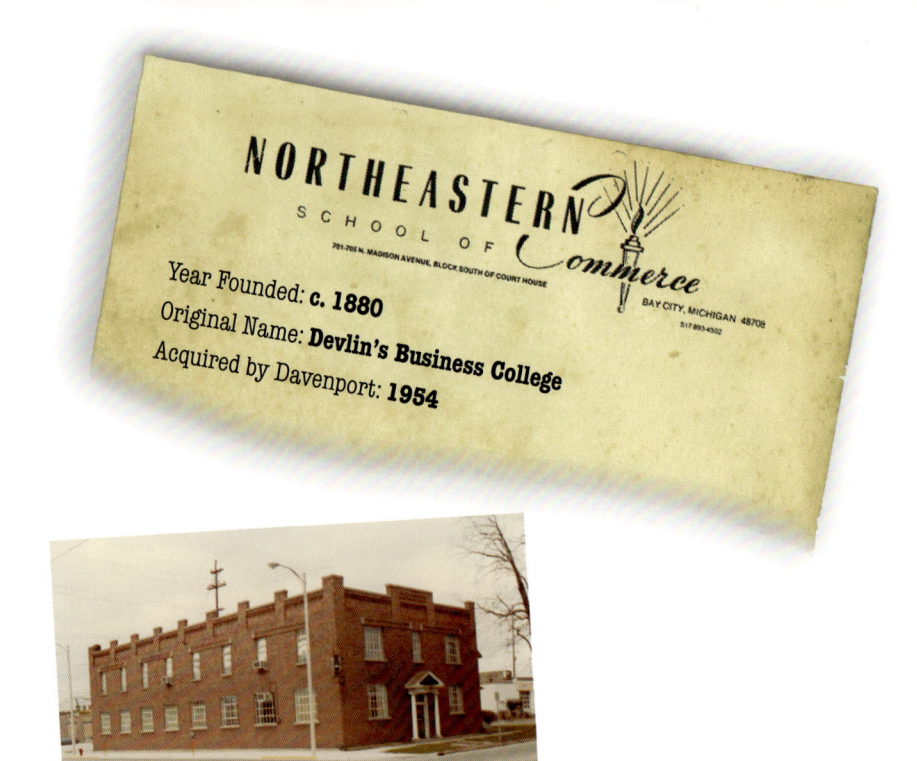

NORTHEASTERN SCHOOL OF Commerce
Year Founded: **c. 1880**
Original Name: **Devlin's Business College**
Acquired by Davenport: **1954**

THE BUSINESS INSTITUTE of SAGINAW
BOARD OF COMMERCE BUILDING
SAGINAW, MICHIGAN
Year Founded: **1907**
Original Name: **Bliss-Alger College**
Acquired by Davenport: **1957**

SAGINAW BUSINESS INSTITUTE. The final piece in the 1950s expansion drive, Saginaw Business Institute entered the Davenport system in 1957. Organized in 1907 as Bliss-Alger College, the school was originally designed for the express purpose of training commercial teachers rather than office employees. Cofounder Frederick Bliss had perfected a curriculum known as the "Bliss System of Actual Business," which became widely used in high schools and business colleges throughout the country. The school acquired a national reputation through Bliss's textbooks.

The college was sold in 1928 and renamed the Business Institute. After decades of success, the school regressed, filed for bankruptcy, and closed in 1954.

The demise was not permanent. The Muskegon School of Business (now Baker College) revived the shuttered institute before selling to Davenport in 1957. It remained an operating unit of Davenport Schools, Inc., for four decades, changed its name in the 1980s to Great Lakes Junior College, and expanded into several Thumb-area communities. Eventually it relocated its main campus from downtown Saginaw to Midland, merged with Davenport College in 1996, and became part of Davenport University.

(Top) Saginaw Business Institute in 1962. The downtown campus was relocated to Midland and renamed Great Lakes Junior College in 1986. (Far left) The present Davenport University Midland campus.

258

THE BUSINESS INSTITUTE

MICHIGAN BUILDING
220 BAGLEY AVENUE
DETROIT 26, MICHIGAN

PHONE WOODWARD 2-8536

Year Founded: **1850**
Original Name: **Goldsmith Business College**
Acquired by Davenport: **1954**

DETROIT COLLEGE OF BUSINESS. In 1954, M.E. Davenport purchased the Business Institute of Detroit and revised its name to Detroit Business Institute. Aside from being one of the oldest and largest private business colleges in the country, DBI held a vital asset not shared by Davenport's other component schools: its original 1850 charter permitted bachelor's degrees. It was a provision the century-old school had never activated, but M.E. Davenport and son-in-law Robert Sneden realized its potential. By operating DBI as a separate for-profit corporation, Davenport could keep intact the original charter. This would not only prove its value at DBI itself, but eventually would relay that impact to the home campus in Grand Rapids.

After receiving accreditation as a junior college of business in 1961, DBI became Detroit College of Business. School leaders acquired the former Henry Ford Community College campus in Dearborn and transferred its new collegiate division to that location. (The original diploma-certificate unit remained in downtown Detroit and was later sold to Lear-Siegler, Inc.)

A century of managers and mergers preceded Davenport's 1954 acquisition, which finally put "Detroit" into the school name.

According to records, Henry Ford was enrolled in an accounting class at the Business Institute in 1884, while working as an engineer at Detroit Edison Company. "I studied accounting," Ford later said, "but I learned method." Perhaps his Business Institute training contributed to Ford's development of the modern assembly line in 1909—the epitome of method applied to process.

DISTINGUISHING DAVENPORT

DISTINGUISHING DAVENPORT

Davenport University in Dearborn became the state's largest independent college in 1985, with the purchase of the old Detroit College of Business.

Detroit College of Business

- Issued its charter in 1850.
- Acquired by the Business Institute in 1906
- Purchased by M.E. Davenport in 1954. The school also had campuses in Grand Rapids, Lansing, Bay City, Saginaw, Kalamazoo and Battle Creek.
- Operated from the Michigan Theater Building on Bagley Avenue in Detroit. The school was moved to its Dearborn location in 1962, with the purchase of a former Henry Ford Community College building at Oakman and Michigan Avenue. The new campus was rechristened the Detroit College of Business.

In 2008 the Dearborn campus—site of the original Detroit College of Business—was sold. To serve its southeast students, a new location was established in Livonia (lower right), while the existing Warren location (below) underwent major improvements.

In 1966, DCB received accreditation as a senior college of business, becoming the first Davenport-affiliated unit to offer the bachelor's degree. Students at other Davenport locations—including the main Grand Rapids site—were eligible to transfer to the Detroit campus and pursue a four-year degree. Eventually, Detroit's upper-level division was introduced at Davenport College in Grand Rapids, allowing students there to complete a bachelor's degree at the main campus.

Detroit College of Business converted from proprietary to nonprofit in 1968. With all of its schools now following a nonprofit model, the Davenport organization had taken another step in its journey from "career school" to institution of higher learning.

In 1985, DCB merged with Davenport College and went on to become part of Davenport University.

FLINT

Davenport had a presence in the city of Flint beginning in the early 1970s with a branch location of the Detroit College of Business. A new Flint location was operated from 2004 to 2015, at which time DU classes were relocated to the University Center of Mott Community College.

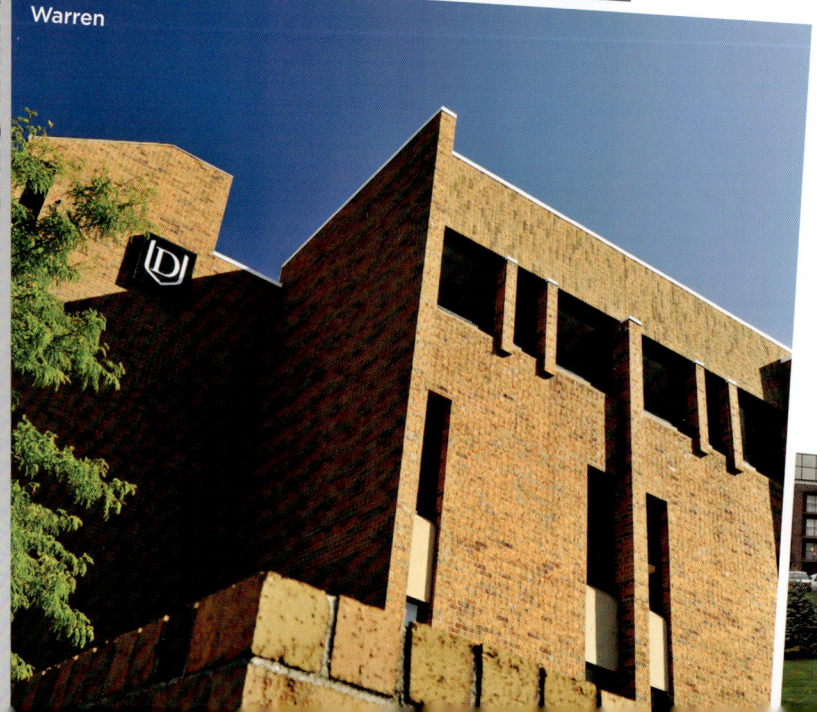

Warren

HOLLAND

Davenport's first lakeshore location opened in 1989 in a rented classroom site. A permanent campus site was obtained on the grounds of the Prince Corporation, which generously donated half of the designated 10-acre property. The new facility would ultimately serve up to 1,200 Davenport students while also providing educational and training programs for Prince employees.

CAREER CENTERS: (Indiana and Grand Rapids)

Beginning in the 1980s, Davenport introduced "Career Centers" that offered certificate training formats—one year or less—in word processing, accounting, and legal and medical secretarial skills. South Bend, and Merrillville, Indiana were chosen as pilot locations for their proximity to the larger metropolitan areas of Chicago and Detroit. They proved popular for employers looking for a certain skill set and with students seeking a specialized credential to enter the workforce quickly. Additional sites were created in Mishawaka, Goshen, and Hammond, as well as a Career Center in Grand Rapids itself. Eventually, the Indiana locations expanded their program offerings to include the associate and bachelor's degrees.

By the early 2000s the Centers had been discontinued, but for more than 20 years the sites contributed to Davenport's phenomenal growth.

BATTLE CREEK

In 1990 Davenport acquired Argubright College in Battle Creek, which began its affiliation with the college as a Career Center. Later a new campus was constructed offering regular degree courses. The Battle Creek Campus was closed in 2015 as Davenport began to transition out of associate degrees and most students in that market took their coursework online.

An iconic name in American commerce received training at Parsons. In 1880, W.K. Kellogg completed the normally year-long "commercial paper" course in a record three months. Kellogg went on to establish the Kellogg Corn Flake Company—the beginning of a breakfast empire.

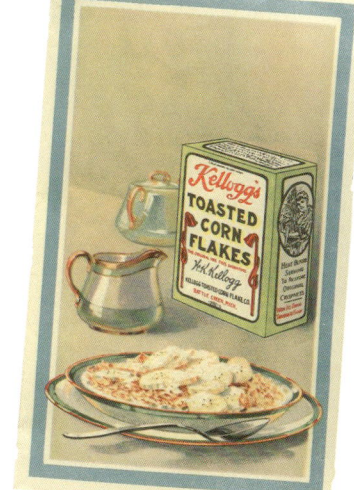

DISTINGUISHING DAVENPORT

The Davenport Classroom

The role of college and university faculty typically involves three concentrations: teaching, scholarship, and service, each shaped by institutional culture and mission. Because of its specialized nature, the Davenport brand of "practical education" has always combined theory and practice. Traditionally, faculty members were selected precisely for their experience as professionals in the business world.

As Davenport advances as a university, research and service roles for Davenport faculty continue to expand, while the teaching role itself has become more formalized. Advances in learning method—especially in the utilization of technology—require continual refinement of instructional method and delivery. Congruently, Davenport faculty are increasingly engaged in secondary research, often focused on new pedagogical strategies both in-seat and online. Involvement in professional organizations related to their disciplines is also expected of instructors, along with service to the university and to their communities.

Twenty-first century educational theory increasingly recognizes the principles of real-world relevance and intentional learning—tenets already deeply embedded in Davenport's approach.

> "We are very proud of our faculty. They are authors, Fulbright scholars, consultants, innovators, business leaders, advisors, and mentors. Our instructors are accomplished and have real-world experience."
> —Davenport University President Randolph Flechsig

Thirty-year classroom veteran Mark Griffin: "I still consider that my most important responsibility is to serve students in the classroom by preparing them for outstanding professional careers." Griffin is an associate professor of accounting and finance.

Two major initiatives are dedicated to helping faculty develop their craft: the Center for Teaching Excellence, a physical and virtual faculty collaborative, and the Wynalda Teaching and Learning Institute, an annual faculty learning conclave. Both provide guidance in interdisciplinary instructional delivery, opportunities for collegial learning and mentoring, and year-round connection to the entire university community.

(Opposite) With help from instructor Betty Deindorfer, students work at autotutor machines, used to improve math and English skills. Launched in 1969, Davenport's College Achievement and Transition program (CAT) was the first organized effort to help students perform at college level.

In the decades since, Davenport has been committed to developing tutorial programs, self-paced learning labs, freshman seminars, orientation courses, study skills training, and early alert programs. It offers these services not only for the sake of its students, but because it helps the institution improve retention and graduation rates.

Learning to Learn: Starting Prepared, Finishing Strong

From its founding, Davenport had practiced an open-admissions policy. This was long considered beneficial both to the college and to society, often tapping unrealized potential and offering a path to higher education that might otherwise be unavailable.

"A founding principle of Davenport University is that we give everybody wanting an education an opportunity to prove he or she can succeed," stated the 2001 president's letter to the Davenport governing board. "Opportunity is central to our mission and at the core of our beliefs."

It became increasingly apparent, however, that the philosophy and intent behind open admissions was becoming burdened. At Davenport and elsewhere, students were entering college with greater deficits in basic skills. In many cases performance challenges were deferred clear through high school graduation, which transferred the responsibility to colleges. Worries mounted not only about a growing diversion of resources toward developmental academics, but also the diminishing return for those students who continued to struggle despite support. The damage to the resources of both could no longer be denied; it was time for Davenport to question whether open enrollment was as viable in the 21st century as it had been in previous eras.

To consider a shift away from such a core principle was dismaying and unsettling for many at Davenport. But even its deepest beliefs about student potential could not keep pace with the realities of declining student preparedness. Leaders made the difficult decision in 2006 to revise the school's open admissions policy. (This was also the year the state of Michigan began implementing more rigorous high school graduation standards designed to reduce the need for remedial intervention at the college level). Incoming freshmen were required for the first time to submit ACT scores. Minimum thresholds were also established on the COMPASS basic skills assessment tests required of all first-time freshman-level applicants.

While this meant that some applicants were not accepted into Davenport, admissions standards did not mitigate the school's commitment to encouraging individual student success. Neither did it compromise its expectations for educational performance. Since students with barriers to learning are at greater risk of leaving college without a degree, commitment to developmental education becomes both a moral imperative and a matter of organizational integrity. Academic assistance, including individualized counseling and tutorials, remained mandatory for those scoring in the lower ranges on the COMPASS tests. Benchmark goals built into a specified timetable help students sustain their academic performance.

Service and Scholarship: Veterans at Davenport

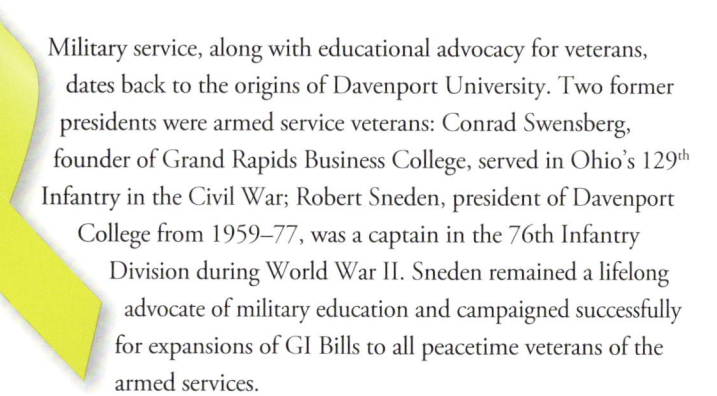

Military service, along with educational advocacy for veterans, dates back to the origins of Davenport University. Two former presidents were armed service veterans: Conrad Swensberg, founder of Grand Rapids Business College, served in Ohio's 129th Infantry in the Civil War; Robert Sneden, president of Davenport College from 1959–77, was a captain in the 76th Infantry Division during World War II. Sneden remained a lifelong advocate of military education and campaigned successfully for expansions of GI Bills to all peacetime veterans of the armed services.

For decades, Davenport has allocated staff resources to military admissions and advising. Full-time administrative positions, staffed by veterans and dedicated exclusively to the educational needs of military students, were created in the 2000s. Online courses allow active-duty students to take classes even during deployments. Tuition reductions are available for veterans, active service members, active duty reservists, and their spouses and dependants. Student Veterans of America, an on-campus organization dedicated to educational and employment support, has maintained a Davenport chapter since 2010. Additionally, the university has been designated repeatedly as a Military Friendly School by veterans organizations that rank educational commitment to military students.

Generations of veterans (like these enrolled at the Lansing campus in the 1990s) continue to receive educational support through legislation passed with the help of Davenport president Robert Sneden...a veteran himself.

In the mid-1960s, Sneden joined educators from across the country to petition Congress for wider-reaching measures that would extend benefit eligibility to peacetime members of the armed services. Previous measures—in place for nearly 20 years—limited benefits to those who served during wartime. This had disqualified Cold War military personnel from receiving any assistance, even while military service remained compulsory.

These efforts led to the Veterans Readjustment Benefits Act of 1966, which amended the "serving in wartime" designation and extended tuition aid to all military personnel serving at any time.

In the 1970s, Davenport established its Outreach Program, which offered flexible class schedules to veterans. The federal Help through Industry Retraining and Employment (HIRE) program of the post-Vietnam War period awarded Davenport a grant to coordinate employment assistance, training, and placement for veterans.

Veterans' Day observations are an annual event at Davenport. Displays and demonstrations, such as the landing of this Blackhawk helicopter (piloted by Army National Guard Captain Trish Barker, a Davenport MBA candidate), invite the public to honor America's military.

Serving in combat areas and other threatening situations can strongly affect concentration, perceptions of safety, and other sensory orientations. To optimize students' comfort and performance, Davenport developed a specially designed study room in the Margaret Sneden Library to provide an atmosphere of quiet privacy for veterans to study. (Right) A DU naval veteran marks where he served on a deployment map in the study room.

DISTINGUISHING DAVENPORT

Afterword

On January 19, 2016, Davenport University kicked off its 150th Anniversary celebrations with the unveiling of a new history wall in the Robert W. Sneden Center, the premiere of our 150th Anniversary video, and the launch of our 150th website. The Davenport story they all share is expanded upon greatly in this book. It is a story of innovation and constant transformation in response to the changing needs of the marketplace.

My predecessors understood and embraced change, constantly looking to the horizon to see how this institution would need to evolve to remain relevant. This resulted in the development of new curricula, achieving valuable higher learning accreditations, transitioning to nonprofit status, establishing new campus locations, pioneering online learning, and so much more.

The focus has always been on our students and helping them to achieve their career and life goals through their education. Our quality initiatives today are about continuously improving student outcomes so that even more lives are transformed through a Davenport education. I am confident that our focus on quality today will have positive outcomes for our students, employers and communities for generations to come.

Richard J. Pappas, Ed.D.
President
Davenport University

Acknowledgements

This project owes much to and has benefitted immeasurably from many resources. An abundance of source material and artifacts available through the university archive—launched in 2010—contributed greatly to the book's presentation and extended its interest and range of appeal. Many university alumni responded to requests for memorabilia; generous contributions of personal mementos, keepsakes, and photographs have enhanced this second edition beyond expectations.

The book team:

Writing/Research/Editing: Thomas Brown Ed.D., Margaret (Peggy) Moceri,

Project Management: Peggy Moceri, Susan Bakkila

Creative Director/Designer/Photography/Photograph Retouching: Susan Bakkila

Graphic Design: Hilary Embrey *Photograph Retouching:* Morgan Moallemian

University Archivist: Jennifer Morrison

Contributions to this history went far beyond the principal players. Dr. Barbara Mieras, Robin Luymes, and Jennifer Morrison spent innumerable hours reviewing chapter drafts. Many people made available their perspective and insight, giving generously of their time for interviews and responses to inquiries. For their assistance we most gratefully acknowledge: Kathy Aboufadel, Irene Bembenista, Chris Bill, Ken Bovee, Ron Draayer, Randolph K. Flechsig, David Fleming, Tracey Graham, Mark Griffin, Betty LaCroix, Wilbur Lettinga, Paul Lowden, Donald W. Maine, James Meyer, Donna Milham, Richard Pappas, Todd Pitts, Aaron Sagraves, Wayne Sneath, Kathy Sneden, Terri Tomasczek, Roger Vander Laan, David Veneklase, Mike Volk, and Kathy Yared.

Thanks are also due to the History and Special Collections Department of Grand Rapids Public Library and the Willard Library in Battle Creek for providing images and additional research. For their assistance and access to the *Grand Rapids Press* Archives, we express appreciation to curators Dale Robertson and Alex Forist.

Credit for the book's title belongs to Jennifer Morrison, Davenport University Archivist. Indexing and proofreading was provided by Mary Kat Workinger.

The book is typeset in Garamond and Gotham type families.

Special Note:

The graphic insignias used in each section of the book are recreations of designs found in the elaborate wood- and tilework at the former T. Stewart White estate, which was known as Warren Hall when Davenport's campus was located in Heritage Hill on Fulton Street.

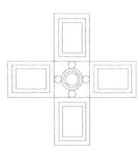

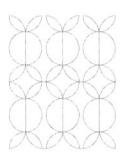

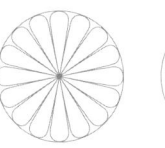

Funded by a grant from the M.E. Davenport Foundation in advance of Davenport University's sesquicentennial year, this volume is part of a comprehensive and ongoing commitment to recognize and preserve the history of Davenport University. Other supported projects within the grant included the establishment of a university archive and a permanent history wall exhibit.

Partial List of Works Consulted

Editor's note: A select bibliography is not a complete record of all works consulted, but indicates a representative range of material contributing to the content of the book.

BOOKS

Baxter, Albert. *History of the City of Grand Rapids*. Chicago, Munsell Publishing Co., 1891.

Educators of Michigan, J.H. Beers & Co., Chicago, IL., 1900.

Logan, Thomas H. *Almost Lost: Building and Preserving Heritage Hill*. Traverse City, Arbutus Press, 2004.

Miller, Jay & Hamilton, William. *The Independent Business School in American Education*. New York. Gregg Division, McGraw Hill, 1964.

Petrello, George J. *In Service to America: AICS at 75*. McGraw Hill, Inc., New York. 1988.

Schmidt, June, and Jennings, Carol. *Chronology of Business Education in the United States 1635–1990*. National Business Education Association, Reston, VA., 1990.

Richard W. Schwarz, *John Harvey Kellogg, M.D.: Pioneering Health Reformer*, Review and Herald Publishing Association, 2006.

Tuttle, Charles Richard. *History of Grand Rapids*. Tuttle & Clooney, Grand Rapids, MI., 1874.

PERIODICALS & NEWSPAPERS

Grand Rapids Democrat
Grand Rapids Herald
Grand Rapids Press
Grand Rapids Business Journal

OTHER SOURCES

Gould's *Peoria City Directory*, David B. Gould, Publisher, Peoria, IL., 1887.

Holland's *Grand Rapids City Directory*, Western Publishing Co., Chicago, IL. 1867.

DAVENPORT UNIVERSITY PUBLICATIONS

Students' Life, 1924–1969
Davenport Digest, 1970–1995
Davenpress, 1979–1993
Davenport University Magazine, Fall 2000–Winter 2007
Davenport University Review, Spring 2007–present

WEBSITES

Lyndon Baines Johnson Library and Museum. *www.lbjlibrary.com*

Accrediting Council for Independent Colleges and Schools. *www.acics.org*

Higher Learning Commission. *www.hlcommission.org*

College Bound Network. *www.collegebound.net*

ARTICLES

Delaney, Robert, "Ending tuition grants opposed," *The Michigan Catholic*, February 2010.

Voelker, Paul F. "Schools Should Serve Society," *Journal of Educational Sociology*, Vol. 8, No. 7, March 1935.

SCHOLARLY RESEARCH

Selmon, John. "Change and Persistence in an Independent Non-Profit College: A Case Study." Ph.D. diss., Eastern Michigan University, 2001.

Sneden, Kathleen. "The Independent Postsecondary Education Institution: An Adaptive Organization." University of Southern California, 1982.

Photo Attributions

All of the images in this book are property of the Davenport University Archives* or private collections, except for those listed:

Baxter, Albert. History of the City of Grand Rapids.
The Institution Debuts: p. 11, Conrad Swensberg.

Grand Rapids Public Library
History and Special Collections Department
The Institution Debuts: p. 14, Luce Bldg; p. 15 Ledyard Bldg.; p. 16, Conrad Swensberg; p. 19, Stickley Chair Factory; p. 20 Norcross Building, Lyon Street; p.21, J.F. Klingensmith & F.L. Brooks; p. 22, view of Monroe Avenue, 1890s. *A New Beginning:* p. 36, view of Monroe Avenue, 1920s; p. 74 group photo; p.79, IBM exposition. *From Institute to College:* p. 110, President Lyndon Johnson signing ceremony; p. 112, Congressman Gerald Ford mobile office; pp. 114-15, Monroe Avenue nighttime, Vandenberg Plaza renovations, Kent County Airport, Calder stabile, G.R. City Hall. *Coming of Age: Growing Toward a University:* p. 160, Monroe Avenue renovation.

Gould's Peoria City Directory
The Institution Debuts: p. 11, Aaron Parish.

iStock by Getty Images
The Institution Debuts: Ancient Email, p. 13, Tarinoel; Antique Car, p. 29 and 259, FullValue. *Coming of Age: Growing Toward a University:* 1980s Retro Cell Phone, p. 135, Tim Zillion; Web Hand Plain, p. 176, EGM; Power Book, p. 183, Slobo; The New Millenium: HTML Code, p. 195, Goldmund Lukic; World Trade Center Rubble, p. 197, Terraxplorer; Working Woman on Laptop, p. 200, spxChrome; *Vision for Continued Excellence:* Diploma, p. 249, Blackred.

Library of Congress
The Institution Debuts: Pinkerton, Lincoln, and McClernand, p. 13.

Shutterstock
The Institution Debuts: 1900 San Francisco Quarter, p. 13, Russell Shively; Old Antique Typewriter with Black Keys, p. 25, Arunas Gabalis. *A New Beginning:* Old Violin, p. 48, Oleg Kozlov.

The Right Place, Inc.
Coming of Age: Growing Toward a University: p. 183, all photos.

Thinkstock by Getty Images
The Institution Debuts: Paperclip, p. 23, Emarto. *A New Beginning:* Old Airplane, p. 29, Bombaert; Vintage Briefcase, p. 39, Miiicha; Stock Certificate, p. 39, Qingwa; USA Postage Stamp Women Support War Effort, p. 53, TonyBaggett; World War II Ration Book, p. 53, Nick Cook. *From Institute to College:* JFK Postage Stamp, p. 97, Dimitris_k; Accredited Stamp, p. 107, Aquir; First Man on the Moon, p. 115, Steve Mann; Vintage Machine, p. 133, Hemera Technologies; Calculator, p. 133, Davincidig; Vintage Mobile Phone, p. 135, Arijuhani. *Coming of Age: Growing Toward a University:* Classic computer with keyboard, p. 151, Anthony Hall; CD, p. 151; Checklist, p. 185, Alexsl. *The New Millenium:* New York City Manhattan Skyline, p. 197, Rabbit75_ist; Old Abandoned Building, p. 220, Ingram Publishing. *Vision for Continued Excellence:* Internet, p. 221, Bagiuiani; Group of young people using smart phones, p. 221, Michael Jung; Fibre Optical, p. 249, Gunnar3000.

Veer/ United Glory International/ Getty Images
The New Millenium: Two Men Sitting at Desk and Computer, p. 195, Corbis Photography.

The university extends its gratitude to the History and Special Collections Department of Grand Rapids Public Library and to The Right Place, Inc., for their generous cooperation in sourcing and providing photographs for this book.

---

*Created in 2010 by a grant from the M.E. Davenport Foundation, the Davenport University Archives collects, organizes, preserves and shares material that documents the history of Davenport University. For more information, go to *http://libguides.davenport.edu/archives*.

Index

Photographs and illustrations indicated by bold italics

Academic Center
    Heritage Hill campus, 115, 120-21
    Sneden Academic Center, Robert W., 127, 138, 153, *153*,
        162, 167, 196
    See also DeVos, Richard M. and Jay Van Andel Academic Center
Accreditation, 85, 106-107, 135, 166-67.
    See also North Central Association
Accrediting Commission for Business Schools, 106
Accrediting Council for Independent Colleges and Schools
    (ACICS), 107
Administration Building, 120-21.
    See also Cook Administration Building
Admissions policy, 263
    in nursing program, 212
    process improvement and, 228
    effect of university consolidation on, 194, 263
    at UGR, 54
Adult Accelerated Career Education, 176-77
Adult education, 254
Albom, Mitch, 180, *180*, 181, 242, *242*, 243
Alma, Michigan, 254, 255
Alpha Iota sorority, 44, 82, *83*, 133, 165
Alumni Association, 129, 133
Amway, 97, 203
Anderson, Charles ("Andy"), 127, *127*
Anderson Student Center, 127
Aquinas College, 13, 198
    UGR and, 58, 70-71
Argubright Business College, 32, 177, 261
Arts and Sciences, College of, 199, 230
Assoc. of Independent Colleges and Schools (AICS), 40
Assoc. of Independent Colleges and Universities of Michigan, 189, 219
Athletics, 46, 82, 116-17, 146, 161, 214, 224
    baseball, 236, *237*
    basketball, men's, 46, *46-47, 65,* 82, *82*, 117, 148, 161, 215
    basketball, women's, *65*, 197, 198, *198*, 215, *236*
    bowling, 82, 117
    championships and conference titles, 236, 237
    cheerleading, 82, *82*, 116-17, *116*, *236*
    cross country 117
    Farmers' Insurance Athletic Complex, 235, 236, *236*, 247, *237*
    fight song, 60
    football, 62-63, 165, 201, *201*, 236, *236*
    golf, 82, *82*, 116-17, *116*, 146
    Great Lakes Intercollegiate Athletics Conference, 241
    hockey, 197, 198, *198*, *237*
    intramural sports, 158, 214
    lacrosse, 215
    mascot
        Lancers, 57, *57*, 60
        Panthers, 46, 100, 116, *116*, *198*, *232, 247*
    Michigan Business School League, 46, 117
    National Association of Intercollegiate Athletics, 197, 224, 237
    reinstated at Davenport, 197-98
    rugby, 237
    school colors, 46, 100
    soccer, 215, *236*
    softball, 82, *82*, 117, *117*, 236
    suspension of, 146
    tennis, 82, 117, *117*, 236
    Wolverine-Hoosier Athletic Conference 197, 198, 237
    Wolverine League, 82
    women's athletics, 116, 158, 224, 236-37
        Title IX, 146
Attendance Centers, 149, 175, 254
Bad Axe, Michigan, 177, 254, 255
Baker College, 32, 257, 258
Barker, Trish, 265
Barrows, Jack, 201, *201*
Battle Creek, Michigan, 72, 168, 261
Bay City, Michigan, 131, 137, 177, 252, *253*, 254-55, 258
Bay City Business College. *See* Northeastern School of Commerce
Bernero, Virg, *247*
Bissell Carpet Sweeper Company, 16-17, *17*
Bliss-Alger College. *See* Saginaw Business Institute
Board of Advisors, 108-109
Board of Control, 131, 134, 164
Board of Trustees, 194, 216, 229, 241
    first African American appointed to, 145, *145,* 151, *151*
    family control, transition from, 131, 134, 135
    and Lettinga Campus approval, 202
    Margaret Sneden's service on, 164
    Robert Sneden's service on, 135, 139
    Vision 2015 and, 226
    Vision 2020 and, 240
    women appointed to, 145, *145*
Boji, Louie, *247*
Bork, Louis, 258
Boshoven, Steve, *247*
Bovee, Kenneth C., 209, 216, *216*, 225

275

Index

Braden, Dallas, 201, *201*
Bradshaw, Terry, 243
Bronner, Wallace ("Wally"), 243, *243*
Bronner Excellence in Business Award, 243
Brooks, Frank L., 21, *21*, 22
Brown, Thomas 182, 204, *204*, 213
Buchwald, Art, 181, *180*
Burns, Donna, 170, *170*
Burt, John R., 243
Bush, Laura, 243, *243*
Business education, history of, 144, 250
    accreditation in the, 107
    in Grand Rapids, 14
    technology's role in, 24, 25, 35, 106, 255
    women in, 12, 25, 35
Business Professionals of America, 208
Business School. *See* Maine School of Business, Donald W.
Buzzitta, Louis V., 237
Buzzitta Scholarship, Louis V. and Catherine, 237
Calvin College, 13, 52
Candlestone Inn, 151-152, 161
Carey, Tom, 175, *175*
Carter, Barbara, 212
Canepa, John C., 243, *243*
Caro, Michigan, 177, 254, 255
Career Centers, 151, 153, 254, 261
Cawood, Matthew, 177, 193
Center for the Study of Emergency Medical Services.
    See Emergency Medical Services Program
Chamberlain, Wallace, 108, *108*, 131
Charter, Class "A", 36
Clark, George ("Potsy"), 62-63, *62*, *63*
Cogbill, Alexander *247*
College Achievement and Transition Program, 262
Colizzi, Donald, 148-149, *148*, 177
Commitment to students
    faculty's, 262
    M.E. Davenport's, 33, 48, 88
    Mabel Davenport's, 33
    Richard Pappas on, 246, 247
    Conrad Swensberg's, 14
    at UGR, 52, 53
    Ty Wessell's, 102-103

Community commitment, 14
    M.E. Davenport and, 53, 91-92
    Joseph Hager on, 109
    Heritage Hill renovation, 122-123, 210
    small business, support of, 167
    volunteer time-off policy, 204
    in West Michigan, 157, 234
Comparing Davenport to Michigan colleges, 54, 56, 106, 228, 240, 254
Continuous Quality Improvement, 240, 246
Cook Administration Building, Peter C., 196, 207
Cook Center for Graduate Studies, Peter C., 207, 225, 234, *234*
Cook Excellence in Business Award, Peter C., 181, 207, 242, 243
Cook, Peter C., 181, *181*, 207, *207*, 242, *242*
Cook Residence Hall, Peter C. and Pat, 205, 207, *209*
Dale Carnegie Course, 79, *79*, 137
Daley, Karen and Shannon, *247*
Davenport Business Institute. *See* Davenport Institute
Davenport College (DC), 108-109
    enrollment, 118 (1966); 130 (1971); 156 (1982); 168 (1985);
        182 (1999)
    faculty, 81, 83, 101, 130, 182
    tuition, 130 (1971) 156 (1982), 182 (1999)
Davenport Educational System (DES), 148, 177, 188, 254
    adult education and, 254
    transition to university, 179, 184
Davenport, Forrest, 29-30, *30*
Davenport Foundation, *160,* 178, 181, 212
    founding of, 143, 160-61, 165
    Wilbur Lettinga and, 173
    Barbara Mieras and, 178-179, 193, 196
    scholarship support from, 139, 160, 164, 181
Davenport Business Institute (DBI), 29-30, 32, 34
    enrollment, 34 (1918); 85 (1957); 83 (1950); 101 (1960)
    faculty, 30-31, 34
    founded, 29
    McLachlan merges with, 36-39
    tuition, 83 (1950), 101 (1960)
Davenport Learning Network, 176, 178, 183, 197
Davenport, Mable Engle, 29, 31, *31*, *32*, *33*, *115*
    death, 91
    early life and education, 33
    Mable Engle Hall, 159
    marriage and family, 29, 30

Index

Davenport-McLachlan Institute (DMI), **75**
    enrollment, 40 (1928); 75 (1945)
    faculty, 40, **49**
    student expenses, 48
    tuition (1928), 40
    UGR, relationship with, 56, 67, 71
Davenport, Michael Edward (M.E.), **86**
    character of, 48, 88-89, **89,** 92, **92**
    on education and citizenship, 53
    civic leadership of, 91, 92, **93,** 115, **115**
    Peter Cook and, 207
    death, 86, 91
    early life and education, 29, **29,** 91
    marriage and family, 29, 30, 70-71, 74, 90-91, **90-91, 164**
    Woodbridge Ferris' influence on, 28
    at GRBC, 30, **30,** 31, **31**
    Grand Rapids, move to, 28, **27, 28**
    on Malcolm McLachlan, 36-37
    management style of, 88, 89
    and Robert Sneden, 75, 85, 96
    students, commitment to, 88, 89
    at UGR, 53, 62-63, **63**
    at Valley City Commercial School, 22, **22**
Davenport Online. *See* Davenport University Online
Davenport Schools, Inc. (DSI), 131, 135, 139, 149, 256
    dissolved, 103
    multi-campus concept, 252
Davenport University
    first commencement, 214
    consolidation of DES into, 183, 184, 192, 193, 194, 196
    enrollment, 206 (2003); 234 (2011)
    faculty, 206, 225, 226, 234
    tuition, 206 (2003), 234 (2011)
Davenport University Online, 175, 177, 197, 200
Davenport, Warren, 70-71, **70, 71, 74,** 91, **91**
Davis, Julia, 177
Dearborn, Michigan, 166, **168,** 169, 212, 254, 259, 260
DeBoer, James, 131, 229, **229**
DeBoer, Joy, 229, **229**
Degrees, diplomas, and certificates, 106, 151
    Accountancy and Business, 40, 130
    Accounting, 230
    Administration, 40
    Arithmetic, Practical 14
    Bookkeeping, 14
    Business Administration, 166
        MBA, 195, 230, 234
    Business Management, 130, 156
    Civil Service, 40
    Commercial Teaching, 40
    Composition, 14
    Computer Programming, 130, 156
    Data Processing, 133, 163
    Emergency Medical Services, 143, 151-52, 154-55, **154**
    Fashion Merchandizing, 156
    General Business and Advertising, 40
    Gregg Shorthand and Touch Typewriting, 40, 58
    Health Informatics and Information Mgt., 230
    Hospitality Management, 152, 156
    Marketing, 130, 156
    Music, 40
    Nursing, 154, 212, 230
    Occupational Therapy, 230
    Penmanship, Practical, 14
    Pharmacy, 54, 57, 69
    Physical Therapy, 230
    Real Estate and Insurance, 101
    Retail Management, 101
    Sales and Marketing, 101
    Secretarial Science, 40, 83, 101, 104-05
    Technology Management, 230
    Transportation and Distribution, 101
    Urban Education, 230
    Word Processing, 106, 153, 156, 163, 261
Deindorfer, Betty, 262, **263**
DeJourno, Philip, 108
DeLuc, Don, **247**
DePree, Max, 3
Detroit Business Institute. *See* Detroit College of Business
Detroit branch campus, 240
Detroit College of Business, 119, 164, 166-67, 254, **259**
    acquired, 168-169, 259, 260
    bachelor's program affiliated with, 166, 169, 259
    and Henry Ford Community College, 259, 260
Development, 85, 115, 126-127
    Charity Golf Classic, 155
    fund drive, employee, 160
    Investing in the Vision campaign, 240
Devlin's Business College. *See* Northeastern School of Commerce
DeVos, Richard M. and Jay Van Andel Academic Center, 203, **203**, 205, **205**
DeVos, Betsy, 243, **243**
DeVos, Doug, 243

Index

DeVos, Richard ("Dick"), 97, **183**
    Cook Award recipient, 181, **181**
Dewey, John, 53, 57
Distance learning, 176, 200, 264. *See also* Davenport University Online
Distinguished Alumni Award, 133, 173
Diversity
    first African American graduate, 238
    board of trustees, first African American member of, 145, 151
    Diversity Council, 246
    Diversity, Equity, and Inclusion, Office of, 239
    enrollment, 239
    Inner City Education Program, 113
    Minority Student Union, 151
    physically challenged students, 164
    Vision 2020 and, 240
Division Ave. (12 S.), 83, 101
Dobbs, Lou, 243
Draayer, Ron, 208
Dyer-Ives Foundation, 113
Eberhard, L.V., 29, 108, **108**, 131
Ehlers, Vernon, 225, **225**
Elkins, Larry, 117
Emergency Med. Services, Ctr. for the Study of, 143, 151-52, 154-55, **154**
Employee development. *See* Learning Academy
Mable Engle Hall, 122, **122**, 159, **159**, 170
Mable Engle Program of Nursing, 212
Engler, John, 174, **174**
Enrollment, 133, 166. *See also under individual institution names*
EPIC Award for Excellence, 231
Excellence in Business Award. *See* Cook EIB Award; Bronner EIB Award
Excellence System, 171, 201
Executive 100, 146, **172**, 180-181, 243
Executive cabinet, 129. *See also* President's Cabinet; Executive council
Executive council, 132. *See also* President's Cabinet
Extracurricular activities, 38, 41, 44, 80-81, 131, 158-59
Facilities, **35**, 41, **41**, **55**, 77, 131, 153, 162, **162**, 232
Faculty
    and accreditation process, 106, 166-67, 196
    Center for Teaching Excellence, 262
    commitment to students, 8, 22, 120, 262
    and Davenport Success System, 171
    employee fund drive, 160
    quality of, 262
    senate, 132
    and university consolidation process, 196, 199
    at Valley City Commercial College, 28, 31

Ferris, Woodbridge N., 28, 257
Field, E. Malcom, 243
Financial aid, 88
    and accreditation, 107
    at Davenport-McLachlan, 48
    federal grants and loans, 118
    Michigan Tuition Grant program, 110-11
Fleming, David, 194
Flechsig, Randolph, 197, **201**, 218, **218**
    chancellor at DES, 192-93, **192**, 197
    at DU, 192, **202**, **214**, **217**
        accreditation process, 192-94, 196, **196, 219**
        resignation from, 211, 216
    early life and education, 192, 218
    Framework for Success, 194
    at Great Lakes Junior College, 192, 218
    professional associations, 219
Flint, Michigan, 169, 175, 254, 260, **260**
Ford, Gerald R.
    at UGR, 62-63, **63**, 112, 113, **112-113**, 201, **165**, 201, **201**
    Peter Cook and, 207
Ford Memorial Scholarship, Gerald R., 201
Founding, anniversary of, 118-119
    100th, 157
    125th, 174-75, 177
    150th, 3, 267
Henry Ford Community College, 259, 260
Foreign study. *See* Study abroad
Fountain Hill Apartments. *See* Florence Woods Hall
Fountain St. (14), 74, **75**
Framework for Success, 194, **194**
Frey, David, 243
Fulton St. (2), 75, 76-78, **76-78**
Fulton St. (415 E.), *See* Heritage Hill campus
Fundraising. *See* Development
Garber, Richard J., 243
Gaylord, Michigan, 175, 254
Global Campus, 240
Goshen, Indiana, 254, 261
Gough, Reid, 211, **213**
Gould, Erma, 49, **49**, 78, **78**
Governing board. *See* Board of Trustees; Board of Control
Graduate placement. *See* Placement
Graduate School. *See* Sneden Graduate School
Graham, Tracy D., 235

278

Index

Grand Rapids Business College (and Telegraphic Institute), 12-14, **14**, 21, **21**
    under M.E. Davenport, 30
    enrollment, 13, 14 (1866)
    faculty, 19
    motto, 18
    A.S. Parish and, 19
    tuition (1866), 14
Grand Rapids Business Journal, 231
Grand Rapids City College, 54
Grand Rapids College of Applied Science. *See* University of Grand Rapids
Grand Rapids Community College, 29, 54, 67, 134
    Heritage Hill campus purchase, 123, 210, 232
Grand Rapids Evening Leader, 18, 19
Grand Rapids Herald, 16, 17, **17**, **20**, 21
Grand Rapids Junior College. *See* Grand Rapids Community College
Grand Rapids Press, 21, 93, 123
Grand Rapids Telegram-Herald, 12, 16
Grand River Valley Review, 69
Grand Valley State University, 97, 255
    Davenport affiliation proposed, 134
    Emergency Medical Services Program, 143, 152
Grant, Hazel, 238
Great Depression, 39, 48-49, 52, 62, 74, 88, 102
Great Lakes Intercollegiate Athletic Conference, 241
Great Lakes Junior College, 139, 148, 165, 177
    Davenport and, 177, 212, 218, 254
    Randolph Flechsig and, 192, 218
    nursing program, 212
Gregg Shorthand Course, 40, 58
Gregg, John Robert, 23
Griffin, Mark, 205, 262, **262**
Giuliani, Rudy, 243
Hackett, Jim, 243
Hager, Joseph A., 109, **109**
    board of trustees chair, 131, 145
Hammond, Indiana, 254, 261
Hauenstein, Ralph, 242, **242**, 243
Health Professions, School of, 154, 182, 199, 206, 234
Heaney, H. M., 31-32, **31**, **32**
Heaney's Commercial College, 32, 74
Heritage Hall, 122, **123**
Heritage Hill campus, 118, 120-125
    closing, 202-03, 210, 211
    GRCC purchase of, 123, 210, 232
    move to, 115, 120
    See also under individual building names

Herman Miller, Inc., 3
Herpolsheimer's, 22, **22**
Higher Education Act, 250-51
Higher Education Newsmaker of the Year, 231
HIRE program, 264
Holland, Michigan, branch campus, 168, 175, 177, 261, **261**
Holmdene. *See* Lowe Estate
Holtz, Lou, 243
Hooker, Bob, 242, **242**, 243
Hopkins, Claude, 13
Howell, Arthur E., 31-32, **31**, **32**, 257
Howell's School of Business, 32, 257
Hunt, Helen, 243
Hunting, John, 113
Idema, Walter, 29
Imperato, Pamela, **240**
Inner City Education Project, 113
Institute for Professional Excellence, 234
Izzo, Tom, 242, **242**, 243
Jandernoa, Michael J. and Sue, 243, **243**
Janeway, Elliot, 180
Jordan College, 175
Kalamazoo, Michigan, 131, 137, 143, 149, 156, 252, 254, 257, **257**
Kalamazoo Business College and Telegraph Institute. *See* Parsons Business School
Kalamazoo Valley Community College, 257
Keller, Fred P., 243
Kellogg Community College, 257
Kendall College of Art and Design, 39
Killman, Karl, 117, 146
Klingensmith, John F., 19, 21, **21**, 22
Knight, Brent, **247**
Koppel, Ted, 242, **242**, 243
Korean War, 78
Krueger, Blake W., 243, **243**
Kuyper College, 53
LaCroix, Betty, 133, **133**, **170**
Lansing, Michigan, 131, 137, 156, 168, 177, **235**, 252
Lansing Commercial Institute. *See* LBU
Lansing Business Institute. *See* LBU
Lansing Business University (LBU), 143, 148-49, **256**
Lanting, James and Clarine, 196, **196**
Lanting Welcome Center, 196
Lapeer, Michigan, 254
Learning Academy, 178
Learning Network. *See* Davenport Learning Network
Ledyard Building, 14

279

Index

Leno, Jay, 174-75, *174*
Leonard, Sugar Ray, 243, *243*
Lettinga Auditorium, Wilbur and Sharon, 233
Lettinga Campus, W.A., 123, 172, 205, *205*
    construction proposed, 184, 202
    expansion, 240
    groundbreaking, 202, 203
    opens, 197, 205
    See also under individual building names
Lettinga Entrepreneurial Center, W. A., 123, 161, 167-168, 173, *173*
Lettinga, Sharon, *202*
Lettinga, Wilbur A., *153*, *172-73*, *196*, *202*, *206*, *218*
    board of trustees, 145, *145*, 173
    and Cook Award, *242*, 243
    early life and education, 172
Liberal arts
    College of Arts and Sciences, 199, 230
    M.E. Davenport on importance of, 39
    at Davenport College, 108
    at Davenport Institute, 98
    at University of Grand Rapids, 52-54, 57
Library, 41, 71, 135, *135*, 167, 178, 205
    on Heritage Hill campus, 118, 120
    Margaret Davenport Sneden Library, 162, *162*, 165, 211, *211*
    and University of Grand Rapids accreditation, 56, 70
Livonia, Michigan, 260
Lowden, Paul, 198, *198*
Lowe Estate, *51*, 53, *53*, *56*, 57, *58*, *63*, *66*, 70
Lubbers, Arend ("Don"), 184, 185
Luce Building, 12, 14
Lucid Secretarial School, 74
Ludington, Michigan, 254
McBain, Robert, 131
McLachlan Business University, 21, 23, 34, 36, *36*
    DBI, merger with 36, 39
McLachlan, Malcolm, 21, 36, 37, *37*
    M.E. Davenport's respect for, 36
Maidlow, Spencer T., 243
Maine, Kathy, *243*
Maine, Donald, *144*, *161*, *174*, *181*, *240*
    and baccalaureate accreditation, 143, 166-67
    civic leadership of, 183, *183*, 188-89
    on competition, 175
    and Peter Cook, *242*
    and DES, 177
    as Davenport president, *135*, 142-45, *142*, 169, *169-70*, *201*
    on diversity, 151, *151*
    early life and education, 186, *186-87*, 189
    25 Goals list, 143, 166, 185
    honors and awards, 186, 189, *243*
    leadership style, 3, 188
    retirement, 183-84, *184,* 188, *189*
    and Robert Sneden, *138*, *143*
Maine School of Business, Donald W., 188, 197, 204, *240*, 241
Maine Street, 188, 189
Make a Living, Make a Life, Make a Contribution, 39, 53, 204, 241
Margaret Hall, 122
Mathis, Ralph, 145, 151, *151*
Meijer, Doug, 206, *206*
Meijer, Frederik, 181, *206*
Meijer, Lena, 206, *206*
Meijer Residence Hall, 206, *206,* 211
Mendola, James, 169, *169*
Merlotti, Jr., Frank, *240*, 241
Merrillville, Indiana, 167, 254-55, 261, *261*
Metal Office Furniture, Co. *See* Steelcase
Meyer, James, 195, 202, *202*, *218*, 219
Michigan Assoc. of North Central Colleges (MANCC), 56, 68
Michigan Business Education Assoc., 137
Michigan Business and Normal College, 32
Michigan Business Schools Association, 137
Michigan Performance Excellence Award, 241
Michigan Tuition Grant Program, 110-11, 138
Midland, Michigan, 148, 177, 212, 214, 234, 254, *258*
Mieras, Barbara, *184*, *201*
    awards and honors, 179, *179,* 243, *243*
    at Davenport
        admissions and marketing VP, 178, *178*
        advancement VP, 193, *196*, *202*
        and Holland campus, 175, *175*
        president, 177-78
        university foundation president, 193, *196*
    early life and education, 178
Minorities. *See* Diversity
Mishawaka, Indiana, 254, 261
Muskegon Business College, 32, 257
Music, 40, 41, 44, 48
Myners, Lillian, 83
Myners Hall, 123, *123,* 158, 170
Name changes (in chronological order), GRBC to VCCS, 21;
    VCCS to GRBC, 30; GRBC to DBI, 29, 34; DBI to DMI, 36, 39;
    GRCAS to UGR, 57; DMI to DI, 74; DI to DC, 97, 108-109;
    DC to DU, 179, 184
Nat'l Assoc. of Accredited Commercial Schools, 36, 40, *40*, 107

Index

Nat'l Assoc. and Council of Business Schools, 138
Nat'l Assoc. of Independent Colleges and Universities, 251
Nat'l Assoc. of Intercollegiate Athletics (NAIA), 197, 219, 224, 237
Nat'l Business Teacher's Association, 137
Nazareth College, 175
Norris Building, 34
North Central Assoc. of Colleges and Schools (NCA), 106-07, 119, 127, 131-32, 135, 138
    baccalaureate degree accredited by, 166-68
    and Davenport Learning Network, 183
    and Detroit College of Business, 168
    and online learning, 176
    and university accreditation, 184, 193, 194, 199
Northeastern School of Commerce (NSC), 258, *258*
Northwestern Michigan College, 175
Oleske, Denise, 213
Open House One Hundred, 157
Organization type
    independent, 250
    nonprofit, 84-85, 87, 229
    private, not-for-profit, 246, 250
Paone, Frank, 169, *169*
Pappas, Richard ("Rick") J., *240*, *244*, *245*
    civic leadership of, 247
    and Cook Award, *243*
    Davenport president, 216, *224*, 225, *225*
    early life and education, 244
    education philosophy, 225
    honors and professional organizations, 246-247
    on leadership, 246
    and process improvement, 228
    Vision 2015, 226-27, 228, 231, 235, 246
    Vision 2020, 240, 241
Parish, Aaron S., 18-19, *19*
Parson's Business School, 143, 148-149, 257
Philbin, Regis, 243
Phillips, Richard, 243
Phi Theta Pi fraternity, 44, 66, *68*, 69, *69*, *100*, 118, 137
Phoenix Furniture Company, 16-17
Placement, 78, 208, 228
    Employment Guarantee, 231, 235
Porter, Donald, 108, 131

Practical education, 15, 19, 39, 48, 98, 250
    faculty commitment to, 262
    and the Great Depression, 48
    and Student Success Skills Survey, 171
    at UGR, 52, 53, 57, 71
    in *Vision 2020*, 240
    Paul Voelker on, 72-73
Predictive curricula, 56, 144, 211, 214
    and computers, 163, 176, 200
    Success System and, 171
Presidential succession (in chronological order)
    M.E. Davenport to Robert Sneden, 87, 96
    Robert Sneden to Donald Maine, 103, 134, 142-43
    Donald Maine to Randolph Flechsig, 184, 192
    Randolph Flechsig to Michael Volk, 216
    Michael Volk to Richard Pappas, 224-25
President's cabinet, 129, 132, 204
Prince Corporation, 261
Process improvement, 228
Publications, 45
    Aeonian, *61*
    Davenport Digest, 133, 143, *143*
    RetroSpectus, 100, *100*
    Student Life, *45*, *76*, 100, 104, 128
Putnam Building, 36, *36*
Quartey, Kojo, *213*
Regency Apartments. *See* Residence halls, Heritage Hall
Residence halls, 87, 118, 205, 209
    Cook Hall, 205, 207, *209*
    Engle Hall, 122, *122*, 159, *159*, 170
    Heritage Hall, *123*, 170
    Margaret Hall, 122
    Meijer Hall, 206, *206*, 211
    Myners Hall, 123, *123*, 158, *158*, 170
    South Hall, 232, *232*
    Wessell Hall, 122
    Warren Hall, 87, 100-101, 106, 118, 122, *122* 124-25, *124-25*, 170
    Woods Hall, *123*, 170
Retention and graduation
    Clifton Wonders and, 129
    Framework for Success, goals in, 194
    student performance and, 228, 236, 262-63
Rinker, Linda, 230
Rohm, Dexter, 117, *148*, 148-149, 257
Roker, Al, 242, *242*, 243
Russell, Mark, 146, 181

Index

Russert, Tim, 243
Saginaw, Michigan, 131, 137, 139, 177, 218, 252-54
Saginaw Business Institute, 167, 258, **258**
Schmiedicke, Robert, 98, **98**, **102**, 129, **129**
Scholarships
    Louis and Catherine Buzzitta, 237
    endowed fund, 240
    Davenport Foundation and, 160, 181
    Jenny Engle, 212
    Excellence in Business Gala and, 181, 242
    Gerald Ford Memorial, 201
    golf fundraiser for, 161
    health professions, 154
    Barbara Mieras support of, 179
    public fundraising drive and, 127
    Dexter Rohm Memorial, 148
    Sneden family and, 164-65
    state scholarship for private colleges, 111
    Ty Wessel endowed, 103
Schrotenboer, Albert, 108, 131
Secchia, Peter F., 243, **243**
Sheldon Blvd. (215), 29, 32, **32**, **34**, 39, 40, 41, **41**, 44, 164, **164**
Sligh estate, 87, 118, 122, **122**. *See also* Mabel Engle Hall
Small business, support of, 123, 167, 173, 241
Sneden Academic Center, Robert W. (Heritage Hill), 127, 138, 153, **153**, 162, 167, 196
Sneden Center, Robert W. (Lettinga Campus), 138-39, **139**, 225, 229, 232, 233, **233**, 267
Sneden Graduate School, Margaret and Robert, 165
    launch of, 182-83
    and Thomas Brown, 204, 182
Sneden Library, Margaret Davenport, 162, **162**, 165
    expansion of, 178
    on Lettinga campus, 211, **211**
    veterans' study room, 265
Sneden, Margaret Davenport, 136, 139, **164-65**
    board of control director, 164
    on board of trustees, 131
    early life and education, 91, **91**, **115**, 164
    honors, 165
    marriage and family, 136, 164
    volunteer work, 165
Sneden, Robert W., **125**, **130**
    and accreditation process, 133-34
    civic leadership of, 138-139
    early life and education, 96, 136-37, **136-37**
    as Davenport president, 96-97, **96,** 98, 108, **108, 111,** 125, **139**
    as DMI faculty member, 75, **77, 79,** 96, 137
    as DMI student, 136
    and M.E. Davenport, 96, 136-37
        vice president under, 85, **87,** 111, 137
    honorary doctorate, 138
    marriage and family, 136-37, 139
    and Barb Mieras, 178
    military service, 97, 136-37, 264
    professional associations, 138
    retirement, 133-134, **138,** 139, **143, 169**
    in Washington, D.C., 110, 138, 264
South Bend, Indiana, 151, 153, 156, 254-55, 261
South Residence Hall, 232, **232**
Speelman, Jacob, 63
Spoelhof, John, **242**, 243
Stauffer, James, 102, 119, **119**
Steelcase, 29, 220, 241
Steil, Glenn and Barbara, 202
Stickley Furniture Company, 20
Stokes, Robert, 113
Student body, 118, 128, 237
    academic performance of, 208, 228, 236, 262-63
    at Davenport Institute, 85
    demographics of, 97, 144, 146, 149, 154
    satisfaction of, 28, 106, 120, 228
    transfer, 193
Student Center (Heritage Hill), 120, 127, 153
Student Center (Lettinga Campus), 206, 211, 215, **215.** *See also Anderson Student Center*
Student Veterans of America, 264
Study abroad, 201
Success System. *See* Excellence System
Swensberg, Conrad, 10, 12, **12, 16,** 16-18, 264
    commitment to students, 14
    early life and education, 16
    educational philosophy of, 13
Technology, College of/School of, 182, 199, 206, 211, 234
Theater, 44
Tomaszek, Therese, 133, 201, **201**
Traverse City, Michigan, 175, 254
Tuition, 48, 76, 101, 110-11, 127, 130, 160. *See also by individual institutions*
    veterans, reduction for, 264
United Business Schools Assoc., 107, 138, 251. *See also* ACIS
University Foundation. *See* Davenport Foundation
University of Grand Rapids, 51-73
    accreditation, 56

Index

admission requirements, 54
athletics, 57, 62-63, 64-65
Davenport-McLachlan Institute, relationship with, 56, 67, 71
degrees offered, 54, 58
enrollment, 54, (1936), 58 (1940), 67
faculty, 54, 57, 58, 67
fight song, 60
Lowe Estate location, **51**, 53, **56**, 57, **58**, **63**, **66**, 70
name change, 57
opening, 52, 54
and practical education, 52, 53, 57
student life, 55, 57
student publications, 61, 64
tuition, 58
and World War II, 66-67, 69
University School. See Arts and Sciences, School of
Urban Education, College of, 230-31, 239-40, 247
Valley City Commercial School, 8, 21-22
    faculty, 19, 28, 30
Valley City Milling, 16
Van Andel, Carol, **240**, 243, **243**
Van Andel, Dave, 243, **243**
Van Andel, Jay, 97, 203, 205
Van Andel, Steve, 243
Van Dyke, Michelle
Van Gessel, Mike 202, **202, 240**
Vandenberg, Fred, 142, 171, **171**
    on Donald Maine, 184, 185, 188
VanderLaan, Roger, 117, 161, **161**
Vasu, C. Mark, 154
Veneklase, David, 196
Veterans Readjustment Benefits Act of 1966, 264
Veterans' services
    HIRE program 264
    Military Friendly School designation, 264
    study facilities, Margaret Davenport Sneden Library, 265
Viet Nam war, 128
Virtual learning, 176
Vision 2015, 216, 226-27, 228, 229, 233, 243, 246
    Employment Guarantee, 230-32, 235
Vision 2020, 240, 241, 247
Visionary leadership, 144
   and accreditation, 106
   George Clark on, 63
   and Davenport Schools, Inc., 252
   Heritage Hill development, 122-23
   and UGR founding principles, 53-54

Vitale, Dick, 243, **243**
Voelker, Paul Frederick, 52-54, **52**, 56-57, **67**, 72-73, 113, 164
Volk, Michael, **206**, 211, 216-217, **217**
Vos, B. Margaret, 127, **133**
Warren, Michigan, 169, 212, 234, 254, 260
Warren Hall, 87, 100-101, 106, 118, **122**, 122, **124-25**, 170
Wege, Peter M., 29
Wessell Award for Distinguished Employee Service, Tyrus R., 103
    Thomas Brown awarded, 204
    Barbara Mieras awarded, 179
    Roger VanderLaan awarded, 161
Wessell Hall, Tyrus R., 122
Wessell, Tyrus ("Ty") R., **98**, 102-03, **125**, **170**
    on M.E. Davenport, 88
    and founding of UGR, 52
West Shore Community College, 175, 254
White Estate. See Warren Hall
Wolfe, Colleen, 196, **196**, 202, **202**
Wolverine World Wide, 243
Women at Davenport
    board of trustees, 133, 145
    dean of, 133
    gender stereotyping and, 104-05
    president, first woman, 178-79
    Margaret Sneden on, 164
    Title IX, 146
    See also Alpha Iota sorority; Athletics, women's
Wonders, Cliff, 46, **49**, 52, **102**, 129, **129, 170**
Woods, Florence, 123, 170
    Florence Woods Hall, **123**, 170
Wooten, Al, 117
World War II, 46, 55, 65, 66-67, 69, 74-75, 78, 165
Wynalda, Marian Davenport, 91, **91**, **115**, 131, 256, **256**
Wynalda, Martin, 149, 256, **256**
Wynalda Teaching and Learning Institute, 256, 262
Yerrick, Ken, **240**